POETandPAINTER

E. E. Cummings, c. 1923.

POETandPAINTER

The Aesthetics of E. E. CUMMINGS'S Early Work

MILTON A. COHEN

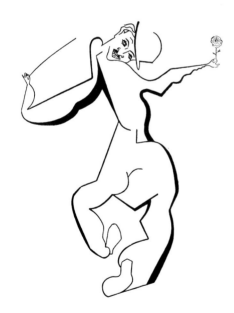

WAYNE STATE UNIVERSITY PRESS   DETROIT   1987

Library of Congress Cataloging-in-Publication Data

Cohen, Milton A.
    Poet and painter.

    Bibliography: p.
    Includes index.
    1. Cummings, E. E. (Edward Estlin), 1894–1962—
Criticism and interpretation. 2. Cummings,
E. E. (Edward Estlin), 1894–1962—Aesthetics.
I. Title.
PS3505.U334Z567 1987   811′.52   87-4991
ISBN 0-8143-1845-2

Grateful acknowledgment is made to the Art Book Publication
Fund, the John M. Dorsey Publishing Fund, and the University of
Texas at Dallas for financial assistance in the publication of this
volume.

To Phillip and Bertha Cohen and to Florence Chasey-Cohen

Contents

Illustrations

Note: Asterisks indicate titles Cummings gave to his own works.

Acknowledgments

■■■■For permission to reproduce E. E. Cummings's paintings and drawings, I wish to thank: The State University of New York at Brockport Foundation, The Memorial Art Gallery of the University of Rochester, the Houghton Library of Harvard University, the Harry Ransom Humanities Research Center of the University of Texas at Austin, Luethi-Peterson Camps, Inc., The Metropolitan Museum of Art, Dr. Rushworth Kidder, and Mr. Bradford Morrow. Cummings's paintings in *CIOPW* are Copyright 1931, 1959 by E. E. Cummings and are reproduced by permission of George J. Firmage.

Quotations from E. E. Cummings's poems in *Tulips & Chimneys* (including *&* and *XLI Poems*), *IS 5*, and *Viva* are used with the permission of Liveright Publishing Corporation:

TULIPS & CHIMNEYS by E. E. Cummings. Edited by George James Firmage. Copyright 1923, 1925 and renewed 1951, 1953 by E. E. Cummings. Copyright © 1973, 1976 by the Trustees for the E. E. Cummings Trust. Copyright © 1973, 1976 by George James Firmage.

IS 5 by E. E. Cummings. Edited by George James Firmage. Copyright © 1985 by E. E. Cummings Trust. Copyright 1926 by Horace Liveright. Copyright © 1953 by E. E. Cummings. Copyright © 1985 by George James Firmage.

Viva by E. E. Cummings. Edited by George James Firmage. Copyright 1931, 1959 by E. E. Cummings. Copyright © 1979, 1973 by the Trustees for the E. E. Cummings Trust. Copyright © 1979, 1973 by George James Firmage.

"So many selves(so many fiends and gods" Copyright 1948 by E. E. Cummings. Reprinted from his volume *COMPLETE POEMS, 1913-1962* by permission of Harcourt Brace Jovanovich, Inc.

"1(a" Copyright 1958 by E. E. Cummings. Reprinted from his volume *COMPLETE POEMS, 1913-1962* by permission of Harcourt Brace Jovanovich, Inc.

Quotations from essays in *E. E. Cummings: A Miscellany Revised,* edited, with an introduction and notes, by George J. Firmage

(New York: October House, Inc., 1965) are reproduced by permission of George J. Firmage.

Excerpts from E. E. Cummings's unpublished papers (including unpublished letters, notes, poems, and drawings) are quoted by permission of The Houghton Library of Harvard University, the Harry Ransom Humanities Research Center of the University of Texas at Austin, the Berg Collections of the New York Public Library, Astor, Lennox and Tilden Foundations, and the E. E. Cummings Trust, © 1979 by Nancy T. Andrews.

On a more personal note, I wish to thank Professor John Crowley, Syracuse University, for his patient and helpful guidance when this book was in its nascent stages; Professor Rainer Schulte, Translation Center of the University of Texas at Dallas, for providing word-processing services; Dr. Rushworth M. Kidder, columnist for the *Christian Science Monitor*, and Mr. George James Firmage, Literary Executor and Attorney in Fact for the E. E. Cummings Trust, for their kind cooperation and assistance; and Dr. Alexander Clark, Vice President for Academic Affairs, the University of Texas at Dallas, and the University of Texas at Dallas, for providing a generous subvention that helped make possible the color reproductions in this book.

Finally, I wish to thank my wife, Florence, without whose unflagging support I could not have seen this book through to publication.

Introduction: The Hidden "Selves" of E. E. Cummings

so many selves (so many fiends and gods
each greedier than every) is a man
(so easily one in another hides;
yet man can, being all, escape from none)

. . . .

—how should a fool that calls him "I" presume
to comprehend not numerable whom?

—E. E. Cummings, *Xaipe*

■■■■ "What every author hopes to achieve from posterity—a hope usually disappointed—is justice." So wrote W. H. Auden. To E. E. Cummings, posterity has been somewhat less than just. It has, of course, long recognized him as one of the premier Modernists—in poetry. His reputation as a structural innovator, a gleeful violator of poetic conventions, is so firm that no high school anthology would be compléte without one of his "poempictures," as he called them.

But Cummings's reputation as a poet has, in itself, distorted a deceptively complex artistic career. For the poems by which posterity remembers him occupied only part of his talents and time—and (according to his first biographer, Charles Norman) the lesser part at that. Two other pursuits together attracted most of Cummings's professional labors throughout his life: painting and aesthetics. About Cummings's painting, Norman writes: "He has painted more than he has written, and he has painted—for more than half a century—with an intense, undeviating passion."[1] One index of this passion is the impressive number of paintings Cummings produced. According to Rushworth Kidder, more than sixteen hundred oils and watercolors were in the Cummings estate, and this does not include the number he had sold during his career.[2]

Why, then, has posterity slighted until quite recently this side of Cummings's artistry?[3] Certainly not from any coyness in Cummings's professional—and professed—identity. Regardless of what others may have thought, he considered—and called—himself a "poet & painter" from the outset of his career.[4] More important, he behaved like one. He exhibited his paintings frequently in the early years (1916–27): at the yearly exhibitions of the Society of Independent Artists (hereafter: Independents); at the Penguin and other Modernist galleries; in the *Dial,* probably the most respected journal of modern arts and ideas in the twenties, where Cummings displayed a score of line drawings and several oils; in a book of black and white reproductions of his work in the late twenties published in 1931 and entitled *CIOPW* (standing for charcoal, ink, oil, pencil, watercolor); and in numerous one-man shows in New York, Rochester, and elsewhere in the ensuing decades. As if the exhibitions were not proof enough, many of Cummings's catalog statements (some later published in art journals) reassert his identity as a painter, such as one that begins: "For more than half a hundred years, the oversigned's twin obsessions have been painting and writing."[5]

At first, it appeared that *both* of Cummings's "twin obsessions" would be recognized. As he began to paint seriously in 1917, he made contacts with such prominent Modernists as Albert Gleizes, Joseph Stella, and Walter Pach and adopted Gaston Lachaise as his mentor and friend. Gleizes, Pach, and Lachaise all praised his abstractions at the 1919 Independents. More impressive still, in every Independents exhibition that he entered from 1919 to 1924, Cummings's abstractions—competing each year with over a thousand other canvases for critical attention—received mention by journalists covering the shows. Finally, his line drawings in the *Dial* kept company with the likes of Picasso, Braque, Derain, and Lachaise and were seen by a readership obviously sympathetic to Modernism in all the arts. With such a prominent start, why did Cummings's reputation as a painter fail to take off?

There is no single answer, only a number of competing explanations. The most obvious one is that his painting was increasingly eclipsed by his poetry. As a Modernist painter, Cummings was only one of many, and to an unpracticed eye, his work did not differ all that much from other "Post-Impressionist" painting.[6] In any case, the seismic shocks of Modernist painting had registered several years earlier at the Armory Show. But as a poet, Cummings had indeed "done something FIRST," as he boasted in a letter to his father.[7] The innovations of his poems sparked immediate and lasting controversy even among self-styled Modernists; and with controversy, Cummings's poetic reputation grew. By 1924, although he still considered himself "primarily a painter," he was already "better known as a poet and novelist" to a journalist reviewing his painting.[8] By 1926, he had published four substantial and provocative books of poetry (*Tulips and Chimneys, &, XLI Poems,* and *is 5*), participated in another (*Eight Harvard Poets*), and published poems regularly in such avant-garde journals as the *Dial* and *Broom.* Even had his early paintings been capable of stirring such continuous controversy, they received no exposure comparable to that of his poems.

By the end of the twenties, moreover, Cummings's painting offered little to arouse controversy. He had changed both his art and his aesthetics in the late twenties towards what was, superficially at least, a more representational style. The disparity between his increasingly "abstract" poetry and his increasingly "representational" painting puzzled critics of his later one-man shows and led them to assume that poetry was Cummings's vocation, painting his avocation. Typical of this attitude was Henry McBride's comment in a review of Cummings's one-man show in 1949: "So he is a personage of known [literary] stature and *the paintings he does in his off moments* and now shows . . . could be less than they are and yet take considerable rank for their association interest."[9] Such a misconception, repeated often enough, must surely have biased critical judgment of Cummings's achievement as a painter. Cummings was painfully aware of his increasingly one-sided image, and quite possibly, this awareness sapped his efforts to establish himself as a painter, made him less aggressive in seeking out exhibitions and in keeping up his contacts in the art world. In an unfinished draft of an autobiographical sketch, "The Fable of a Painter Who Was a Writer—True Story," the narrator confides to a friend why he never tried to get an uptown exhibition: "they'd think I was a writer. [. . .] they'd think I wasn't a painter."[10]

Perhaps what the narrator *really* feared was that "they" would think he was not a very *good* painter. This final possibility must be faced squarely, but it can be seen in two ways. After 1927, Cummings found the representational mode more aesthetically and personally satisfying. But his critics generally did not. Was it true, as Rushworth Kidder has suggested, that in "renouncing abstract art, Cummings also renounced his standing with the critics of his day"?[11]

Was his painting simply so outŕe that it precluded serious consideration? Cummings himself suspected the critics of this bias, and his suspicion fueled his rancor against "nonobjective art" in the forties and fifties—even though his own art was by no means as representational as it has been portrayed.[12] Or did his later painting, in its drive for spontaneity and expression, lack what one critic called "a solicitude for craftmanship as such"?[13] Was it largely second rate?

While to some extent this question is clouded by one's preferences regarding abstraction and representation, it seems fair to say that a sizable portion of Cummings's later work *was* second rate: produced too quickly and too profusely, lacking a rigorous and confident technique. As subsequent chapters argue, Cummings's later aesthetics largely permitted this slackness. His subjectivity often lacked the rigor of an external standard to counterbalance and restrain his spontaneous excesses.[14] And his iconoclasm, furthered by the ignorance of the critics, encouraged the dangerous tendency of painting to please only himself, of self-indulgence. Thus, both the reasons posed above—the one-sided reputation that may have biased the art critics and inhibited Cummings's efforts to establish himself publicly as a painter, and the unfashionableness and frequent self-indulgence of the later painting—figured in the neglect of Cummings's "other" career.

What is sad about this neglect is that even if some of the later work is forgettable, much of it is not and deserves another look. And the early work—the more significant, in my view—certainly held its own among the works of other American Modernists at the time of its exhibition. Would it not do so in retrospect?

More important, Cummings's painting is closely related to his poetry, and both his poetry and painting derive from his aesthetics. The visual quality of his typographical innovations has long been observed, but is nowhere better expressed than by Cummings himself in a letter to his editor: "What I care infinitely is that each poempicture should remain intact. Why? Possibly because with a few exceptions, my poems are essentially pictures."[15] Critics recognized this connection as early as 1923;[16] but only recently have there been serious attempts to examine it. If one is to understand fully Cummings's poetics, therefore, one must appreciate its relation to his techniques of painting—and to the common source of both: his aesthetics. This study examines the relationship among the three in his early work.

A far more hidden side of Cummings—but this one concealed by his own choice—was his life as an aesthetician and intellectual. From reading Cummings's many poems and essays that praise feeling, intuition, and spontaneity while they damn thinking, analysis, and calculation, one would never suspect that this self-proclaimed romantic was an indefatigable note-taker, a systematic thinker who developed his own aesthetics and philosophies to guide his art, and an intellectual whose boundless interests included all aspects of the arts, Eastern and Western philosophy, religion and metaphysics, psychology, the occult, and even that realm he publicly ridiculed, the sciences.[17]

A vast and vigorous mental life—and virtually secret! But secret was the way Cummings wanted it. He permitted no one, not even his roommate in the early years, to see his work in manuscript.[18] More private still were the notes that revealed not just his poetic techniques (which would, after all, produce a finished work), but his less structured thoughts, aesthetic speculations, and self-analyses.

Why Cummings preferred to remain a closet intellectual is a mystery. Perhaps he felt that his intellectual practices violated his aesthetic philosophy of feeling and spontaneity and would therefore undercut his image as a romantic who distrusted thinking. Perhaps intellectualism was too reminiscent of Cummings's father, a prominent Unitarian clergyman, whose dominance Cummings struggled to resist in his early years. Perhaps, also, he did not wish to reveal moments when his mind was less than certain, when it asked questions without having answers, when it dared to be wrong. For certainly, these notes show a mind as searching and self-critical in its private musings as it appeared unwavering certain and self-congratulatory in its public pronouncements.

Whatever Cummings's reasons, he at least did not destroy the evidence of his private thoughts. In fact, he seems to have preserved every scrap and envelope on which he ever jotted a thought or sketched a picture (e.g., fig. 1)—almost as if he wanted his secret life to be discovered. His papers, now at Harvard University's Houghton Library, have been called "perhaps the largest collection in existence of the papers of an American writer."[19] The collection is indeed prodigious and includes manuscripts and typescripts of all Cummings's poems, essays, and plays (published and unpublished); numerous fragments and drafts of plays; voluminous correspondence to and

Fig. 1.
Note on recognition, c. 1921-23. The E. E. Cummings papers, the Houghton Library, Harvard University. By permission of the Houghton Library. Copyright 1982, The E. E. Cummings Trust.

from Cummings; his library of books at the time of his death; over nine thousand loose drawings (besides scores of sketchbooks); juvenilia; college notebooks; and thousands of pages of loose notes and notebooks.

These last-mentioned notes are of particular importance in what they reveal about Cummings's intellect and aesthetics. Exhaustively comprehensive, they span the life of a creative mind from its first artistic stirrings (his parents apparently saved every one of young Estlin's scribbles), to the last thought Cummings penned in his notebook on the day of his death at sixty-eight. The sheer volume of these notes is intimidating and their condition often forbidding (especially the early notes that Cummings often scrawled on scraps of paper). But they are invaluable for anyone interested in Cummings's opinions on art, artists, and authors, in his aesthetics and techniques of painting and poetry, in his philosophy of life, in the Renaissance breadth of his mind, or even in the private thoughts of this essentially private person. One cannot help but wonder at the vitality of the mind that produced them: to follow its varied interests, intensive investigations, and farflung inquiries is a fascinating experience. Inevitably, this secret cache changes one's estimate of the man whose public persona critics have often, and with some justification, characterized as narrow and nonintellectual.

But the notes contain more particular rewards. Rushworth Kidder has aptly termed them "Cummings's workshop in which he developed, articulated, and illustrated his aesthetic theories."[20] They were also Cummings's classroom, for—apart from some relatively unimportant college courses in art history and poetry writing—Cummings never received formal training in the arts. He taught himself the fundamentals of two arts by analyzing and testing the ideas and techniques of others that interested him: philosophical ideas of subjectivity, feeling, and self-expression and technical theories of perception, movement, color, three-dimensional form, and (in the early thirties) figure drawing. His notes are both the laboratory and record of these investigations and experiments.[21]

Not surprisingly, the character of the notes changed as Cummings himself changed. The early notes look outward to assimilate the dizzying variety of Modernist styles and aesthetics, to glean from each ideas and techniques congenial to Cummings's own proclivities, and to determine just what those proclivities were. The later notes—

after 1930, say—look increasingly inward; they speculate less on the elements of craft, more on the values and philosophy Cummings lived by. While the range of their worldly interests broadens from the more technical concerns of the early notes, their function narrows, often serving as a sounding board for Cummings to refine his philosophy anew or reinforce his opinions. But like the early notes, the volume of these notes never diminished.

For Cummings, it seems, was never without a pencil in his hand, a notebook in his pocket, to jot down a thought, a line of verse, a quick sketch and later work it into an idea, a poem, or a painting. John Dos Passos writes of their strolls around Greenwich Village and the Lower East Side of New York during which Cummings "would be noting down groups of words or little scribbly sketches on bits of paper."[22] Significantly, these little scribbles were closely entwined with the composition of his paintings and poems. Many notes are illustrated (e.g., fig. 1) or share space with drawings; some drawings bear notes on technique; and many drawings are spattered with paint or sprinkled with fragments of poetry (e.g., fig. 2). The interchange between notebook and canvas or typewriter was fluid and continuous. Indeed, we have no better image of this symbiosis than Cummings's own self-portrait in *Him* (I, iv), as the playwright who is ever jotting thoughts into his notebook and who even shares with the audience one note (quoting almost verbatim from Cummings's unpublished notes) on the kinetic nature of reality.

Tied as these notes were to the practical business of formulating principles to guide his painting and poetry, there were yet periods in Cummings's early career when circumstance directed his labors *primarily* to note-taking and aesthetics. The first such period occupied his senior and M.A. years at Harvard. During that time, Cummings fulfilled course assignments with several essays on aesthetic subjects that interested him: "The New Art" (1915), a survey of the avant-garde in several arts which he later shortened for his commencement address; "The Poetry of Silence" (1915) on Chinese and Japanese poetry; "The Significance of El Greco" (1915); and "The Poetry of a New Era" (1916) on Imagism. Some of the Harvard notes, however, arose not from course requirements but from Cummings's personal need to comment on modern art, artists, and aestheticians, e.g., "The Latest *BLAST*," Cummings's reaction to the bombastic journal of the English Vorticists.[23] In both cases, Cum-

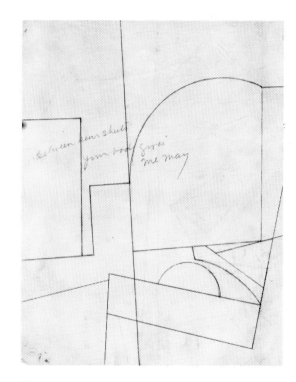

Fig. 2
Linear-geometric abstraction, c. 1921–23, pencil drawing. The E. E. Cummings papers, the Houghton Library, Harvard University. By permission of the Houghton Library. Copyright 1982, The E. E. Cummings Trust.

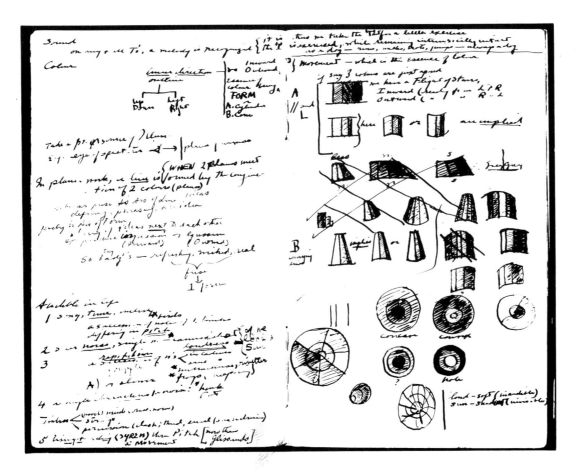

Fig. 3.
Note on color, sound, etc., c. 1921–23. The E. E. Cummings papers, the Houghton Library, Harvard University. By permission of the Houghton Library. Copyright 1982, The E. E. Cummings Trust.

mings's writings provide comprehensive evidence of the artists and styles he had assimilated, of the cast and depth of his views, and of the genesis of his own aesthetics.

Cummings's imprisonment by the French at La Ferté-Macé in the fall of 1917, which became the subject of his first book, *The Enormous Room* (1922), marks another period of intensive notetaking. As he writes his father, from prison, he made the best of his time: "Our life here is A1. Never have I so appreciated leisure. I continually write notes on painting, poetry, and sculpture, as well as music; and the Muse herself has not been unkind. My days . . . remind me of the mental peregrinations of your favorite Socrates, insofar as they have already illuminated many dark crannies in the greatest of all sciences—Art."[24]

Still another productive imprisonment was Cummings's military service at Camp Devens (July 1918–January 1919). Between drills and endless K.P., he found time to write hundreds of pages of notes and at least a dozen poems that he later collected in *Tulips & Chimneys.* A final burst of prolific note-taking in the early years occurred during Cummings's stay in Paris from May 1921 to December 1923. Living alone and seeing friends only sporadically, Cummings had ample time to ponder aesthetics. As chapter 1 will show, this was a time in Cummings's painting for taking stock and reconsidering his techniques through hundreds of experimental drawings. His voluminous notes of this period, easily dated from their French watermark, provide the theoretical complement to these visual studies.

The method of these notes, particularly the Parisian ones, belies Cummings's frequent sallies against analytical thinking. Typically, he approached a problem Socratically and dialectically, first by asking a basic question and then by breaking down the answer into primary categories or elements that often oppose each other. In one typical page of notes written en route to Europe in 1921 (fig. 3), Cummings analyzes the propensity of color to effect two types of motion, two-dimensional ("outline") and three-dimensional ("inward outward").

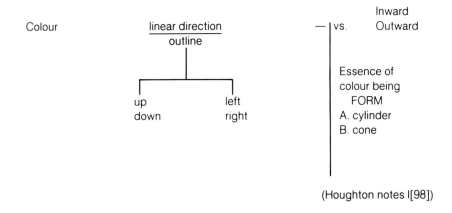

(Houghton notes I[98])

This distinction helped lead him to a concept of three-dimensional form in his early painting achieved by juxtaposing colors that moved "inward" with those that moved "outward." The page continues with notes comparing poetry and prose in terms of plane and line, distinguishing between elements of noise and music, and relating motion to color and shape. The range and interconnectedness of these notes are characteristic of Cummings's aesthetic inquiries.

There is nothing particularly new or sophisticated in these analyses. On the contrary, they represent elementary discoveries worked out with painstaking thoroughness by a young artist bent on teaching himself the fundamentals of his crafts. What *is* important is the close relationship these notes bear to the techniques in Cummings's early painting and poetry. The fundamental premise of this book is that such a relationship does exist and that many of the techniques in the early poetry and painting, while not always directly analogous to each other, grew out of the aesthetics Cummings developed in his notes.

In determining Cummings's aesthetics from thousands of pages of notes, essays, letters, poems, and paintings, my method of research was inductive. My presentation of these ideas, however, is deductive. That is, in each chapter, I begin with an aesthetic problem important to Cummings, review briefly his intellectual and aesthetic sources, and describe the solutions to the problem he formulated in his writings. Then, I examine the poetic and painterly techniques Cummings devised to realize his aesthetic theory and analyze sample paintings and poems to demonstrate these techniques.

The chapters are arranged hierarchically in a kind of pyramid, beginning at the apex with Cummings's philosophical aesthetics of wholeness and feeling that govern the other aesthetics (chap. 2), moving down to the more technical aesthetics of perception (chap. 3), form (chap. 4), and motion (chap. 5), and concluding with Cummings's more speculative and largely unrealized theories of analogues among the arts (chap. 6). To provide a context for the paintings discussed elsewhere in the book, chapter 1 offers an overview of Cummings's painting, early and late, and considers the major influences on his early art and aesthetics.

Given the limitless possibilities in discussing three separate practices, some necessary limitations have been imposed. First, only Cummings's early work, from 1916 to about 1927, is considered (except in chap.1, where discussion of the later painting puts the earlier work into a clearer perspective). The year 1927 is a logical stopping point for several reasons. By then, the structural and visual techniques in Cummings's poetry had all appeared, although they would be extended and refined in later years. More important, the late twenties and early thirties marked a turning point in Cummings's painting, his aesthetics, and his weltanschauung. Aesthetically, he resolved the interesting and fruitful tension between the subjectivity of his personal philosophy and the objectivity of his painting. What resulted was a more unified, though in many ways less interesting, aesthetics of subjectivity, self-expression, and spontaneity.

Cummings's personal life also changed in these years. Following the upheavals of two divorces (1924–25 and 1932), his father's sudden death (1926), his psychoanalysis (1928–29), and a distasteful but illuminating trip to Russia (1931), Cummings grew far more conservative politically, more isolated from his times and milieu, and more closed in on himself intellectually and spiritually. With his successful third marriage to Marion Morehouse in 1934, he settled into an increasingly domestic and restricted routine.[25] In all realms, then, his gaze turned inwards. To a student of Cummings's aesthetics, the early years—years of high-spirited exploration, of open-minded inquiry, and of stylistic experiments—are not only vital to understanding the formation of Cummings's aesthetics but also fascinating in their expansive and undogmatic search for these principles.

Not all dimensions of Cummings's aesthetics are considered, however. His kinship with nature and the spiritual values he developed later in his life, while important, are beyond the limits of this investigation. Except for chapter 6, I have confined myself only to those early aesthetic ideas that appear to lead directly to artistic techniques.

Beyond demonstrating the relationship between Cummings's theory and practice, I hope in this study to enlarge Cummings's reputation as an artist and aesthetician, perhaps even to provide a measure of the "justice" that posterity has denied him. In surveying Cummings's painting, I present a side of his artistry that, while occupying an entire half of his creative life, has not received enough critical attention. If successful, I will show that Cummings was not simply a poet who "also painted,"[26] but was, like Rossetti, an artist of two equal callings, a "poet & painter." I hope, further, to encourage more interest in Cummings's painting and particularly in his early abstractions, both for their notable, if all too brief, impact on the New York art world of the early twenties and for their aesthetic parallels to his poetry. Finally, I propose to challenge the image that

Cummings himself encouraged, that of the romantic who opposed intellection as vigorously as he praised feeling, by arguing that the cerebral self he left in shadows assumes the dominant role in shaping his early work. Redefining his creative identity, in turn, permits a revaluation of his art. For Cummings's romantic persona has worked against his critical standing by prompting some influential critics to gauge his typographical innovations as little more than the capriciousness of an enfant terrible who never grew up.[27] If Cummings can be seen as having striven for a coherent and unified system of aesthetics—despite his failure to reconcile his public and private selves —then his poetic inventions fall into place as the means through which he realized his aesthetics and expressed his themes. And the young artist who wrote that art "was the greatest of all sciences" may come to appear in exactly the scientific guise he so ridiculed later in his life: as a scientist of aesthetics.

Plate 2.
Noise Number 1, 1919, oil on canvas,
36 × 36 in. Courtesy of SUNY College
at Brockport Foundation. Photograph
by Earl Kage, Museographics.

Plate 1.
Sound Number 1, 1919, oil on canvas,
35 × 35 in. The Metropolitan Museum
of Art, Bequest of Scofield Thayer,
1982. (1984.433.8) Copyright © 1985
by The Metropolitan Museum of Art.
All rights reserved, The Metropolitan
Museum of Art.

Plate 4.
Seated red-headed nude, c. 1920s, oil on cardboard, 17 × 9 in. Courtesy of SUNY College at Brockport Foundation.

Plate 3.
Sound Number 5, 1920, oil on canvas, 42 × 36 in. Courtesy of SUNY College at Brockport Foundation.

Plate 5.
Noise Number 13, 1925, oil on canvas,
59½ × 43 in. Private Collection, New
York.

Plate 7.
Posed woman: eyes half-closed, n.d., oil
on cardboard, 17½ × 8½ in. Private
Collection.

Plate 6.
Anne in blue hat at table, c. 1926–30,
oil on cardboard, 17½ × 8½ in. Cour-
tesy of SUNY College at Brockport
Foundation. Photograph by Earl Kage,
Museographics.

Plate 8.
View from Joy Farm: Mt. Chocorua,
1941, oil on canvas, 38 × 48 in. Private
Collection.

Plate 9.
Flowers in a vase, n.d., watercolor on
paper, 12½ × 9½ in. Courtesy of Martin and Allegra Allen, Boston.

Plate 10.
Landscape with stormy sky, n.d., watercolor on paper, 8½ × 11 in. Private Collection.

Plate 11.
Self-portrait in blue tie, 1958, oil on cardboard, 14 × 8½ in. Collection of R. W. Davidson.

Plate 12.
Flowers and hat: Patchen Place, c. 1950, oil on canvas, 44 × 33½ in. Courtesy of SUNY College at Brockport Foundation.

Cummings the Painter

1

A complete study of Cummings should take penetrating account of his painting and drawing, and no estimate of his literary work can begin without noting the important fact that Cummings is a painter.

—Gorham Munson

E. E. Cummings who referred to himself as "a draftsman of words," wanted to be known also as "an author of pictures." Why he wanted serious consideration as an artist is one of the mysteries that will be the province of future Ph.D. students.

—Brian O'Doherty

■■■■The gulf between the opinions quoted above (from 1923 and 1963, respectively) offers a succint comment on how Cummings's reputation as a painter has fared with the critics and public. In 1923 —probably for the last time during his life—he was considered an artist of *two* equally important and intricately related disciplines. By 1963, his painting was dismissed as an avocation. Scarcely before it had begun to gain public recognition, Cummings's career as a painter faded into obscurity. The oils and line drawings he displayed in the *Dial* during the twenties, the 1931 book of black and white reproductions of his art (*CIOPW*), his numerous exhibitions and one-man shows in the years following—none of these was sufficient to rekindle the flame to more than a brief and distorted flicker. Yet, however little his painting failed to take hold publicly, it continued undiminished privately as a vital part of the artist's daily life for over half a century. It existed not as relief or diversion from the poetry, but as a complement and co-equal to it, a different and challenging medium through which Cummings could express feelings and aesthetic ideas analogous to and sometimes identical with those he put into his poems. Munson's 1923 caveat was thus remarkably prescient: to grasp and gauge the aesthetics and artistry of this "poet & painter" in their entirety requires a careful look at this career that "wasn't"— if only to understand more fully the career that was.

Tracing Cummings's development and career as a painter, however, is by no means easy, not only because so much of his work was private—undated and uncataloged—but also because the painter, like the poet, worked in several modes and styles and developed along several paths at once. To simplify matters, we can roughly divide his paintings into two disparate periods, early (1915–26) and late (1927–62), a division corresponding to marked changes in Cummings's attitudes towards nature and abstraction, in his technique, and in his goals and values as an artist.

The Promising Modernist: 1915–26

Even as a child, Cummings seemed always to be working with a pencil or a paint brush. When he was not composing poems, he was drawing elephants, or knights, or flowers. As he matured, he bypassed formal instruction with a Cézannesque disdain for the academy and determined to teach himself the fundamentals of his craft.[1] At Harvard, he studied a bit of art history and, more important, became au courant with all the modern styles and theories he could encounter. Profoundly impressed by the 1913 Armory Show in Boston (especially by Brancusi's *Mlle. Pogany* and Duchamp's *Nude Descending a Staircase*),[2] he attended numerous exhibitions in New York and Boston during the teens and snatched up the few existing books on modern art he could find, such as Arthur Jerome Eddy's *Cubists and Post-Impressionism* (1914) and Willard Huntington Wright's *Modern Painting: Its Tendency and Meaning* (1915).[3] As one of the Harvard aesthetes of the midteens, Cummings was particularly fortunate in having knowledgeable friends—notably S. Foster Damon, Scofield Thayer (figs. 10, 33) and Edward Nagel (stepson of the Modernist sculptor Gaston Lachaise)—from whom he could glean the latest developments in the arts.[4] And whether he stood before a Cézanne or read an analysis of it, Cummings responded immediately and continuously in extensive notes describing his emotional reaction to what he saw and read, analyzing the dynamics of the canvas, the painter, or the style, and working out his own aesthetic principles. All the while, he was drawing and painting.

Soon after completing his M.A. at Harvard, Cummings found a studio in New York in January 1917 and began to paint seriously.

At the same time, he worked at his poetry intensively and even briefly essayed a nine-to-five job—his last—at the booksellers P. F. Collier and Sons. One might therefore assume that painting was more his Sunday pastime than serious vocation. But Cummings's letters to his parents from New York are not those of a dabbler or dilettante. He speaks of painting "8–12" each night and claims (with only a trace of hyperbole) that his painting "consist in the mental concentration equivalent to 80 weeks" at his daytime job.[5] His roommate in the years following, William Slater Brown, confirms that Cummings was "painting all the time."[6] His brush was stayed only by his two war-related stints: as a volunteer in the Norton-Harjes Ambulance Service and guest of the French prison bureaucracy (April–December 1917) and as a draftee in the U.S. Army (July 1918–January 1919).

That Cummings took painting seriously becomes clearer in light of his literary achievements in the early twenties. In February 1920, the first of his critical essays, "Gaston Lachaise," appeared in the *Dial*; others followed. In 1922, *The Enormous Room*, a lengthy prose narrative of his World War I imprisonment, earned him considerable recognition and praise. A year later appeared his first large collection of poems, *Tulips and Chimneys*, fueling an already heated controversy over his innovative style. With these accomplishments behind him, and with the callings of novelist, critic, or poet his for the choosing, Cummings could still write his father in December 1923: "am still convinced that am primarily a painter."[7]

Because his parents were not so convinced, Cummings's letters to them from New York and Paris in these years pointedly devote far more detail to painting than to the prose-writing his parents urged on him.[8] They often bristle with declarations of his professional independence.

> I wish, my chère maman, you could give o'er the (Father born methinks) idée fixe of Prose Superiority; womenandchildrenfirst style! Just why it should seem impossible to an intelligent not to say sensitive person or persons that colour, shape, rhythm, music being built for human beings reveal each other chiefly in mutual explorings—I can't conceive. Must I roar out that there are, live, eat, exist persons of {sensitiveness intelligence} to whom the (as you infer) un-thorough-bred branches of my interest (e.g. poetry, painting) in life liberty and the

p.o.h. appear as a more formidable achievement than prose? Or does the penchan[t] for running somebody else's mentality strike deeper than aught else within the pat⎫ soul ⎫
⎬ernal ⎬ ? Not so forsooth![9]
mat⎭ heart⎭

To his sister, Cummings simply stated: "I started, some years ago, against the continuous advice of my elders, to paint as I saw fit."[10] Neither his parents' well-intentioned meddling, nor the public's indifference, nor the critics' coolness would dampen that determination for the next forty years.

Cummings's early painting reflects the artist's thorough sympathy and identification with the avant-garde of his day and with the aesthetics of abstraction. In 1918, he described his work as "organizations of colour and line, presentative, semi-abstract, and abstract. Figures often taken in design, more often machinerish elements. There are some 'types.'"[11] This requires some translation. "Organizations of colour and line"—itself a précis of Modernist painting—shows Cummings's essentially formalist conception of his own work regardless of whether the subject matter was representational ("presentative") as in *Pornic* (fig. 12), semiabstract as in *Nude on a Precipice* (fig. 24), or abstract as in *Noise Number 1* (plate 2). "Figures taken in design," likewise, suggests that a recognizable subject, whether human or mechanical, was merely a starting point—the "raw material" as he put it later—for a stylized "design." Among Cummings's numerous drawings, some (e.g., fig. 4) are clearly "machinerish" in a fashion not unlike the Dadaism of that time. Others merge human and machine into biomorphic figures (fig. 5), or blend figure and ground into a unified design (fig. 6).[12]

Cummings shared the Modernist's ambivalence toward the object. He was fascinated by its "thinginess"—its planes and lines, solids and hollows—so temptingly transmutable into an abstract design. But he distrusted its perceptual magnetism, the destructive dominance it exerted over a work's complete configuration. Hence, while he experimented with many ways of rendering or concealing the object, his early sympathies and most diligent efforts were towards abstraction. While still at Harvard, he declared with youthful absolutism: "Nothing can be more vile than to imitate Nature. The means (technique) of the Artist is Geometry. . . . Art is capable of expressing everything abstract. Motion, sound, smell, taste, syncopa-

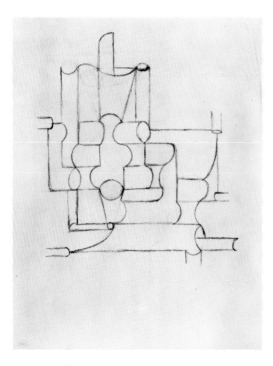

Fig. 4.
"Machinerish" tubes, c. 1921–23, pencil drawing, The E. E. Cummings papers, the Houghton Library, Harvard University. By permission of the Houghton Library. Copyright 1982, The E. E. Cummings Trust.

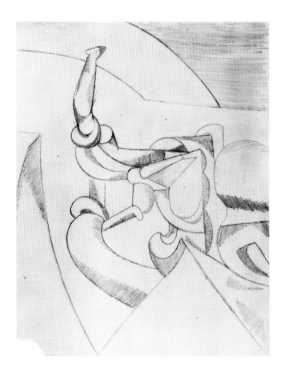

Fig. 5.
Biomorphic figures, c. 1921–23, pencil
drawing, The E. E. Cummings papers,
the Houghton Library, Harvard University. By permission of the Houghton Library. Copyright 1982, The E. E.
Cummings Trust.

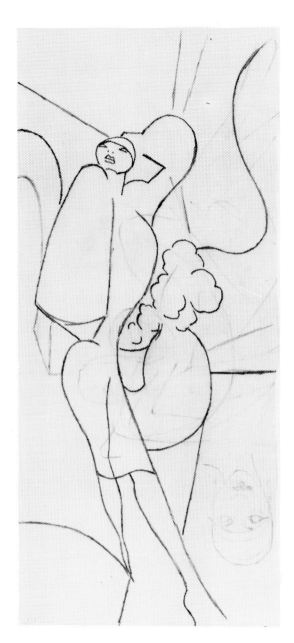

Fig. 6.
Figures merging with background,
1920s, pencil drawing, The E. E. Cummings papers, the Houghton Library,
Harvard University. By permission of
the Houghton Library. Copyright
1982, The E. E. Cummings Trust.

tion, etc. are Its goal, i.e. Beauty" (Houghton notes, bMS Am 1892.7[149] nos. 1-2). A decade later, he had not moderated his views. He still objected to the secondhand nature of representational painting; a painting could not be "itself" if it was "of" something else: "The only thing which a p[ainting] can be is itself—an integration by means of colour. . . . [A]n arrangement of pure colours, a juxtaposition [of] cones, cylinders, cubes, or a progression of planes suggests everything to me" (Houghton notes, I [39] nos. 110-11).[13]

Even before he began to see the ideographic possibilities of words, Cummings was submerging the figures of his painting into a design. A drawing of Scofield Thayer (fig. 7), dated October 1915, becomes a pinwheel of flat, curving planes dividing Thayer's profile, Janus-like, into opposing directions. By 1917, abstraction had become complete. An untitled pastel sent to a Wanamaker's Gallery exhibition in April presents "a juxtaposition of cones"—albeit a crude one—as its subject. No doubt, Wanamaker's rejected it.

Even in his most abstract work, however, Cummings did not wish to cut all ties with the recognizable world. To do so would run counter to his profoundly sensuous attachment to nature. Rather, he believed (as Picasso later put it so well), "You must always start with something. Afterward you can remove all traces of reality. There is no danger then, anyway, because the idea of the object will have left an indelible mark."[14] In Cummings's work, that "indelible mark" sometimes evoked considerable tension with the final, abstract design, beguiling the viewer to reconstruct—or misconstruct—lines and planes into their figurative origins.

In 1918, for example, he delightedly recounts just such a misreading by no less seasoned a Modernist than his friend and mentor, Gaston Lachaise. In one painting that Cummings titled *Traffic*, whose "forms are exclusively inorganic," Lachaise saw "the playing of joyous kids." In another, which Cummings called *Brooklyn Bridge*, Lachaise saw "a woman, perhaps Astec Woman" and "Saw 'so leede' [solid] in it which I must have mistaken for a bridge!" More important for Cummings, Lachaise "honoured me by seeing a fitness of form-to-colour in it."[15] Praise from someone of Lachaise's stature— and from one whose opinion Cummings valued above all others— played no small role in encouraging the young painter to continue.

Perhaps because Lachaise inveighed against descriptive titles at this meeting, Cummings subsequently dropped from his abstrac-

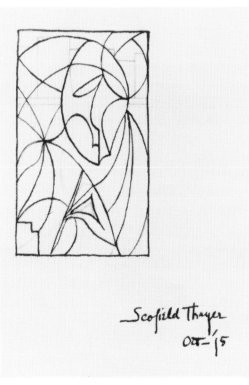

Fig. 7.
Scofield Thayer, October 1915, ink drawing. The E. E. Cummings papers, the Houghton Library, Harvard University. By permission of the Houghton Library. Copyright 1982, The E. E. Cummings Trust.

tions such spoofing subtitles as *Soft Shell Crab Defending Its Young* and restrained his fancy to the cryptically synesthetic titles *Sound* and *Noise*, numbering them sequentially.[16] Privately, and with his characteristic blend of irreverent humor and self-deprecation, he accepted his father's nickname for the abstractions, "crazy quilts," an apt description of their patchwork of planes.[17]

There was nothing offhand, however, about Cummings's attitude toward these *Sounds* and *Noises*. He conceived them in minute detail (fig. 8) and painted them with great care, often working and reworking a canvas over several months. As a series, they mark Cummings's highest achievement in the early period, both artistically and critically, and hence deserve careful consideration. Essentially, they were guided by three aesthetic principles (which subsequent chapters

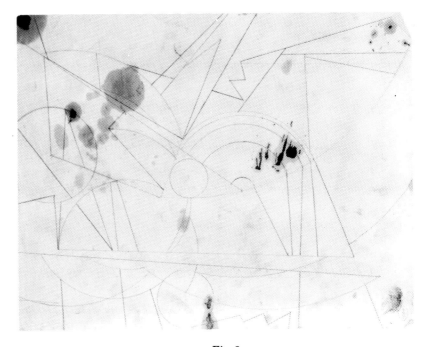

Fig. 8.
Study (for *Sound Number 2?*), c. 1919, ink drawing. The E. E. Cummings papers, the Houghton Library, Harvard University. By permission of the Houghton Library. Copyright 1982, The E. E. Cummings Trust.

will examine in detail): perceptual integrity that subordinates recognizable figures to the work's complete configuration; structural solidity and depth achieved through carefully planned interactions of colors and planes; and dynamic rhythm running through and unifying the separate parts. All three principles bear on the broader aesthetics of interrelatedness—wholeness—as Cummings himself makes clear. In a letter home, he compares his painstaking composition of *The Enormous Room*, paragraph by paragraph, to "the same way that a 'crazy quilt' is made so that every inch of it seems good to me. And so that if you put your hand over one inch, the other inches lose force. And so that in every inch there is a binding rhythm which integrates the whole thing and makes it a single moveing [sic] thinginitself."[18] In his notes, he asserts repeatedly the interrelatedness of parts as a quality central to both poetry and painting: "a painting, a poem should be like a pile of jackstraws: a heap of strains, of stresses, enormous and minute, each necessarily and incredibly through its neighbor related to and responsible for an . . . entirety fortunately existing through the impossibility of a single dislocation or subtraction" (Houghton notes, I[27] no. 3).

Fig. 9.
Small's, mid-1920s, oil on cardboard, 17 × 8½ in. From *CIOPW.* Copyright 1931, 1959 by E. E. Cummings.

These interdependent stresses and rhythms are evident in each of the *Sounds* and *Noises*. All are aesthetic battlefields, pitting colors, lines, and planes against each other; but each maps out its own conflict of motifs and hues. The early abstractions of 1919 (already far beyond the crude 1917 pastel) emphasize weighty conflict, as tumbling circles collide in *Sound Number 2* (fig. 31), while sweeping crescents and pod-shapes of bright orange, red, and yellow cut into straight-edged planes of recessive dark green and blue in *Noise Number 1* (plate 2). By the end of the series in 1924–25, the fulcrum has shifted more to graceful, rhythmic flow, as serpentine curves meld into each other in *Noise Number 12* (fig. 22), and spirals burgeon forth in *Noise Number 13* (plate 5). Unlike his later work, Cummings applies his paint here in uniformly flat textures that emphasize planes as they efface individual brushstrokes; hence, the dynamism of these works derives from the careful *arrangement* of conflicting planes, lines, and colors, rather than from the textural *act* of painting them.

Devoted as he was to his *Sound* and *Noise* abstractions, Cummings had too much to learn about painting to limit himself to one style and medium only. His reference to "presentative" and "semi-abstract" painting confirms that he moved freely among several styles, media, and degrees of abstraction in the conventional genres of portraiture, still life, and landscape. Caricature was a particular favorite. The challenge of compressing character and motion into a few telling—and exaggerated—details appealed to the artist fully as much as it did the poet of *is 5*. In paint, however, Cummings's caricatures are labored and sometimes embarassing, such as the dancing blacks in *Small's* (fig. 9), named after a Harlem club he frequented in the twenties. Here, as in *Harlem* and *straw-hat nigger* (*CIOPW*, pp. 43, 76), the distortions are both expressionistic and racist (rolling eyes, wide lips, flashing teeth)—the same mentality that deforms his poems about "niggers" and "kikes."

In the challenging medium of line drawing, on the other hand, his talent for caricature and compression succeeds handsomely, perhaps because the medium requires economy as well as spontaneity. An unpublished drawing of Scofield Thayer (fig. 10) highlights Thayer's distinctive upraised eyebrow and tiny, bow mouth. Thayer, in turn, recognized Cummings's talent in this medium and published twenty-two of his line drawings in the *Dial* between 1920 and 1927. Of these, the best is *Charles Spencer Chaplin* (fig. 11), which Hilton Kramer called "a minor graphic masterpiece."[19] With a marvelously fluent line, Cummings fuses several features of the comedian: his forlorn shuffle, with the legs and feet seeming to fold into each other; his tragicomic nature in the rose and cane, the ingratiating waiflike smile and the subserviently bent head; and his nimble dexterity both in balancing the rose and in seeming to come towards the viewer in his top half and move away in his bottom half—exactly as a colleague of Chaplin's recalls him: "I can't once remember him *still*. He was always standing up as he sat down, and going out as he came in."[20]

Another successful medium—and one that remained so throughout Cummings's career—was watercolor. It required light, quick brushwork and a delicacy of color that gratified Cummings's talents (not least because it bypassed his coloristic weaknesses in the more deliberate medium of oils) and must have seemed a welcome relief from the massive and painstaking *Sounds* and *Noises*. His *Pornic* (fig. 12), a view of a town in southern France where he vacationed in 1922, pays an obvious debt to Cézanne in its motif and structure and yet, in the fanciful sky, expresses Cummings's own subjectivity.

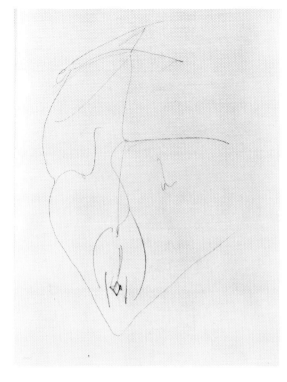

Fig. 10.
Scofield Thayer, before 1923, pencil drawing. The E. E. Cummings papers, the Houghton Library, Harvard University. By permission of the Houghton Library. Copyright 1982, The E. E. Cummings Trust.

Fig. 11.
Charles Spencer Chaplin, 1924, ink
drawing. From *CIOPW.* Copyright
1931, 1959 by E. E. Cummings.

Fig. 12.
Pornic, 1922, watercolor on paper, 10½
× 13½ in. Collection of R. W. Davidson.

Pornic's derivativeness, however, suggests how profoundly Modernist styles and artists influenced Cummings's early painting. It could scarcely be otherwise for someone lacking a traditional grounding in older styles and thoroughly imbued with what he called "the modern spirit." His early notes and essays are filled with references to the painters, styles, and works he most admired. Indeed, the very abundance of this evidence complicates the attempt to determine influence, since no one style dominated Cummings's painting, and since his praise and practice do not always coincide. The final test, of course, is in his painting, which, when cross-referenced with his notes, reveals four major influences: Cézanne, the Synchromists (Morgan Russell and Stanton MacDonald-Wright), the Cubists (primarily Picasso and Gleizes), and the Futurists (particularly their American counterparts, Joseph Stella and John Marin).

Of these diverse sources, Cézanne without doubt exerted the greatest influence on Cummings's early painting, aesthetics, and even professional identity. Cummings's admiration began early and bordered on hero-worship. As he wrote an unnamed correspondent (Scofield Thayer?) in a 1917 notebook: "Permit me to astonish you further by declaring that at the present fortunate moment, my conviction of Cézanne's unparalleled greatness as a painter remains absolutely unshaken."[21]

Cummings studied Cézanne's painting both at the 1913 Armory Show in Boston and at New York galleries in the teens. Equally important, he read several important analyses of Cézanne's techniques. Willard Huntington Wright's *Modern Painting* presented a masterful and authoritative account of how Cézanne used color to achieve three-dimensional form, which Cummings adapted to his own aesthetics of "seeing around" form. Sometime after 1920, he translated into rough English Julius Meier-Graefe's *Cézanne und sein Kreis*—an index of his hunger for material about the painter, but an exercise from which he probably gained little. His most important source was a collection of Cézanne's aesthetic opinions (almost certainly Émile Bernard's *Souvenirs sur Paul Cézanne*)—opinions that recur often in Cummings's notes and inform several aspects of his early aesthetics.[22]

One item that Cummings found immediately useful was an inventory of the master's palette:

These colors find direct expression in Cummings's own painting, as he reveals in a letter to his mother, dated 3 March 1922: "in great part I've been using the world famous Cézanne palette [. . . .] but employing it not à Cézanne in his watercolors—feeling me out with it, rather; me times water times paper times de jaune so to speak!"[23] Even allowing for the subjective liberties Cummings took in "feeling [himself] out with" Cézanne's palette, there are striking tonal similarities between, say, Cummings's watercolor *Pornic*, painted only a few months after the letter quoted above, and Cézanne's 1906 watercolor *Way to the Woods*. In both, light greens and yellows dominate, while blue-grays and hints of crimson provide contrast.

Cézanne's abandonment of one-point perspective, his leaning figures, and his discontinuous lines, inform several of Cummings's early paintings. In *Anne in cloche and gray dress* (fig. 50), the figure's off-center tilt into the picture derives from the asymmetrical positioning of Madame Cézanne in several later portraits (e.g., *The Yellow Armchair*). In Cézannesque fashion, the table in Cummings's *Open window* (fig. 13) lacks a fourth leg; and the ceiling and floor lines slant off-kilter to emphasize the planes of the window and view.

Finally, Cézanne's motifs and formal arrangements appear in Cummings's work—sometimes with embarrassing fidelity. *Pornic*, for example, portrays the same hillside town crowned by a church campanile, with masses arranged in vertical tiers, that Cézanne depicts in *La Gardanne*. And Cummings's *View from Joy Farm* (plate 8), in which the foreground tree frames the distant mountain, pays direct homage to the Cézanne *Mont Sainte-Victoire* in the Courtauld Institute, a work Cummings saw and admired. Like Cézanne, he returned repeatedly to the motif of the distant mountain.

Ultimately, Cézanne's influence transcended motifs and aesthetics to shape Cummings's very identity as an artist and innovator. For as he struggled to throw off the hands of tradition that would restrain his ideas and his life—the received wisdom of a Harvard education, the approved morality of Cambridge, the suitable careers his parents urged on him—Cummings turned to Cézanne. A long letter

Fig. 13
Open window, 1922, oil on canvasboard, 18 × 14½ in. Private Collection.

to Rebecca Cummings, in which Cummings reaffirmed his determination to paint, closes with a quotation of Cézanne's advice to Bernard: "Now the theme to develop is that—whatever our temperament or power in the presence of nature may be—we must render the image of what we see, forgetting everything that existed before us. Which, I believe, must permit the artist to give his entire personality whether great or small." Below the quotation, Cummings repeated: "forgetting everything that existed before us."[24] If he were to assert his own personality as an artist, Cummings knew he would have to forget not only the bourgeois respectability that would stifle his career and his perceptions, but also the artistic propriety that would inhibit his innovations. It is no coincidence, then, that the young poet bent on exploding the conventions of poetry should dedicate the very earliest of his demolitions, a sheaf of experimental poems begun in 1916, to the French painter who broke so decisively with the conventions of Western painting.[25]

The Modernists who developed and extended Cézanne's innovations also influenced Cummings. The Synchromists—Morgan Russell and Stanton MacDonald-Wright—demonstrated how large color planes, when juxtaposed, can create the push and pull of three-dimensional form. Cummings learned of their work through the writings of Willard Huntington Wright (Stanton's brother and publicist of the movement) and probably attended the important Forum Exhibition of Modern American Painters in 1916, which featured several Synchromist works. Like Russell's *Synchromie in Orange: To Form*, Cummings's *Sound Number 5* (plate 3) abstracts a human torso in contraposto pose into large planes of bold, single colors.

From Henri Gaudier-Brzeska, Albert Gleizes, and Picasso, Cummings derived his early preference for planar structures. While still at Harvard, he encountered Gaudier-Brezska's opinions and sculptures through the short-lived journal *BLAST*, and through Ezra Pound's memoir of the sculptor; quotations from the sculptor's manifesto on Vorticism soon appeared in Cummings's notes: "For as Gaudier says, 'lines are nothing, there are only planes.'"[26] Gleizes, Picasso, and Cubism in general are somewhat deceptive in their influence. While Cummings admired Cubism's structural integrity and the three-dimensional solidity it conveyed without resorting to trompe l'oeil effects, he found the style too static and ponderous: it "administers an overdose of architecture to the human form," he wrote in 1918. Its "neglect of the colour element" denies it both the dynamism and the emotional impact of color. If Cubism began as a "repunctuation of the vitalities" of painting, Cummings noted, it "ends in a cold and frozen grammar[.]"[27] Because he once referred to himself as a "specialist in Cubism," however, some literary critics have accepted his self-designation at face value. But in these years, Cummings bandied stylistic labels with insouciance; and a glance at his early abstractions shows that only one, the *Sound Number 1* (plate 1), adopts a Cubist motif and planar schema.[28] Identifying Cummings's aesthetics with *any* single group is a mistake, because even in college Cummings had formed a lifelong distrust of the group mentality, which he considered merely a "concentrated defense" against critics and (in the case of the Cubists and Imagists) "inclined to petulance, over-aggressiveness, and insistence that they only are the priests of their particular art."[29] Then, as always, his sympathies were with individuals, in this case Picasso and Gleizes. He considered Picasso the "world's greatest living painter" and respected his "elimination of trivial pretty [and] charming (emotions)" from his pictures and his ability to convey *directly* "sensations of Weight, Solidity, Depth (hugeness[).]" Cummings's poetic tribute, "picasso," enacts these qualities and concludes with the highest compliment, "you hew form truly."[30]

Cummings's admiration for Gleizes developed simply from his access to the latter's art and criticism. Besides coauthoring one of the first analytical books on Cubism, Gleizes was prominently mentioned in A. J. Eddy's *Cubists and Post-Impressionism*. Indeed, his *Man on a Balcony* (reproduced in Eddy) may well have inspired the facial faceting of Cummings's *Scofield Thayer* (fig. 33). Gleizes' presence in New York from 1916 to 1920 made his recent abstractions of large, colorful planes set at dynamic angles easily available to Cummings and may have informed similar features in Cummings's work. Cummings finally met Gleizes in 1919 and basked in the latter's praise of his *Noise* and *Sound* entries at the 1919 Independents. For his part, Cummings considered Gleizes in 1919 "probably the most individual though somewhat cold, abstract painter in America."[31]

The appealing dynamism of Gleizes' later works suggests another major influence on Cummings: Futurism. Its "worship of speed," as Cummings put it, appealed to his own love of motion and provided a necessary antidote to Cubism's "cold and frozen grammar." While Cummings's debt to Futurist aesthetics is considered in chapter 5, his relation to two painters inspired by Futurism, Joseph Stella and John Marin, should be noted.

Cummings had ample opportunities in the teens to study Stella's first great work, *Battle of Lights, Coney Island* (1913-14). Its tumult of lights and tracks, rides and people, perhaps inspired Cummings to go to Coney Island in 1918 to capture "colour and motion."[32] Certainly, the tangle of serpentine and jagged lines and elliptical curves in *Battle* anticipates those in Cummings's *Noise Number 5* (fig. 16), painted only a few months after Cummings met Stella in 1919. Similarly, the thrusting diagonal tubes and circular forms in many of Stella's works of the late teens (e.g., *The Gas Tank*) prefigure a similar emphasis on diagonals and spirals in Cummings's *Noise Number 13* (plate 5).

John Marin's influences is more amorphous. Although Cummings does not mention Marin in his writings until 1925, his lavish praise then (America's "greatest living painter")[33] suggests an earlier acquaintance. The two artists shared several interests. They both loved the motifs of the Brooklyn Bridge and, especially, of the Woolworth Building. Indeed, Cummings's kinetic descriptions of the building in his 1918 poem and 1925 essay ("Anyone who has stood just across the street from the Woolworth Building and watched it wriggle upward like a skyrocket") seem a verbal accompaniment to Marin's quivering watercolors and etchings of the same motif.[34] Similarly, Marin's writhing and caving skyscrapers in *Movement, Fifth Avenue* anticipate the tilting pieces of cityscape in Cummings's *New York, 1927* (fig. 23). Finally, both artists recognized the necessity of subjective emotion in their work: Marin in his widely read catalog statement of 1913,[35] Cummings in his "conversion" to a more emotive style of painting at the very time, 1926-27, when he praised Marin's work and painted *New York, 1927*.

A paradoxical split between Cummings's life and art can be seen in the contrasting influences of Gaston Lachaise and the German Expressionists. Lachaise was a revered friend and artistic father figure to Cummings. The young painter's letters home in the late teens describe at length visits to Lachaise's studio, his work in progress, his visits to Cummings's studio and opinions of Cummings's work—all expressing the highest respect for Lachaise's talent and artistic probity.[36] Yet, except for some drawings of women (e.g., figs. 45, 48) with proportions akin to Lachaise's *Standing Woman*, Cum-

Fig. 14.
street, c. 1926–30, oil on cardboard, 17 × 8 in. From *CIOPW.* Copyright 1931, 1959 by E. E. Cummings.

mings's work shows little evidence of the sculptor's stylistic influence. Perhaps the very intimacy of their friendship, as well as the difference of their media, precluded a more technical influence from developing. Even Cummings's long article on Lachaise for the *Dial* in February 1920 generally avoids direct analysis or criticism and addresses instead qualities of the sculptor that express Cummings's own philosophical aesthetics of spontaneity, childlike naïveté, and "intuitional" intelligence.

Conversely, the Expressionist painters receive almost no mention in Cummings's notes and essays; yet many of his works, early and late, show Expressionistic motifs and techniques. *Street* (fig. 14), for example, recalls Munch's *The Cry* in the street's severe foreshortening and eerie desertedness. And the garish, undated *Figure sketch* (fig. 15) resembles a prewar Kirchner (e.g., *Potsdam Square*) in its shocking red and green juxtapositions, in the woman's long-necked angularity and detached stare, and in her oddly outlined eye and breast. While Expressionistic works and reproductions were certainly available to Cummings, it is possible that his later aesthetics of subjective feeling and expressive exaggeration simply coincided with, rather than assimilated, Expressionism.

Finally, Dadaist influence on Cummings's aesthetics has recently been asserted by Dikran Tashjian, though with inaccurate evidence and questionable logic.[37] It is possible, though, that Cummings briefly flirted with Dadaist aesthetics, both in his "machinerish" drawings (figs. 4, 5), reminiscent of the Mechanomorphism of Duchamp and Picabia in the midteens, and in such non-sequitur poems as "Will i ever forget that precarious moment?"[38] But as Tashjian concedes, Cummings did not practice artistic destruction for its own sake, as the Dadaists had.[39] Rather, his violations of tradition presume a constructive end: to fashion new patterns from the rubble of old ones.

Form this plethora of influences, it is apparent that Cummings's early painting and aesthetics were not beholden to any one style exclusively. As Cézanne lent numerous ideas about color and form (extrapolated in the planar structures of the Cubists and the colors of the Synchromists), the Futurists, Stella and Marin offered examples of dynamism. But the whole here equals more than the sum of its parts, and Cummings's early painting is no mere "pastiche of Modernist derivation," as Hilton Kramer unfairly dismissed it.[40] For while it absorbed all of these influences, it retains its own individuality in the way that it transforms them, through Cummings's sensibility, into a unique whole: "me times water times paper times de jaune." His paintings cannot be mistaken for someone else's.

Certainly, the *Sounds* and *Noises* were not considered "derivative" when they first appeared. Indeed, their meteoric flash through the avant-garde world of postwar New York suggests just the opposite: that they impressed contemporaneous viewers with their distinctiveness and originality. The first of the series, *Sound* [Number 1] (plate 1) and *Noise* [Number 1] (plate 2), appeared publicly in March 1919 at the exhibition of the Society of Independent Artists, a huge yearly event that was, like its French prototype, open to all comers.

Amidst a sea of representational painting, Cummings's "spinning jerking and generally petulant chromatic planes" (as he described them) created an immediate stir.[41] One of the journalists covering the exhibition singled out his abstractions—from the many hundreds of works on display—for special praise: "the brilliant sally in color by Mr. Cummings will greatly impress those who have arrived at an appreciation of the abstract in art."[42] His friends were impressed with both the painting and its public reception. Lachaise was already an admirer; now Mrs. Lachaise praised his works and asked Cummings: "How does it feel to be the sensation of the Independent? That's what everyone is telling me." The best compliment, however, came from a painter of sterling Modernist credentials, Albert Gleizes. Eagerly, Cummings relayed the response to his parents.

> You may be glad to know that Gleizes (the "first cubist"—probably the most individual, though somewhat cold, abstract painter in America, and—after Picasso—best known among painters of a type—was (to use Lachaise's phrase) "*TAKEN OUT OF HIS FEET*" by the two things of mine at the Independent. According to Nagel, he said later on that they were the "best things in oil" that he had seen "in America." Mr. [Walter] Pach, the director [of the Independents], was (as you may imagine) highly pleased; and said very pleasant things à propos when Nagel and I came to take away our things. . . . Since, I have been asked to exhibit, free of charge, at a small pseudo-gallery [the Penguin Gallery] in Washington Square.[43]

It was an auspicious beginning, and, buoyed by this praise, Cummings must have redoubled his efforts; for by the following year the numerical sequence of his abstractions shown at the 1920 Inde-

Fig. 15.
Figure sketch, c. 1920s, tempera on cardboard, 17 × 8 in. Copyright 1982, The E. E. Cummings Trust.

Fig. 16.
Noise Number 5, 1919–20, oil on canvas, 40½ × 40½ in. Courtesy of SUNY College at Brockport Foundation. Photograph by Earl Kage, Museographics.

pendents had reached five: *Noise Number 5* and *Sound Number 5.* Although he had labored long over the *Noise* (fig. 16)—perhaps too long—Cummings jokingly dismissed it in letters home as "Chop Suey" and "more like a seethe of indigestion than anything thinkable."[44] He was right. It is the least typical—and weakest—of the series, shapeless in structure, muddily colored, and smothered in swirling lines. Its companion piece, *Sound Number 5* (plate 3), on the other hand, is a solid work, balancing planar abstraction against its figurative origins, warm against cool colors, and rounded against angular planes.

The response to these works at the 1920 Independents must have surpassed Cummings's most hopeful daydreams: reviewers from four newspapers mentioned his work. One called the paintings "a striking bit of post-impressionism."[45] Another recommended that Cummings's work be included in future exhibitions of abstract art.[46]

The most detailed—and, for its time, remarkably open-minded—review appeared in the *Evening Post*.

> E. E. Cummings entitles one of these [abstractions] "Noise Number 5" and the other "Sound Number 5." Of the two, we preferred the noise; both of them are interesting. Of course, these irregular patterns of sharp positive color are banners of a small army of theorists, and the theories will either entrance you or set your teeth on edge, according to the bias of your theories. But if the paintings can be looked at with the eye, if they can be seen as frankly as one sees the pattern of a roll of linoleum, they are bound to be admired.[47]

As his letters home reveal, Cummings delighted in being recognized, especially when he could ruffle some feathers. In fact, his desire to shock derived from the same impulse as his determination to innovate: a gleeful rebellion against established authority—the father figure—whether it was representational painting ("I hope to scare a few people out of their wits[?]—at any rate!"), conventional poetry ("It is a supreme pleasure to have done something FIRST"), bourgeois taste (with the new *Dial*, "We are due to wake up some (Stoopid) nth power people,croyez moi!"), American capitalism (he continually tweaked his father about Bolshevist successes in the 1919 civil war), or finally the father himself (in the son's repudiation of a "respectable" career and middle-class propriety).[48] Mischievous, even adolescent, as the personal motive may have been, however, doing something "FIRST" took work, and Cummings addressed himself to his avant-garde labors with professional seriousness.

By February 1921, Cummings had produced at least fifteen major abstractions, for his entry at the Independents that year was entitled *Noise Number 10*. This work, too, received critical notice, albeit a cool one: apparently the *Evening Post* reviewer had grown tired of the "linoleum school."[49] Still, to be recognized at all in these exhibitions of several hundred paintings was a minor feat for a new artist, and Cummings was mentioned each year he exhibited. More impressive, still, was the high opinion of such recognized Modernists and discerning critics as Gleizes, Pach, and Lachaise. If these artists could look at Cummings's work professionally and like what they saw, then Cummings was indeed on the verge of widespread recognition. Developed further and exhibited prominently, his *Sounds* and *Noises* promised to establish him in the forefront of American Modernism.

Fig. 17.
Saxophone player, c. 1921-23, pencil drawing. The E. E. Cummings papers, the Houghton Library, Harvard University. By permission of the Houghton Library. Copyright 1982, The E. E. Cummings Trust.

But the promise was never realized. Shortly after he finished *Noise Number 10* in 1921, Cummings sailed for Europe and settled in Paris for the next few years. During this time, though he produced india ink drawings, watercolors, and small oils (e.g., *Open window*, fig. 13), he appears to have painted very few *Sounds* and *Noises*. (His next reference to one, *Noise Number 12*, comes in March 1924, after he returned to America.) And while his friends in America submitted his watercolors to at least one exhibition in his absence, Cummings's major abstractions were not shown in these years.

The three-year hiatus in the series is curious. Perhaps not having the ready showcase of the Independents dampened Cummings's enthusiasm for producing these large oils. Then, too, for someone living on a tight budget, large canvases were expensive and difficult to ship abroad. But a more significant reason for the dearth appears in his letters home referring to the hundreds of drawings he was then producing. And, in fact, the Houghton Library's collection of Cummings's drawings contains several score from the Paris years.[50] Many extrapolate from Cubism and Mechanomorphism (e.g., figs. 17, 18) or explore ways of infusing dynamism into planar structures (fig. 19). Here and there, figurative sketches appear in these years—shaded drawings, often labored and pedestrian, such as one of his sister, Elizabeth (fig. 20), and sometimes a pointedly succinct line drawing (fig. 21)—showing that Cummings also kept his perceptual and manual skills limber. The bulk of the Paris drawings, however, appear to be abstract studies, stylistic exercises and experiments, that correspond to the extensive notes Cummings made then while thinking through his aesthetics. Perhaps after the continuous outpouring of abstract oils from 1918 to 1921, Cummings now felt the need to take stock, to return to "school" on the linear and structural elements of his art. Moreover, in Paris he had easy access to the work of his favorites: Cézanne, Picasso, Duchamp, and Brancusi. The sketch pad was a convenient place to work out compositional ideas gleaned from Bernheim-Jeune and the Luxembourg.

But as he rethought the aesthetics of his painting in a room in Paris, Cummings's literary reputation in America suddenly blossomed with the publication of *The Enormous Room* in 1922 and *Tulips and Chimneys* in 1923. Poems and essays in such highly regarded little magazines as the *Dial* and *Broom* further established Cummings's literary persona as enfant terrible and provocative innovator. As he prepared to return to America in December 1923, Cummings

Fig. 18.
Mechanical figures in planes, c. 1921–23, pencil drawing. The E. E. Cummings papers, the Houghton Library, Harvard University. By permission of the Houghton Library. Copyright 1982, The E. E. Cummings Trust.

Fig. 19.
Curving solids (Eiffel Tower?), c. 1921–23, pencil drawing. The E. E. Cummings papers, the Houghton Library, Harvard University. By permission of the Houghton Library. Copyright 1982, The E. E. Cummings Trust.

Fig. 20.
Elizabeth Cummings, 1920s, pencil drawing. The E. E. Cummings papers, the Houghton Library, Harvard University. By permission of the Houghton Library. Copyright 1982, The E. E. Cummings Trust.

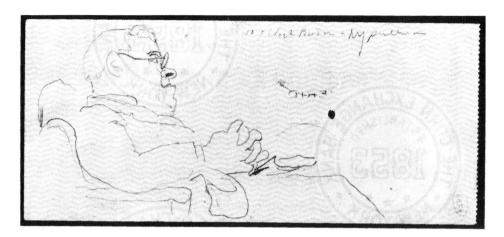

Fig. 21.
10 o'clock Boston–N.Y. Pullman, 23 October 1925, pencil drawing. The E. E. Cummings papers, the Houghton Library, Harvard University. By permission of the Houghton Library. Copyright 1982, The E. E. Cummings Trust.

Fig. 22.
Noise Number 12, 1924, oil on canvas, 50 × 40 in. Photograph: Harry Ransom Humanities Research Center Art Collection, The University of Texas at Austin.

still considered himself "primarily a painter." Without his quite realizing it, though, the literary controversy aroused by his writing (and the dearth of his exhibited painting) had begun to constrict his public identity to "poet and novelist."[51]

Even then, Cummings did little to reverse this increasingly one-sided image, settling for a place in the yearly Independents rather than aggressively pursuing exhibitions of his painting. This diffidence is particularly ironic because his painting had matured, benefiting from his Parisian study. *Noise Number 12* and *Noise Number 13* (fig. 22, plate 5) are markedly superior to the earlier abstractions in their fluency of line, their concentrated force, and their distinctive blend of planar weight and dynamic turbulence. *Noise Number 12*, for example, appears to grow out of a Cubist-influenced drawing (fig. 17) of a black saxophone player. Both works feature a horn as their central motif. The painting, however, develops into a visual metaphor for jazz itself: flowing, twisting, and jaggedly syncopated rhythmic lines, silhouetted hints of faces and hands making music, toes tapping,[52] and in the telescoping figure filling the lower-right quadrant an image of a biracial figure (one light arm, one dark one)—or a gramophone horn—springing forth to sing its soul.

Once again, Cummings's entry to the Independents made the papers, this time taking the story's lead: "One of the hundreds of paintings now being hung . . . in preparation for the opening of the eighth annual exhibition of the Society of Independent Artists . . . is described by its artist, E. E. Cummings, better known as a poet and novelist, as "Noise No. 12". . . . none of [the other "noisy" works] are as carefully and correctly named as the work of Mr. Cummings."[53] But now, the review darkly foreshadowed the context of all future reviews: "better known as a poet and novelist." The appearance of three new volumes of poetry in 1925–26 (&, *XLI Poems*, and *is 5*) virtually cemented Cummings's public identity as poet. By contrast, his entry at the 1925 Independents, the superb *Noise Number 13* (later to become his best-known abstraction), was virtually ignored by the critics. The "twin" spheres of his art no longer shone equally: as his poetry grew ever brighter in the eyes of his public, his painting quietly faded into the penumbra of the poetry.

Why did Cummings not work harder in the midtwenties to give his painting the same public recognition that his early poetry received? Personal reasons were partly responsible. A painful and protracted divorce from his first wife, Elaine Orr, in 1924–25, and his father's sudden death in 1926, left Cummings dispirited, less sure of himself in these years—hardly disposed to promote his painting in public. But aesthetic reasons were probably the dominant factor. By 1926, Cummings was no longer satisfied with Modernist aesthetics of geometric abstraction and emotional objectivity. To search for exhibitions at this period of aesthetic uncertainty must have seemed unwise—and trivial amid a greater search for the aesthetics and styles that would redefine his identity as a painter.

The Retiring Subjectivist: 1927–62

On 4 October 1926, Cummings wrote to his mother: "Hope soon to resume Painting but in a new direction." A few days later, apparently responding to her question, he added: "I don't know myself what 'painting in a new direction' means—since it hasn't yet begun. But it must mean something new!"

The "new direction" soon took shape in *New York, 1927* (fig. 23), a large oil that superimposes a naturalistic nude over a Marinesque background of tilting buildings, smokestacks, and organic shapes. A similar merger of concrete and abstract appears in another twenties oil, *Nude on a precipice* (fig. 24), in which the abstract, organic shapes at left humorously imitate the nude's curves and angles. But the nude is clumsily rendered, and the two modes coexist uneasily. Clearly, Cummings was searching for a new way of reconciling

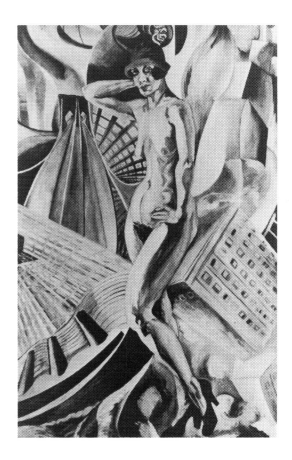

Fig. 23.
New York, 1927, 1926–27, oil on canvas, 67 × 42 in. From *CIOPW*. Copyright 1931, 1959 by E. E. Cummings.

Fig. 25.
Sky over Paris, c. 1932, oil on canvas,
28 × 32 in. Courtesy of SUNY College
at Brockport Foundation.

Fig. 24.
Nude on a precipice, mid-1920s, oil on
cardboard, 21½ × 17½ in. Courtesy of
SUNY College at Brockport Foundation.

abstraction and representation; but finding the right mixture was difficult. *Sky over Paris* (fig. 25), probably dating from the early thirties, offers a quite different fusion: naturalistic representation and
expressionism. Over a carefully detailed view of Parisian rooftops
swirls an El Grecoesque sky in turbulent yellows and mauves.

The course of Cummings's "new direction" was indeed uncertain and produced, as the later painting reveals, not one route but
several. Yet the aesthetic philosophy underlying it was remarkably
unified. To understand it, we must first consider what drove Cummings from Modernist abstraction. First, Modernist aesthetics was
not of his own devising, although he had appropriated it in unique
ways. Its derivativeness was increasingly incompatible with Cummings's need for uniqueness, for a distinctly personal approach to
painting. If in 1922 Cézanne's palette governed his self-expression,
by the 1940s his goal was "to get my own colours (i.e. expressive spiritually to me alone) my own palette; instead of merely swallowing another's (e.g. Cézanne's)—which he made for purely personal (e.g.

sculptural) purpose. Also, instead of borrowing direct from the tubes, to invent" (Houghton notes, I[55]5[82]).

Equally important, Cummings sensed a rift between Modernist aesthetics of objectivity, calculation, and detachment, and his personal and philosophical values of subjective feeling, spontaneity, and self-expression—values informing such lines as: "let's live suddenly without thinking." In charting his "new direction," Cummings wanted to align his painting to his philosophy of subjectivity. Thus, although it occurred amid a general repudiation of geometric abstraction both at home and abroad in the midtwenties, Cummings's "new direction" evolved from personal needs, followed its own paths, and was guided by the painter's aesthetics of subjectivity.

To see how the new aesthetics worked, consider the problem of dynamism, a quality Cummings valued in all of his art. In his early *Sounds* and *Noises*, he had striven for a "binding rhythm" to connect the parts. Yet, his deliberate technique, in carefully arranging those parts and in applying the paint slowly and evenly, lent no motion to this rhythm, no spontaneity. To convey motion in much of his later painting, Cummings was far more spontaneous, using faster, looser brushwork, rougher textures, and often impastoed strokes. *Sea* (fig. 26) and *portrait—hair* (fig. 34) are good examples of this new style, as are the oils in *CIOPW*.

The spontaneity of this technique captured the immediacy of experience Cummings was after. To convey motion, he would not simply paint a subject *in* motion, but *create* motion by making "the paint fly"[54]—an idea that anticipates the action painting of Abstract Expressionism. Spontaneity also permitted Cummings maximum self-expression. In a note dated 1 April 1940, he summarizes the change.

long ago i found out that my forte (as a painter) was

slapstick	vs.	miniature
"hardi"	vs.	painstaking
violence	vs.	measurement
SELFexpression	vs.	capturing (an *Im*pression of) the object
verb	vs.	noun

i guess i owe this discovery to Delacroix's inveighing
against Detail ('painting is the art of omitting['])

(Houghton notes, I[55] no. 87)

Fig. 26.
sea, 1944, oil on canvasboard, 12 × 16 in. Courtesy of SUNY College at Brockport Foundation.

A few months later, still musing on his style, he writes:

July 27 '40
   apparently I've found my style in painting
   —it's NOT
         painstakingly washed flat surfaces sans
            brushstrokes
         fine camel's hair delineation[?]-by-outline
         building up a careful sum out of parts
it's chunking ahead with a big brush held loosely
& loaded with paint.
Out of the crisscrossings, ''mistakes'', etc.
a picture Builds itself—chiefly INWARD, thru GREYS
                          (Houghton notes, I[55] no. 55)

"Chunking ahead" with impastoed brushwork produced an intentionally loose structure; grays, moreover, muddied Cummings's palette. Painted with anything less than absolute confidence, such a style can seem shapeless, muddled, and self-indulgent—and, in fact, a sizable number of Cummings's canvases in this style are just that. But when the intensity of Cummings's emotion toward his subject infused this expressionistic looseness, the result could be "violent" indeed, as *Posed woman: eyes half-closed* (plate 7) demonstrates.

The "spontaneous" style also generated the many fine water-colors Cummings painted of Mount Chocorua, e.g., *Landscape with stormy sky* (plate 10). Watercolor, in fact, was probably Cummings's most successful medium in the later period, for it encourages just those qualities Cummings now sought: speed, spontaneity, and self-expression conveyed directly through color and brushstroke. In its blending and overlapping of transparent colors, moreover, watercolor allowed Cummings subjective latitude, particularly in conveying the varied and rapidly changing hues of the sunsets over Mount Chocorua.

The changes in Cummings's later painting surpass style alone, however. In a sense, they reflect changes in his philosophy that go above and below the visible world: "below," because of his profound interest in Freud and psychoanalytic theory; "above" because of his growing need to transcend the material world for the spiritual. As psychoanalysis encouraged him to look deeper into himself, an emerging concern with spiritual values beckoned him to look beyond: "a release for me (in painting) via The Dream? this would free me from representative colors—which, in turn, I feel, would free me from literal forms."

> problem
> to create (*not* represent) an incident—via paint
> (NOT PICTORIAL REPRESENTATION)
> hue . . . . will take me out of the jail of anatomy
> into lyricism . . . into actuality (Spirit—the beautiful)
> (Houghton notes, I[55] nos. 86, 108, 70)

This search for new realms of expression was part of what soured Cummings on geometrical abstraction: "it leads nowhere," he explained to Charles Norman.[55]

The "underside" of Cummings's subjectivism—his interest in dreams and psychoanalysis—may have inspired the fantastic landscapes and murky moonscapes of the late period. In *Man worshipping moon* (fig. 27), for example, the brooding colors combine with impastoed brushwork to produce a disturbing, nocturnal vision.

Fig. 27.
Man worshipping moon, n.d., oil on board, 15 × 8 in. Courtesy of SUNY College at Brockport Foundation.

These late moonscapes (some no more than a sliver of white on a dark ground), are indeed dreamy and tie Cummings loosely to Surrealism. But where the representational Surrealists were more literal in dredging the unconscious for Freudian imagery (Dali) or for double entendre (Magritte), Cummings's canvases remain "dreamy" without being dream depictions, subjective without really probing the unconscious. As self-expressions, they reflect—but seldom transcend—the artist's mood vis-à-vis his subject. Thus, while they eschew Surrealist didacticism, they are prone to the flaccid sentimentality of an artist who cannot get beyond his own emotions.

In one major style of the later painting, however, Cummings *did* transcend the solipsism of subjectivity. When he put aside the palette knife and the big brush and lightened his colors, he could turn out such finely detailed, naturalistic renderings as *Portrait of the artist's mother* (fig. 28), *Flowers and hat: Patchen Place* (plate 12), and the *View from Joy Farm* (plate 8). Carefully planned and precisely painted, these canvases seem to belie Cummings's aesthetics of subjectivity and spontaneity. More paradoxical, still, is how successful these naturalistic pieces are. And the success came not by accident. In the early thirties, for example, Cummings took a leaf from Da Vinci and Michelangelo and undertook an exhaustive study of human anatomy, covering hundreds of pages with drawings of musculature and bone structure—practice that shows in the fine contouring of Rebecca Cummings's face.

Yet, for all their apparent objectivity, these naturalistic canvases emerged from the deeply subjective sensibility that Cummings brought to all of his late work and especially to his paintings of nature. As Loren MacIver has aptly written, he does not just paint nature, he celebrates it: "his works revere."[56] The *Self-portrait with sketchpad* of 1939 (fig. 29) conveys this reverence, mingled with sensuality, with such immediacy as to be a kind of spiritual credo. The bare background tree curves and twists like a female torso (nature was always a "she" to Cummings) and lifts one protective arm to shelter—and caress—the artist.

The painter, himself, did not identify his late work with representational art, but rather, at right angles to both pure naturalism and pure abstraction: "Were I a critic, should probably add that 'academic' (i.e.un-) art resembles every good coin, which it isn't, in having two sides. One side can be called 'photographic realism' or even 'naturalism'; the other, 'nonrepresentational' or 'abstract' sic 'paint-

Fig. 28.
Portrait of the artist's mother, 1942, oil on canvas, 13 × 16 in. Copyright 1982, The E. E. Cummings Trust.

ing.' And your stupid wiseguy doing his worst to deny Nature equals your clever fool who did his best to possess Her."[57] Thus, to describe Cummings's late painting merely as a change from abstract to representational oversimplifies its complexities and overlooks its subjective aesthetics and expressionistic features.[58]

What *did* change markedly between the two periods was Cummings's regard for nature. Where the *Sound* and *Noise* abstractions repress or conceal the material subjects that inspired them, the later works confront and present nature directly, bouncing off of it, so to speak, to express something deeper. In one sense, nature's function has not changed: it is still a means, not an end. Where once it was a buried spur to "organizations of colour and line," now it is a visible means to self-expression at once subjective and spiritual.

Expressionism, quasi-Surrealism, Naturalistic representation —Cummings's later painting embraced all of these divergent styles, shifting restlessly among them without ever finally settling on one. Indeed, how could such intangible aesthetic goals as "self-expression" and "actuality" dictate any one style? Stylistic freedom, moreover, may have been precisely what Cummings wanted: Guided only by his subjective response to a motif, he was free to paint as his mood of the moment demanded. Such freedom comes at a price, however. Working in several styles, Cummings did not truly develop through one, nor did he make one recognizably *his* style.

Perhaps this refusal—or inability—to settle on a single style accounts for the critics' coolness to the later period fully as much as do Cummings's lapses into sentimentality and his iconoclastic divergence from the dominant styles of the day. For unlike his poetry, the late paintings offered no easily recognizable features by which critics could "place" him. Inevitably, perhaps, they concluded that poetry was Cummings's vocation, painting his avocation. McBride's remark in 1949 about "the paintings he does in his off moments" typified this attitude.[59] Nearly twenty years later, Hilton Kramer continued the myth, noting that "the small public that was aware of his paintings . . . regarded them as an interesting but unimportant product of the poet's leisure" and that Cummings's work "was only rarely exhibited in his lifetime."[60] In fact, Cummings exhibited his painting at least thirty times during his life (see Appendix).

The misconception of Cummings's seriousness—growing stronger with each repetition—disfigured critical judgment of his painting. Critics were puzzled, for example, by the apparent disparity

Fig. 29.
Self-portrait with sketchpad, 1939, oil on canvas, 43 × 31½ in. Harry Ransom Humanities Research Center Art Collection, The University of Texas at Austin.

between his "abstract" poems and his "representational" paintings. (They need not have been so confused had they compared the romantic themes of both arts: transcendent subjectivity in nature and love.) Nevertheless, in reviewing Cummings's 1934 exhibition, Henry McBride grumbled: "You could never imagine [the paintings] to be by the author of 'Eimi.' They are thin, uncertain, and separated by some curious wall of inhibition from the medium."[61]

In characteristic rebuttal, Cummings parodied his critics' befuddlement in an imaginary dialogue between artist and critic.

> [Your poetry and painting are] very different.
> Very: one is painting and one is writing.
> But your poems are rather hard to understand, whereas your paintings are so easy.
> Easy?
> Of course—you paint flowers and girls and sunsets; things that everybody understands.
> I never met him.
> Who?
> Everybody.

The "interview" concludes with the artist resolving to live in China, "where a painter is a poet."[62]

For his American critics, however, Cummings could apparently *not* be both painter and poet. Generally, they shared the same impressions of his later work, while differing sharply in their approval or disapproval. The paintings were "delicate," "fragile," "charming," "discreet," "refined," sometimes even "mysterious," but technically "inhibited," lacking in "boldness," in "determined purpose," in a sure handling of craft.[63] What one critic of the 1949 exhibition mildly applauded as "a romantic feeling [in the painting] that infuses the early work *Tulips and Chimneys*," a critic of the 1963 retrospective castigated as "devotion to the pretty that sends one back suspiciously to his poetry which favored repetition of "soft" words (such as "flower") more than it should. . . . In the art [this sentiment] is there to see in all its embarrassing earnestness."[64]

Only once did a critic (the mercurial Henry McBride) claim that "E. E. Cummings the painter could have had a career of note independently of E. E. Cummings the writer."[65]

And how did Cummings respond to these stubborn misconceptions about his vocation as painter, to the unflattering comparisons of his painting to his writing? Largely by withdrawing gradually from public exhibitions and by seeking safer havens when he did show. Following several exhibitions in the early thirties (and McBride's demeaning comparison of his painting to *Eimi* in 1934), Cummings did not have another one-man show until 1944. After his 1949 exhibition (and another distorted McBride comment about painting in "his off moments"), Cummings exhibited outside of New York, often in Rochester, home of his close friends and patrons, Sibley and Hildegarde Watson. Like the painter of his autobiographical fable,[66] Cummings was tired of being treated as an interloper from another discipline and simply avoided the painful occasions of this misconception: the New York "uptown" gallery shows that would make his painting seen—and misconstrued. "The gallery lads," he observed peevishly, "are a bunch of punks."[67] In avoiding the galleries, of course, he guaranteed his public obscurity as a painter.

If he no longer cared what the New York critics thought, Cummings still had to satisfy himself, however. And as this 1940 note reveals, his self-criticism could be stringent.

> what i now seek to master is expressing myself
> thru a person in the way(Tao) i 'feel to do' (as
> Lachaise, bless him! would say) through nature
> so far,
>> the presence of a person has resulted in an object.
>> i.e. I get lost (immersed,buried) in Detail.
>> Result—compromise=confusion
> but perhaps i'll win yet! esperons.
>> (Houghton notes, I[55] no. 55)

Whether or not he finally did "win" in mastering his self-expression, Cummings was convinced that the aesthetics he had come to shape in his later period expressed his mature temperament and philosophy as an artist. By these deeply personal standards, he guided his painting for the rest of his life.

Aesthetic Underpinnings: Wholeness and Feeling

2

Whereas the mind's function is to take apart, to distinguish between, to separate, break up, analyze, poets work and play as whole human beings.

—E. E. Cummings, Houghton notes

Wholeness

▬▬▬Of the many thousands of pages of notes on the arts that E. E. Cummings wrote, the one that best seems to embody his early theories is a tiny scrap (fig. 30) buried in a folder dated 1921–23.[1] On part of it, Cummings typed:

	(pure form) is natural to everybody in a dream state. [. . .]
	Meaning=a poise, 2 factors are the Heard or Seen word (eg Bad) & the
	Unseen Unheard(Good) ie, language based on ANTI-THESES (good-bad) on
	Syntax (position) & on Grammar[.]
THE	Nonsense, eg "a good, bad men" : the awake =
PUN	Form (seeing all of a vase, the Behind) : the dream.
	development of language. . killing of Homogeneity
	(buffalo drawing is writing, "-alo"=the tail)
when	the Need for art is when(because) original Homogeneous
Drawing	(both sides of vase at once) lost, in the awake. Hence
was	great artists of all ages have felt urge to make the vase
language	appear as if we experienced the Behind,ie Form; or a Presence.

(Houghton notes, I[25] no. 136)

In a kind of conceptual shorthand, this note condenses aesthetic theories Cummings was then working out, theories of homogeneity, verbal and visual language, perception and three-dimensional form, feeling and thinking, and consciousness and the unconscious. A good place to begin is with Cummings's view of language and homogeneity.

"When drawing was language," i.e., when language was ideographic, the picture symbol was closer to its referent than the later alphabetical symbol was to its referent. Because it is a picture, the ideogram has physical presence and aesthetic worth. It appeals to the eye: Seeing it, one simultaneously *envisions* its referent. The alphabetical symbol that supplanted it is not pictorial and appeals only to the mind. It thus requires a mental translation from symbol to referent; and in the gap caused by this conversion, the close proximity that once existed between symbol and referent—their homogeneity—is lost. Modern language, instead of visually being something itself, only refers to something else.

In another note, probably written before 1923,[2] Cummings expanded this idea. He copied and footnoted a passage from A. A. Brill's *Psychoanalysis* that traces the transition from pictorial to alphabetical language.

> With the advance of civilization the alphabetic symbols lost their original meaning and became consonants and vowels. Symbols, therefore, represent a lower form of thinking[a] for they identify objects which have only a very remote analogy. Children and primitive races still make use of this form of expression. Thus a child calls a stick a horse simply because it can ride on it.[b] The analogy between[c] the stick and horse is very remote indeed. As the child grows older and becomes able to discriminate and compare[d] it no longer forms such vague analogies[e].[3]

Cummings disagreed wholeheartedly with Brill's explanation and tore it apart in his footnotes on the same sheet (lettered and edited here).

a. they *did not represent* anything, they *meant.*

b. a child *feels* what it is taught to call "horse" i.e. "horse" = verb. horse *means* (is felt by child to Be) the verb, to ride, a degree of IS, or motion. The child declines[?] the noun, or stick, in favor of the verb. [. . .]

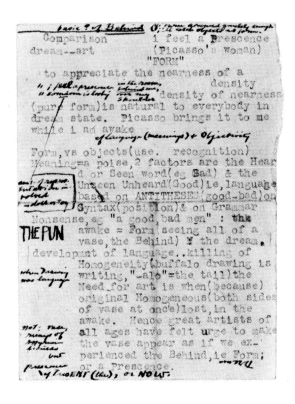

Fig. 30.
Note on form, c. 1921-23. The E. E. Cummings papers, the Houghton Library, Harvard University. By permission of the Houghton Library. Copyright 1982, The E. E. Cummings Trust.

c. analogy = the between (neither a nor b but an interval betw.) The child feels ab as a chord, an entirety—this = what IS. the discrete a AND b come later (thought)

d. substitution (thinking discriminates) for feeling (unites, integrates) [. . . .]

e. no. it makes similes. a (is) LIKE b . . . contrast the stickhorse IS. (not a stick being like a horse.—a stick is not like a horse in any way —i.e. no analogy BETWEEN, analogy between being the LIKE. That is, Stick-Horse(=IS) is purely tactile; Or, if you put *Like* between (making 2 nouns in place of 1 IS) you have absurdity.

(Houghton notes, I[59] no. 70)

The stick-horse is not an "analogy" because the child *feels* stick and horse as *one*; its fusion equals a metaphor ("IS") not a simile ("Like"), one moving verb, not two static nouns. If modern language has lost these felt homogenous fusions by becoming cerebral, then it was up to modern art—poetry, in this case—to restore them. As Barry Marks observes: "Cummings was interested in the wholeness of language and in the full range of its possibilities rather than in its limited, conceptual nature. And this interest produced . . . his attention not only to words and sentences but also to parts of words. . . . He searched the smallest details of language in all its dimensions in his effort to extend the ways in which language could be used to communicate."[4]

But as the two notes suggest, the "killing of homogeneity" sweeps far beyond language and suggests splits between feeling and thinking, dreaming and waking, "pure" form and facade, and subject and object. These dichotomies receive careful analysis in subsequent chapters, but it is useful to summarize here their relation to the problem of wholeness.

In Cummings's footnotes to Brill, "thinking" and "feeling" are at odds, a conflict Cummings proclaimed throughout his life. Thinking analyzes and "discriminates"; it "analogizes," "represents," "substitutes" one thing for another; in sum, it separates "a" from "b" and thus destroys the homogeneity of "ab." Feeling restores that wholeness; it "unites" and "integrates": the child "*feels* ab as a chord." The thinking-feeling dichotomy is thus really twofold: between thinking and feeling, and between the divided results of thinking (a *and* b). It is no accident, then, that those groups who, Brill implies, feel first and think later, the "children and primitive races," are the very ones with whom Cummings most identified himself and the artist. For they are capable of a "homogeneous vision," of a sense of time and space closer to that of the modern artist than to that of the "civilized," thinking adult.[5] In his first published essay, "Gaston Lachaise," Cummings developed his sense of the "child's vision" in order to distinguish the genuine naïveté of Lachaise from such "would-be primitives" as William Zorach:

> the inexcusable and spontaneous scribblings which children make on sidewalks, walls, anywhere . . . . cannot be grasped until we have accomplished the thorough destruction of the world. By this destruction alone we cease to be spectators of a ludicrous and ineffectual striving and, involving ourselves in a new and fundamental kinesis, become protagonists of the child's vision.
>
> To analyze child art in a sentence is to say that houses, trees, smoke, people, etc., are depicted not as nouns but as verbs. The more genuine child art is, the more it is . . . purely depictive. . . . [But] a child['s art] most distinctly is not [secondhand]. Consequently to appreciate child art we are compelled to undress one by one the soggy nouns whose agglomeration constitutes the mechanism of Normality, and finally to liberate the actual crisp organic squirm—the IS.[6]

For Cummings, the "world" that must be destroyed is the civilized world of analytical thinking that keeps us spectators, *outside* the child's art. Once we stop thinking and begin feeling, however, we begin "involving ourselves" and "become protagonists of" the homogeneous kinesis that constitutes the child's vision. Feeling thus leads to two kinds of wholeness: an involvement in the art—a union of subject and object—and a sense of wholeness in the art itself.

Cummings's interest in children as exemplars of wholeness, of course, comes straight out of a Rousseauian romantic primitivism that celebrated the seemingly less complicated worlds of children and "primitive" cultures. Lacking the ornament of overly sophisticated Western art, the art of these "simpler" cultures was thought to convey aesthetic emotion in its clearest, most powerful form. As Cummings defined it in a college paper, "the essential act of 'primitivism' is *elimination*."[7] This simplification, in turn, enabled "primitive" art to convey emotion with such immediacy as to erase all "psychic distance" between artist and subject, to "absorb the spectator, or be absorbed by him in a direct and undifferentiated fashion."[8] Such a union of subject and object appealed to Cummings's aesthetics of wholeness. But at the same time, his sympathy with children—indeed his very subjectivism—was a deeply personal one, emerging perhaps as a reaction to an overbearing father whose breadth of intellect Cummings perceived as intimidating and stifling. Thus, one of Cummings's lifelong personas was "little Estlin," the helpless child whom others must protect and care for.[9] And his poems, early and late, often speak in a child's voice, or portray a childlike wonder at nature.

Significantly, analytical thinking is common to one's waking hours, while the fusions accomplished by feeling (if not feeling itself) dominate one's dreaming. In dreams, elements are free to transcend the linear space and sequential time of daytime logic. Thus, as Cummings's note suggests, what seems nonsensical to the waking mind, "a good bad men," becomes entirely possible in dreams. Such a yoking of opposites is necessary to capture the wholeness of "pure form" and complete meaning, to "see around" an object or a word. A word, for example, might really possess two "sides": a front, or conventional meaning that one sees and hears (e.g., "Bad"), and a back, or antithesis, unseen and unheard (e.g., "Good"). The front may leave a semantic trace of the back on the mind, just as the color red leaves a fleeting afterimage of its complement, green, on the retina. Placed side by side, red and green intensify each other; would "complementary" adjectives ("good bad") do likewise? Would their juxtaposition form a meaning more potent than that of either alone?

The possibilities must have intrigued Cummings, for he developed them into techniques in both his poetry and his painting. In so doing, he sought to unite two entirely different mental states: to bring the murky fusions of the dream world into the harsh sunlight of "the Awake," and to reconcile the "illimitable" unconscious with that "stumbling and thwarted emanation—a silly strutting and dancing upon a tiny platform called 'life,'" the "Conscious."[10] Such a psychic union would, in turn, permit two mergers important to Cummings's art: (1) perceptual wholeness, in which all visible elements in a painting or poem are sufficiently strong to unify the surface and keep the viewer's eye in motion, and (2) formal wholeness, in which the seen front and unseen (but felt) back of an object fused in the viewer's consciousness.

In addition, Cummings pondered a third union, the creative, in which the artist or viewer hurdles the psychic distance separating her from the art work and becomes one with it. In one note, for example, he punningly identified two stages of perception: the eye (or instrument of perception) and the "I" (or consciousness of that perception). Then, as if retreating from his own analysis, he added:

NOTE that here, we have separated 'eye' and 'I' (vs. eye&i) in order to make this comparison, we have divided—analyzed a whole, integer, homogeneity

IT IS THE FUNCTION OF 'ART' TO RESTORE THIS WHOLENESS *INTEGRALITY*

art says—'I' do not 'see,' WITH my 'eye,' 'objects or Things' my eye does not 'see,' WITH my 'I,' 'objects' or Things' but eye-things (subject) me (verb, reflexive)[.]

(Houghton notes, I[111] [1])

Certainly, an ambiguous, perhaps even whimsical, conclusion—but not impenetrable. "Eye-things" fuses the means of perception (eye) with the object of perception (things) into a new subject. "Me (verb, reflexive)" appears to do the same with consciousness (me) and the act of perceiving, only now consciousness *receives* the action (thus the objective case) and the action is reflexive. The perceiver's consciousness has become the beneficiary of his perception: Rather than his doing something to the object (looking at it), the object, via his perception, is doing something to him (changing his consciousness). Considered this way, subject and object seem to overcome their separateness and seem almost to merge as they continuously interact.

In other notes, Cummings envisioned an ideal aesthetic relationship in which the artist and viewer actually become the work of art—presumably, by imaginatively entering into it so thoroughly as to obscure the boundaries separating subject and object. A fictitious dialogue between an "artist" and "poet" (both obviously personas of Cummings), probably written in 1922, has the artist say: "Let us contemplate a picture. These planes writhe. In becoming these planes that is to say this picture one attains the firm and extraordinary dimensions of Alive[.]"[11]

He reached a similar conclusion in notes entitled "Essay." Here, Cummings distinguishes between the painting of "objective reality" before Cézanne, when form and color were separate considerations for the artist and "could not freely interact," and the painting of "subjective actuality" that Cézanne introduced, when "form [. . .] is actually the expression of color." In the first style, the spectator's sense of form comes from the artist's correlation of forms in the painting to forms in the outside world. In recognizing these forms, that is, in referring them to something external, the viewer can remain intellectually "outside" the painting. In the new style, "the spectator as such ceases to exist. In this case, the spectator creates, that is the spectator becomes an artist."[12]

Although the notes do not explain what "becomes an artist" means, one might surmise that the spectator, viewing the new style, can no longer convert the colors and lines of the painting into familiar forms. She must, instead, accept the *un*familiar, unrecognizable forms *on their own terms* as shaped colors. In so doing, she enters more deeply into the work itself by seeing form and color as the artist would. By imaginatively participating in the work, she has become the artist.

Such mergers of "I" and "it" may have been little more than fanciful speculation. Indeed, Cummings designed techniques in his early work, such as complicating surfaces to retard one's recognition of a single subject or theme, and treating prostitutes as things in his sex poems, that *distance* the viewer from the subject of the art work. But there can be little doubt that his theoretical concern with merging subject and object stems from his deeper preoccupation with aesthetic wholeness; and even his distancing techniques aim at a higher form of aesthetic wholeness: the viewer's felt sense of a work's totality. At the center of his early aesathetics, wholeness both transcends and joins all the separate domains mentioned in Cummings's seminal note: language, emotion, consciousness, perception, and structure. The child *feels* the wholeness of "ab," just as the viewer might sense "the Behind" of an object he cannot see, or the reader the antithesis of a word—fusions natural to unconscious feeling, but foreign to conscious, analytical thinking. The artist's task is to capture such dreamlike integrations of the seen and unseen, the front and back, the subject and object in the "Awake" if he would achieve wholeness.

The relationship of these domains to each other, then, is not static but fluid. Such fluidity, or motion, enables an ideogram simultaneously to mean both itself *and* its referent, a perception to move back and forth between perceiver and object. In the stick-horse example,"horse *means* (is felt by child to Be) the verb, to ride, a degree of IS or motion." Similarly, motion could merge the artist and his art:

"Also eerie is his [El Greco's] Homogeneity—having no moving devices (limbs, wings, fins) he himself *is* MOVING (the Verb). . . wholeness, entirely [. . .] he is FLUID "(Houghton notes, I[55] no. 22). As the condition facilitating these identities and transformations, motion became a major technical goal in both Cummings's poetry and painting.

The relationship between wholeness and the various subjects of the preceding pages might be expressed as the diagram shown here.

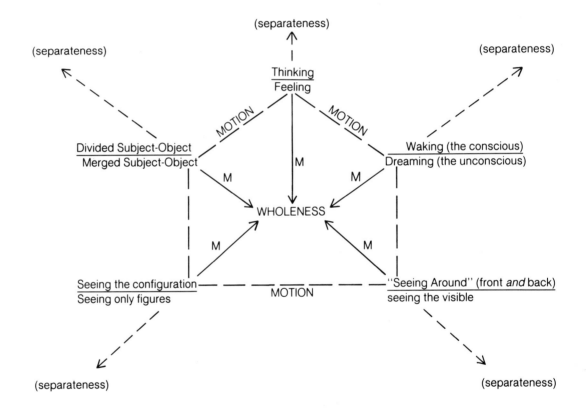

The chapters to follow examine in detail such paths to wholeness as feeling (below), perception (chap. 3), three-dimensional form (chap. 4), motion (chap. 5), and analogues among the arts (chap. 6). But two points should already be apparent about the way Cummings's mind worked. One is that he tended to think dialectically in almost Manichaean oppositions, a habit he changed only slightly in his later years.[13] In each dichotomy, one side is good because it leads to wholeness, the other side bad because it creates separateness. But the latter can hardly be ignored. For thinking, waking, and the tendency to see the object's facade and to stay "outside" the object are natural, everyday conditions, the "givens" an artist begins with. The conditions fostering wholeness are more rarefied; to attain them requires a psychic or imaginative leap. Cummings's techniques aim at effecting that leap, at converting cerebral apprehension of only part of a work into a felt experience of its totality.

Yet, for all his dialectical turn of mind, Cummings made no rigid or categorical distinctions between verbal and pictorial thinking. He could—and did—view words with a painter's eye as well as hear them with a poet's ear. In that charming equation in the seminal note, for example, he could *see* the "alo" of "buffalo" as the buffalo's tail. That Cummings's mind could move so fluidly between the pictorial and verbal, between the temporal and spatial, helps explain his urge to reconcile and equilibrate their differences in his art and makes the painterly qualities of his "poempictures," as he called them, seem an inevitable result.[14]

Feeling

"The artist is not a man who describes but a man who FEELS."
(Houghton notes)

The diagram above shows "feeling" as only one of several paths to wholeness. But its importance to Cummings's aesthetics, art, and lifelong values cannot be overestimated. Indeed, so often did Cummings praise feeling in his notes, essays, poems, and plays, that it might seem at the very center of his aesthetics. Certainly, it is the mental state necessary for wholeness to be realized in all of the other categories of Cummings's aesthetics. Only because it serves as a means to, and facilitator of, the more visionary goal of wholeness, should feeling not be considered the center of Cummings's aesthetics.

For Cummings, "feeling" means both emotion and sensuous perception simultaneously. Sometimes he fuses the two in his notes as "SEE(Feel)"; other notes observe the perceptual root "to see" (*intueri*) in "intuition," a mental action closer to feeling than to thinking.[15] True to form, his own definition of "feeling" is dialectical, opposing feeling to thinking and belief.

Is = the cold 3rd singular of the intransitive verb, to Feel
not to completely feel = Thinking, the participle
incomplete thinking = Belief, the box in which god and all other nouns are kept.

(Houghton notes, I[25] no., 107)

This epigram recurs obsessively in the early notes, in a 1927 article for *Vanity Fair*, ("People who are incapable of thinking only believe"), and still later in *i: Six Nonlectures* (1953).[16] In *The Enormous Room* (1922), Cummings fleshes it out: "There are certain things in which one is unable to believe for the simple reason that he never ceases to feel them. Things of this sort—things which are always inside of us and in fact are us and which consequently will not be pushed off or away where we can begin thinking about them—are no longer things; they, and the us which they are, equals A Verb; an IS."[17]

Note that Cummings equates feeling with verbs, just as he did in his description of children's art. But he realized that the equation was not ideal: "as i use the word Feeling, i am perfectly conscious of its failure which is the failure of a noun, participial at best, to define a phenomenon or verb. it is to this accidental homogeneity to which Feeling refers" (Houghton notes, I[27] no. 3). This awareness did not stop him from making "feeling" synonymous with "IS." In so doing, he linked an affective state of mind to a grammatical part of speech that, in itself, was supremely important to his poetics. For verbs were the pistons that drove Cummings's poetry and created a technique he valued highly: motion. The equation should therefore read: Feeling = IS→Motion. His footnote to Brill above confirms this: "horse means ... the verb, to ride, a degree of IS or motion."

Another significant feature of the "not to completely feel" epigram is that the balance between feeling and thinking leans heavily toward thinking and even more toward belief. Thus, "not to *completely* feel = thinking." Elsewhere, Cummings wrote: "Thinking is the normal state / Feeling the abnormal."[18] Why are thinking and belief so much easier to fall into? Partly because feeling is tenuous: Spontaneous, momentary, and accidental, it can only occur in the present, the "Now." Cummings conveys this tenuousness in a sequence of steps he outlined in seeing a color.

III. for . . . "a simple or pure color sensation" to occur "thinking" [must] abdicate for a fraction of an instant in favor of the sensual enemy or NOW.

IV. the formula for NOW in terms of Then, "I see a color," may be improved as a substitute for NOW. "I have a feeling" is a more precise statement of what happened. Still more precise would be "I Am a feeling."

V. in speaking of this particular kind of NOW, or in terms of Then "color," we may use the phrase "a chromatic Am" with the understanding that Am is the 1st person singular of the intransitive verb To Feel. [. . .]

VII. a chromatic Am conjugates the Human verb [to feel]. For an instant more or less, we are at the mercy of NOW[.]

VIII. [After that instant] Then has again assumed control, reinventing[.]

IX. This noun we go on declining, as if no accident had happened to interrupt.

(Houghton notes, I[27] no. 74)

Feeling's tenuous nowness easily yields to the engulfing thenness of thinking; its spontaneous and accidental nature is no match for thinking's calculation. Yet, for a moment, thinking must be suppressed and feeling prevail for pure perception (seeing the color) to occur. And feeling is not merely a passive condition in which one sees: it actively merges the viewer's consciousness with his perception: "I Am a feeling."

By contrast, thinking dulls one's perception by converting fresh sensations into stale recognition. Before thinking, for example, the eye might see a collection of curves and ovals; roundness and flatness; shadowy voids and gleaming, smooth, hard surfaces; fine, swirling sky-blues and thick, creamy whites. But thinking abstracts these sensations into an "object," then abstracts it again into a recognizable object, e.g., a "vase." For the artist who should be "merely the earth's most acute and wiley observer of everything-under-the sun,"[19] thinking was dangerous—dangerous, especially, in the form of shopworn ideas that separated an artist from his true feelings.

In a letter to his sister from Paris (3 May 1922) brimming with declamatory enthusiasm, Cummings urged her to liberate herself by "putting aside all lackadaisical antique 5th hand notions about 'Beauty' 'Ugliness' 'The Right' 'The Art of Living' 'Education' 'The Best' etcetera ad infin." and continued: "Of this i am sure: nothing 'occurs' to anyone as an *individual*—nothing can possibly enter and be entertained by the mind of anyone except as somebody's *tool . . .* —except:the person or mind in question has FIRST OF ALL, FEAR-LESSLY wiped out,THOROUGHLY AND UNSENTIMENTALLY defecated WHAT HAS BEEN TAUGHT HIM OR HER. In a nutshell; #THE MORE WE KNOW THE LESS WE FEEL!!!!!!!!" Further on, he confided: "For me personally concepts do not exist;but I am going very slowly)by what right do I attempt to *see indirectly*? To, instead of admitting the smell and colour of a swill pail, attempt either to 'enjoy' or 'dislike' it or its multifarious contents?"

This is the language of youthful exuberance, and Cummings knowingly exaggerated: some concepts—Freud's and Cézanne's, for example—not only existed for him, they guided him. But it is also the voice of one who felt that the genteel values of his Cambridge up-bringing and the gentlemanly ideas of his Harvard education were so much cotton batting muffling the sounds and sights and smells of the real world—especially the world of swill pails.

His solution? "NEVER take ANYONE'S word for ANYTHING. Find out *for yourself* !!!!! THE ONLY SINCERITY IS PERSPICUITY." And as for those moldy concepts: "Destroy, first of all!!! . . . TO DESTROY IS ALWAYS THE FIRST STEP IN ANY CREATION."[20] This destruction in no way contra-dicts wholeness. On the contrary, a wholeness based on a new way of seeing and fusing could arise only from the rubble of old ideas, from the wreckage of thought grounded in the logic of analysis, categoriza-tion, and separation. And by 1922, Cummings had long since prac-ticed in his poetry the destruction he preached to his sister.

Besides dulling perception, logical thinking, in its penchant for creating order, also stifles the mind's ability to form easy and wide-ranging association. One artist who captured such associations, Cummings noted, was James Joyce.

Mrs. Bloom chapter (Ulysses)
no punctuation (except huge paragraphs)
ideas follow in associative sequence,
not simply logically—or
IN ALL DIRECTIONS
       but
with the logic of UNconsciousness
just as they really occur,in us,before
artificially ordered(by thinking)

(Houghton notes, I[39] no. 114)

The "artificially ordered" logic, here, is analytical and linear; it separates ideas into the "Sentence unit. (short thought wh. begins & stops)" using conventional punctuation and syntax. By contrast, association—the unconscious mode—moves spatially in all directions and, lacking the interruptions of sentence units, can fuse separate but related ideas. Thus, only in the dream state can one see "*all of a vase: the Behind*"—and thus Cummings's fascination with the dream logic explicated by Freud. Cummings tinkered with his own asyntactical stream-of-consciousness next to his note on Joyce.

> he gave me a hit in the I never woke up until
> Wednesday was Washington's birthdays are bores
> but not as bad as
>   vs.
> 1) he gave me a hit in the HEAD
> 2) I never woke up until Wednesday
> 3) Wednesday(or,which) was Washington's Birthday(sing.)
> 4) Birthdays are terrible bores
> 5) But not as bad as

The example is pedestrian, but the technique of associative fusion produced some brilliant condensations in his poetry (e.g., "buds know better / than books / don't grow" [*1x1*, LIV]), while stream-of-consciousness structure effected such multi-directional marvels as this immersion into the din of McSorley's bar:

> the Bar.tinking luscious jigs dint of ripe silver with
> warmlyish wetflat splurging smells waltz the glush of
> squirting taps plus slush of foam knocked off and a
> faint piddle-of-drops she says I ploc spittle what the
> lands thaz me kid in no sir hopping sawdust you kiddo
> he's a palping wreaths of badly Yep cigars who jim
> him why gluey grins topple together eyes pout ges-
> tures stickily point made glints squinting who's a wink
> bum-nothing and money fuzzily mouths take big
> wobbly foot-steps every goggle cent of it get out ears
> dribbles soft right old feller belch the chap hic sum-
> more eh chuckles skulch . . . .
>
>   (*&*, "Post Impressions," VIII)

To achieve these effects, Cummings did not hesitate to break the linear molds of sentence and syntax, grammar and punctuation—the products of orderly thinking.

Logical thinking also leads to knowing and certainty, and these, Cummings felt, could shrivel the imagination. To demonstrate this, he imagined receiving an unexpected letter and compared its possible contents (the imaginative possibilities flooding his mind) with its actual contents once the letter is opened.

1) Until I open the envelope, I am in control. The envelope stimulates me to imagine a whole series of possibilities, any one of which may or may not be true [. . . .]

2) By the gesture of tearing the envelope, I renounce my imaginative omnipotence. I deliberately place myself at the mercy of fate, I choose to submit to what is outside of me—to something I did not invent: the validity or reality of one out of my collection of possibilities [. . . .]

3) On tearing open the envelope, all doubt disappears: I   read   the message itself—as is . . . . imagination has ceased to function in order that my understanding might take place [. . . .]

Why do I now believe that this one thing, the message, is real?—Why have I forever abandoned the number of possibilities I previously imagined?

Cummings acknowledges that the message's present reality ("this *is*") has pushed the imaginative possibilities into past "might have been." Yet, he is unwilling to let go of those possibilities, for they meant more to him, were more real for him, than the known reality: "Could anything be more real than my state of mind just before opening the envelope? In other words: not the possibilities, but my conception of them, the preclusion of reality was real; just as, now, not this message, but my belief [in] its reality—this is real" (Houghton notes, I[59] no. 11).

How close this is to Keats's declaration, "I am certain of nothing but of the holiness of the heart's affections, and the truth of Imagination"! Close, also, to Keats's "negative capability," that ability to maintain several imaginative possibilities in suspension without an irritable reaching after fact.[21] Undoubtedly, Keats was the primary source of Cummings's affective philosophy. Indeed, Cummings's conclusion to these notes on imagining versus knowing seems almost a précis of the Romantics' reverence of the imagination and the self as its alpha and omega, the screen through which all external reality is filtered. There is something not only subjective but solipsistic about the line, "not the possibilities but my conception of them was real." But solipsism was a price Cummings was willing to pay—and did pay increasingly throughout his career—for what he felt was immeasurably more important: making *his* imagination triumph over the world's reality. The self is thus feeling's rightful home and "selfintegration" its natural consequence, connections Cummings notes often: "whether or no one is a hedonist, we will recognize [when we feel] a spatial movement, a selfintegration of what is equally entire & spontaneous when one least resembles anyone or anything else,when one is purely selfish & distinct—an integer is most complete" (Houghton notes, I[59] no. 80). This is hardly surprising, coming from a poet who wrote in the 1940s:

```
      high
the &    for me is SELF ('the individual or indivisible'
      low
```

and "Every artist's strictly illimitable country is himself,"[22] and whose poems, from the 1920s onward, proclaimed with ever-increasing tenacity the sanctity of selfhood.

Besides the English Romantics, Emerson's transcendentalism has sometimes been identified as the intellectual source of Cummings's subjectivism.[23] The Platonism in Emerson, however, seems closer to Cummings's later, more mystical philosophy of transcendence. Cummings's earlier subjectivity was more earthbound and enjoyed feeling and sensation as ends in themselves, rather than as Platonic emblems of "higher forms" in nature.[24] If any philosopher provided a model for Cummings's "feeling," it was Henri Bergson. Indeed, Bergson's "intuition" works in virtually the same way: it leads one "to the very inwardness of life," whereas "intelligence" allows one to see life only "from outside." Just as Cummings believed that the child's intuitive feeling permitted him to sense time as a homogeneous whole with "no divisions, value or object," Bergson declared that intuition permits the mind to perceive "the continuous fluidity of real time which flows along, indivisible."[25] Although Bergson's name does not appear often in Cummings's early notes, his influence at the time was considerable, and Cummings could scarcely have avoided learning of theories so congenial to his own predilections.[26]

   If thinking was pernicious to pure perception, to spatial associations, and to unbridled imagination, what could one do with it? A colossal paradox underlies this question: Here is a philosopher of feeling whose voluminous notes, carefully reasoned and analyzed theories, and poetic craftsmanship pay great homage to thinking. This deep rift between his aesthetic philosophy and his aesthetic research and practice is an essential fact of Cummings's early aesthetics. For although Cummings believed that aesthetic wholeness must be felt, he could not simply rely on feeling to *realize* various aspects of wholeness in his art. Specific techniques were necessary to convert theory into practice, to concretize the abstractions of perception, structure, and motion in such ways that their wholeness, if achieved, could be apprehended on the canvas or the page. The techniques, in turn, required sound knowledge and research of the fundamental elements of painting and poetry, of how these elements worked individually and in combinations. And both the techinques and their supporting knowledge required careful, analytical thought. As much as he repudiated thinking in his aesthetic philosophy and in the themes of his poems, Cummings could not—indeed, made no attempt to—banish it from the aesthetic investigations and techniques informing his early poetry and painting. That he recognized this paradox in his aesthetics is quite clear. In his essay on Lachaise, he even offers a possible resolution in his precept to thinking people (like himself) who encounter the unself-conscious expression of the child and savage: "[these works] require of us an intelligent process of the highest order, namely the negation on our part, by thinking, of thinking." Such a willed "annihilation" of thinking, he wrote in his Artist-Painter dialogue of 1922, would allow one "To attain I AM [that is, feeling]".[27]

   One may doubt whether this solution of using thinking to stop thinking is possible, but never Cummings's steadfast belief that "feeling is first."

> since feeling is first
> who pays any attention
> to the syntax of things
> will never wholly kiss you;

wholly to be a fool
while Spring is in the world
my blood approves,
and kisses are a better fate
than wisdom

(is 5, "Four," VII)

So begins one of Cummings's best-known lyrics, a quiet and gentle poem, yet intense and direct—and one that neatly embodies the tension between feeling and thinking. Using the conceit of writing, the poem compares feeling's wholeness and vitality in kisses, laughter, and spring, to wisdom's order ("the syntax of things") and death. Between them, there is no contest: kisses are the better fate; feeling is first. "First" because it allows one to feel tactually and completely without the interference of thinking ("wholly kiss");because it lets the blood speak as well as the brain (the wholeness of integration); and, therefore, because it makes one whole (one can *wholly* be a fool in Spring). Punning on "wholly," the poem implies that feeling is holy; the one who feels, a holy fool, a Parsifal, pure enough—unthinking enough—to receive grace.

Thinking, by contrast, is entirely earthbound. It imposes order ("syntax") and limits ("parenthesis")—both arbitrary. The parenthesis, moreover, is artificial, because death, the poem suggests, is not the end: "And death i think is no parenthesis." Appropriately, "death" and "think" are juxtaposed, for thinking is a kind of living death when it chokes off purely sensuous feeling, the spatial arabesques of consciousness, and the spiritual possibilities of a life to come.

But there is another angle to this poem in its tone and apostrophe. The speaker's lover has been crying; his brave assertions are to reassure her that "the best gesture of my brain is less than / your eyelids' flutter," that her feeling is better than his creative thinking.[28] Is the speaker perchance a little guilty about his apparently superior mind? Are his reassurances genuine?

The same questions—and tensions—appear in Cummings's first play, *Him* (1927). "Him" is a playwright: imaginative, whimsical, and cerebral. He is also, like Cummings, an aesthetician who continuously scribbles notes on his philosophy of art. His mistress, "Me," is emotional and intuitive.

Him: Don't you understand—

Me: I don't. I feel. That's my way and there's nothing remarkable about that: all women are like that.

(III, i)

Like the apostrophized lady in the poem, Me feels intellectually inferior to her lover.

Me: I have no mind. I know that. I know I'm not intelligent, and that you liked me for something else. . . . I know perfectly well it's foolish of you to waste your time with me, when there are people who will understand you. And I know I can't because things were left out of me . . . . I've never done anything and I don't believe I ever will. But you can do things.

(III, i)

As if to repress the obvious, Him declares, "you have something I supremely envy. . . . you are something which I supremely would like to discover: Knowing that it exists in itself as I do not exist and as I never existed" (III, i). But Me will have none of it; like the child in Cummings's later allegory, *Santa Claus*, her intuition cannot be fooled.

Think that you fell in love with someone you invented—someone who wasn't me at all. Now you are trying to feel things; but that doesn't work, because the nicest things happen by themselves. You can't make them happen. I can't either, but I don't want to. And when you try to make things happen, you don't fool yourself and certainly you don't fool me . . . . the fact is, you know you made a mistake [about me] . . . . Think what is: think that you are now talking very beautifully through your hat.

(III, i)

"Think" ominously recurs here as the action by which the scales fall from the eyes—and the romance dies. Moreover, Me's urging Him to think is her retaliation for Him's urging Me to *think* of their inevitable death (which she resists): "Only think, dear, of you and me gone, like two kites when the string breaks, positively into nowhere. (Shut like umbrellas. Folded like napkins.)" (III, i). Here again, thinking presages death: the death of feeling, of love (a dissolution of wholeness), and ultimately of life itself. Yet, in *Him*, it seems an inevitable death, this death of illusion and dreams. And only after it, can Him "renovate," and possibly reintegrate, himself (III, v).

A psychoanalytic critic might see these opposing and stereotypical sides of personality—the male-analytical and female-intuitive —as projections of Jung's idea of the animus (the masculine archetype in woman) and anima (the feminine archetype in man) that one must integrate to achieve wholeness. Him and Me fail to reconcile their differences, fail to create what Jung called the "transcendent function." And their failure may reflect Cummings's own inability, in the early years, to sort out these opposing sides of his creativity. For the more he produced aesthetic "gestures" with his brain, the more drawn he was philosophically to his anima, identifying his creativity with the feminine-intuitive side of his mind. In a note dated "April 22 [1945]" he writes with excitement that he had successfuly painted "my first man . . . per se; not [merely] a girl's sexual partner" and mused: "as with any growing, there is *terror* . . . but this time, mild— that I might cease to be a poet, by ceasing to be feminine(!)"[29] Indeed, the feminine principle came to signify, for the later Cummings especially, the spiritual qualities he most valued. In notes dating from the early 1940s, he identified:

the natural ♂
2 worlds—
the supernatural ♀

The "natural," here, means the "reasonable" scientific world of mind and matter. The "supernatural," the realm of spirit and soul, was also the world of "LOVE . . . (Religion) ART *mutual* full, complete (vs partial) WHOLE."[30] On another sheet of the same notes, he compared qualities of the two worlds:

lust (plural)		love (singular)
collective		*individual*
mechanical;law	vs.	organic,LIVING
rigid)dogma		feel (fluent
dead		Alive

conform	Create
. . . .	. . . .
fixed, stopped	Growing, Infinite

(Houghton notes, I[55] no. 108)

One can easily see with which set of values Cummings identified himself and his philosophy as an artist.

What emerges from these examples is an uneasy relationship between thinking and feeling. Feeling, the path to wholeness and the spirit, receives all praise from a thinking mind that seems guilty about its own ability and intent to think analytically, over its failure to be more intuitive and spontaneous (since "the nicest things happened by themselves"). Thinking, as nemesis to wholeness, becomes the target of suppressive techniques—techniques fashioned by those very thought processes! Thus, "the negation . . . by thinking, of thinking." In seeking to turn thinking back on itself, Cummings addressed the *theoretical* problem of reconciling it to an aesthetics of wholeness grounded in feeling, just as he was later to ponder reconciliations of his masculine-earthly and feminine-spiritual sides. But his solution does not address the *practical* disparity between an aesthetic philosophy of subjectivity and an aesthetic practice requiring calculation and analysis. Not until he changed his style of painting in the late twenties does he appear to have brought the two into alignment—in one art at least.[31] Ironically, however, the unresolved tension produced by these divergent sides of himself and his aesthetics may have proved a boon to his art in producing a complex balance between discipline and expressiveness. And where Cummings unified his aesthetic theory and practice, he may have lost in complexity what he gained in consistency: that indefinable energy of contradiction and many-sidedness intrinsic to unresolved tensions.

Perception: Seeing the Whole Surface

3

No true artist would of purpose exclude Anything which he sees.
—E. E. Cummings, Houghton notes

■■■■■ "THE ONLY SINCERITY IS PERSPICUITY," Cummings wrote his sister in 1922, and probably he had in mind the action in this word, "to see through," as well as its subsequent meaning, "lucidity." For acute perception meant as much to this painter and poet as precise expression did—both in the viewer's experience of the finished work and in the artist's experience creating it. This concern grew out of Cummings's philosophical commitment to feeling over thinking, not only because he often equated feeling and perception ("SEE[Feel]"), but also because he felt that ideas, the fruits of thinking, made one "see indirectly," kept one from "admitting the smell and colour" of the phenomenal world.[1] His goal then was to realize in his art the Cézannian "theme" he had quoted—and repeated—in a letter home: "We must render the image of what we see, forgetting everything that existed before us."[2] Once ideas, those "5th hand notions" that block the senses, were safely put aside, he could then begin to discover *how* to see.

His goal was scarcely unique, of course, for the teens witnessed an upsurge of interest in perception, both as an aesthetic consideration and as a physiological and psychological process. Modernist styles as diverse as Pound's Imagism, Apollinaire's "Calligrammes," and Schoenberg's *Klangfarbenmelodie* all appealed directly to one's momentary perception. Pound's writings in the early teens were especially important. Rejecting ideas as vigorously as he was later to embrace them,[3] he stressed the primacy of the image, the self-sufficiency of its instantaneous apprehension. So distrustful was he of the tendency towards abstraction in language, that he often raided the visual arts for tactile metaphors to convey the physicality and spatiality he saw in images. He speaks of "equations . . . in little splotches of colour," of "planes in relation," and states in an early essay: "The 'one-image poem' is a form of super-position, that is to say, it is one idea set on top of another."[4]

Cummings found Pound's poems and theories a guiding beacon. At Harvard, he singled out Pound for special praise in a lengthy essay on the Imagists: "in originality he equals and in ease, as distinguished from facility, he surpasses any of his contemporaries."[5] And although he rightly suspected Pound's self-conscious fulminations as the work of "a born poseur," Cummings fully subscribed to Pound's views on the physicality and immediacy of the image, holding to them faithfully in his own poetry long after Pound had drifted back to ideas in the *Cantos*.

Cummings probably also knew the more extreme example of perceptual poetry in the "Calligrammes" of Guillaume Apollinaire. A few of these picture poems appeared in Alfred Steiglitz's *291* in 1915, followed by other experiments in concrete poetry. Cummings later denied that Apollinaire had influenced him. Yet it seems doubtful, given Cummings's hunger for all things Modernist and his prescient familiarity at Harvard with even such obscure works as *Tender Buttons*, that he would not have seen the easily accessible "Calligrammes" in *291*. To be sure, the two poets differ radically in their comparative respect for the traditional poetic line, as exemplified in their images of rising smoke (fig. 37). Where Cummings's line descends, Apollinaire's follows the shape of his ideograph and defies poetic gravity. Nevertheless, in outstripping even Pound's pictorial notions (and appearing just prior to Cummings's own structural experiments), the Calligrammes may well have pushed Cummings further towards his own poetic style.[6]

That Cummings heeded the examples of these artistic trailblazers is hardly surprising. What is surprising, given his anti-intellectual persona, is his *scientific* interest in perception. Of course, he grew up in the presence of William James, close friend of the Cummings family; and James devoted considerable space to sensation and perception in his *Principles of Psychology* (1890). Although James's conclusion that sensation and perception could not be divorced from thought contradicted Cummings's view, a few of James's ideas relating the intensity of perception to unfamiliarity and to the isolation of pictorial elements directly anticipate Cummings's ideas. More revealing of Cummings's study, however, is a technical source he consulted. In one note central to his perceptual aesthetics appears the name "Bates":

1. A painting appeals to the eye
2. The Eye must move: must be led about
   on a personally conducted tour
        cf. Bates: stopping—
   must stop only to continue,
                fixed focus
   i.e. pause
   must give the sensation of stopping only to
       "   "   "   " proceeding
   THE EYE MUST NEVER STOP

(Houghton notes, I[27] no. 37)

In 1920, William Bates published *Better Eyesight Without Glasses*— just prior to Cummings's most vigorous speculations on the topic.[7] Bates's contention that the eye naturally remains in constant motion and rests for only fractions of seconds probably inspired Cummings's note. Moreover, Bates's assertion that one sees peripheral objects better once "the vision of the center of sight has been suppressed" corresponds to Cummings's own conclusion.[8] His presence in Cummings's notes suggests how seriously Cummings pursued the subject.

If he troubled to read an opthalmologist's theories of perception, Cummings would likely have known of the ideas, just then appearing in English, of the Gestalt psychologists, notably Kurt Koffka's 1922 article, "Perception: An Introduction to Gestalt-Theorie."[9] Gestalt ideas of how one's perception of an entire field depends on the relative strengths of figure and ground parallel Cummings's own notes on figure and ground. There was, then, no shortage of theories and models to guide his interest in perception. Typically, however, he had to formulate in his own terms the perceptual problems that concerned him and to devise his own artistic solutions.

Perception and Recognition

From the outset, Cummings distinguished between perception and recognition. Perception originates in raw sensations: a color strikes the retina; a sound hits the eardrum. As one *feels* these stimuli separately, that is, as one becomes sensuously aware of them, one perceives them. Recognition follows these perceptions and depends on *thinking* to make "sense" of them by joining and filtering them through the memory. In his notes, Cummings puts it this way:

```
we do not see in terms of the recognizable. [...]
we do however see first, remember second (whether
consciously or not) & the        seeing
                       TIMES         [=s recognition]
                              remembering
                                    (Houghton notes, I[25] no. 66)
```

Recognition blurs our perceptions, makes them secondhand experience in several stages. Because it relies on memory, it loses the "nowness" of perceptions, the full force of their immediacy. Moreover, in making "sense" of discrete perceptions, the mind tends to merge them into a figure or structure—a gestalt. This might seem desirable, given Cummings's aesthetics of wholeness. But the gestalt of recognition, Cummings feels, is partial and reductive; it requires only enough perceptions to stir the memory. Additional perceptions become superfluous: "Recognition is concerned with simplifying our existence, reducing-to-lowest-common-denominator the multitudinous complex[? of] impressions or perceptions" (Houghton notes, I[25] no. 109).

In recognizing the content of a painting, for example, the mind discerns a certain number and arrangement of colors, lines, textures, masses, and vacancies from others surrounding them. As the discerned elements coalesce into "object," they become more perceptible. They stand out. The surrounding elements, relegated to the inferior status of "ground" or "context," become correspondingly less perceptible and recede. Memory then screens this emergent figure to determine its place in the known universe based on its appearance, use, context, etc. Such categorical thinking tends to seek out the object's similarities to others of its type more than its dissimilarities, its uniqueness. As Cummings observed: "If 2 people see a 'chair' and only one knows *its use*, their respective seeings will undoubtedly differ as to clarity; the man who is familiar with 'chairs' will see the 'chair' dully, in a rightly mutilated or incomplete fashion. This is not because his eyesight is poorer than his fellow's; it is because 'familiarity breeds contempt.' " (Houghton notes, I[25] no. 159). Thus, the more we recognize an object in our mind, the less we see it with our eye.

Both memory and abstraction, moreover, put space between the perceiver and the source of his perceptions, thus breaking the subject-object wholeness Cummings valued. By recognizing boundaries, a viewer can detach self-awareness from awareness of the object: "this is not I . . . this is an angleworm." But if the object's contours are left ambiguous, "the spectator fills in, completes [the] picture himself [. . .] & he says 'I am a river.' "[10] What permits this perceptual identity between viewer and object is one's *feeling* a perception and identifying oneself with the feeling *before* thinking about it: from "I see a color" to "I have a feeling [of this color sensation]" to "I AM a feeling." Thus, felt perception creates the reciprocal closure of subject and object by letting the viewer penetrate an object's contours to apprehend its essential qualities, as those perceived qualities penetrate and merge with the viewer's self-consciousness. But "logic or thinking reverses a perception by means of an idea."[11]

A few of Cummings's early poems directly assert the primacy of sensations and perceptions over thought, and many show the idea in action. "My mind is" pictures the speaker's mind as something passive and negative, an inert block to be sculpted.[12] The sights and smells come first: these "sensuous chisels" hit the mind (not vice versa) and change it; they make the speaker "squirm," "shriek," and "bellow" in an "agony" of becoming. By having "altered" the speaker, they bring him into his real, feeling self, as a block of stone is sculpted into a work of art.

> nevertheless i
> feel that i cleverly am being altered that i slightly am
> becoming something a little different, in fact
> myself

The delightful synesthetic couplings, "squirms of chrome," "scarlet bellowings," and "lilac shrieks," reaffirm the primacy of sensation: color, sound, and motion. The mind, however, is "irrevocable": if given the chance, it can indeed overwhelm sensations and make the poet long for a time "when my sensational moments are no more / unjoyously bullied of vilest mind."[13]

Some of Cummings's best early poems are verbal portraits: careful and covert observations of people whose physical details are arranged so as to register perceptually before they can be mentally ordered. A young woman hanging washing becomes "the mother of twelve undershirts"—precisely what the speaker sees.[14] To translate the perception to "mother of twelve children" would wilt its freshness and immediacy.

Equally fresh is the first image of "5":

5

derbies-with-men-in-them   smoke Helmar
cigarettes

(XLI Poems, "Portraits," VIII)*

Inverting "men wearing derbies" to "derbies-with-men-in-them" is as startling and unexpected as the punch line of a good joke. But it is also probably the first feature of these men that struck the poet as he watched them sitting together at a cafe. By presenting his perceptions directly, Cummings lets the reader first *experience* the scene before recognizing it.

In recognition, Cummings sees a double threat to his painting and writing: it could interfere with complete perception of both a work's basic elements (words, colors, planes, etc.) and its larger, overall configuration, its wholeness.

"Recognizing" words means mentally translating their symbolic meanings while brushing over their sensuous qualities, particularly their look on paper. Modern alphabets, as they supplanted pictorial ideographs with visually empty symbols, virtually insured this recognition. In a painting, the eye's primal perception of color and space irrespective of boundaries yields all too easily to the mind's orderly grouping of these qualities into shapes and silhouettes. Cummings writes: "a color cannot be recognized. Only a shape."[15] He continues in other notes: "by colors we mean planes irrespective of their edges [. . . .] to recognize is the edge (to give edges to); color is not recognizing [. . . .] color [. . .] then enwraps or contains: what are contained or enwrapped are visible things, are recognizable things" (Houghton notes, bMS Am. 1892.7[68]). Color, in other words, is what the eye sees *before* the mind discerns boundaries or edges. Since color and plane were synonymous to Cummings, the primacy of one meant the primacy of the other: "not Line, but PLANE is first [. . .] a line is the stopping of one colour by the beginning of another."[16] As the mind discerns a line, it begins to recognize: first shapes; then, grouping the shapes and filtering them through the memory, objects.

If recognition puts fences around color planes and saps words of their sensuous potential, it damages a work's wholeness even more. Such wholeness was dynamic for Cummings, both within the work and between the work and the viewer's experience of it. The internal motion occurs when *all* parts of the painting or poem interact freely and equally in a dynamic balance—a "poise"—of conflicting tensions. Indeed, this "binding rhythm," as he called it, was the force that would "integrate" the disjunctive words, lines, and color planes into "a single Moving Thinginitself."[17]

"Binding rhythm" also describes the viewer's perception of a work's wholeness. Cummings sees this perception as a circuit: the eye moves continuously through all parts of a work, apprehending it as a whole. If anything prevents this motion and breaks the circuit, or keeps all the parts from interacting freely, the work's wholeness is shattered. Recognition does just that:

> Recognition is at the expense of movement (homogeneity)
> [. . . . .]
> Cf. in *Sound* a tune
> If we R[ecognize] a tune in a symphony, it gives us pleasure but throws the rest of the music out of focus.

So with a painting: there is a

> mechanism of mind wh[ich] "recognizes"
> a certain amount of space
>   number or arrangement of planes as a "woman"
> Suppose the equivalent space, planes, arrangement *are not* recognized.
> The mind remains in motion, does not stop.
> Moves thru the picture continuously.
>   (Houghton notes, I[39] no. 111ᵛ)

But if the planes *are* recognized:

the painting ceases to be a whole any & each of whose parts are equally *important* & becomes parts[.] a focus (or foci) are established —meaning of course to the exclusion of rest of field[.]

(Houghton notes, I[25] no. 65)

The problem applies to poetry no less than to painting. As recognition may abstract one form, a "woman," from a complex of planes in a painting, so may it select one pattern of meaning from a complex of meanings in a poem. In both cases, the *Gestalten* formed by the viewer and reader are partial and do not account for "every inch" of the work.

The remedies for these perceptual problems were self-evident to Cummings. To sharpen and intensify his viewers' and readers' sensuous perception, he must give them something to see and hear first, while slowing their recognition. He must replenish the sensuous, pictorial content of words and get color planes to interact freely. But equally important, he must prevent his paintings and poems from eliciting an easy recognition of a single subject or meaning at the expense of their complex wholeness.

Perceiving the Parts

GESTURE IN LANGUAGE

Although Cummings felt that modern language had lost much of its original sensuousness, he needed only visit his favorite Syrian restaurant to recapture this neglected dimension—and to inspire his aesthetics. As the locals all around him chatted and ordered in Arabic and browsed through Syrian newspapers, Cummings observed something familiar to many a tourist:

> To someone who does not understand a word of (let us say) Syrian the most ordinary restaurant command such as "give me a cup of coffee" is complete and beautiful.[. . . Consider] the front page of a certain newspaper published in New York by Syrians in the Syrian language. The alphabet of this language being totally unfamiliar to me, recognition in no way obtains. The unrecognizable symbols completely[?] inhibit thinking which permits me to enjoy their sensual significance. The fact that this unrecognizable deployment of black

and white inhibits Thinking accounts for an enjoyment of the page. (Houghton notes, I[25] no. 74).[18]

Cummings called such wholly sensuous language "gesture."[19] Ideographs, calligraphy, a "deployment of black and white on a page" —all could be gestures, even a forbiddingly long series of numbers: "thinking is almost immediately smothered by an unthinkable array of ciphers. Because unthinkable, this array is promptly feelable to the eye—a feeling of unambiguous entireness and bigness."[20] By short-circuiting mental recognition, the gesture could gratify the eye and ear directly and thus recapture the physical immediacy language once possessed in the ideograph. Cummings was not content, therefore, merely to describe perceptions unvarnished by recognition; the words conveying the perception must themselves be sensuous. Thus,

5
derbies-with-men-in-them

has more pictorial immediacy than "five derbies-with-men-in-them." To use themselves up completely as gestures, words must be something visually and aurally before they mean anything semantically; and ideally, the two acts, sensuous and semantic, should reinforce each other.

As theory, this hardly amounts to a new aesthetics for poetry. One of poetry's pleasures has always been its music; and "concrete" poems in the shape of things were being written three hundred years before Cummings's time. But Cummings saw ways of dramatically extending language's sensuous appeal by wrenching nearly all of its established conventions—its syntax, punctuation, capitalization, spacing, and shape—to achieve these visual and aural ends.

Thus, gesture helped to inspire many of the typographical idiosyncrasies for which Cummings's poetry is best known; it even inspired the visual (and untranslatable) titles of such books as & and W . To see gesture working in the poems, we need consider the visual effects of only a few "wrenched" conventions: capitalization, punctuation, and shape.

Capitalization's purpose has always been to emphasize importance. Cummings both extends and hones that emphasis by using capitals more freely and yet placing them more selectively. Consider the poem "it's jolly":

it's jolly
odd what pops into
your jolly tête when the
jolly shells begin dropping jolly fast you
hear the rrmp and
then nearerandnearerandNEARER
and before
you can

!

& we're

NOT
(oh—
—i say

that's jolly odd
old thing,jolly
odd,jolly
jolly odd isn't
it jolly odd.

(is 5, "Two," IV)

Just as the fusion of "nearerandnearerandNEARER" shows the shells
bursting progressively faster, "NEARER" signals a much closer and
louder blast: the capitals explode from the lowercase line with perceptual force akin to the concussion of the shell-burst. Too close! The
exclamation mark interrupting the narrative is an ideograph of the
explosion that kills the speaker. But oddly, he has time to declare his
own death ("& we're / NOT") before trailing off in a kind of postmor-
tem litany on death's oddness from the other side (as a chicken's
heart keeps beating by reflex after the head has been severed). The
capitalized "NOT" signifies the climactic moment of death simply by
standing out—spatially as well as contrastingly—from the lowercase
words.

In "here's a little mouse," capitals convey visual perspective
as well as emphasis:

(with wee ears and see?

tail frisks)

(gonE)

(is 5, "Four," III)

As the mouse scoots away, the reader (like the speaker) sees it from behind, that is, from the back of the word in the emphasized "E" of "gonE." Too, the "E" lingers, as perhaps the afterimage of the mouse would remain on the retina after the mouse has disappeared.

Capitals placed within a word can fashion the double entendre Cummings was so fond of. He cites this potential in an important note on a rather obscure poem in *is 5*, "(as that named Fred," the first lines of which go:

> (as that named Fred
> –someBody:hippopotamus,scratch-
> ing,one,knee with,its,
> friend observes I
>
> pass Mr Tom Larsen twirls among

(is 5, "One," XXIII)

Cummings's note lists four separate techniques at work here: "inversion of normal word order, miscapitalization, imitative punctuation, and the breaking of a word or phrase." For "miscapitalization," he writes:

> mis-capitalization | = pun,
>   (emphasis) *someBody* | compressed
> interior   ":
>   somebody with <u>some</u> body

(Houghton notes, I[59] no. 30)

Using the maximum compression of a pun, the internal capitalization conveys two meanings at once ("somebody with <u>some</u> body").

In the same note, Cummings cites another device for visual gesture, "imitative punctuation":

> imitative punctuation (picture, image)
>   vs.
> grammatical "   (sentence, thought idea)
>   : *one, knee with, its* (vs. one knee with its
>   —no commas

Just as in capitalization, Cummings respects the symbolic and temporal meaning of each punctuation mark: his question marks question, his exclamation marks exclaim, his commas only pause while his periods halt. But he promotes these lowly grammatical servants to full partners with the words in visually and aurally expressing meaning. Thus, the commas in "scratch- / ing,one,knee with,its" imitate the gesture of repetitive scratching—and are perhaps even an ideograph of bent knees.

The variety of gestures Cummings draws from the punctuation mark is remarkable. It can function as a single ideograph, as the exclamation mark signals the fatal explosion in "it's jolly odd"; or it can perform several perceptual duties at once. The exclamation mark in the line "(suddenly-Lights go!on,by schedule" is simultaneously the visual equivalent of "suddenly," of lights in the act of going on, and of the speaker's perceptual surprise on seeing them go on.[21]

A question mark is the wholly visual (and unpronounceable) title of "?";[22] appropriately, it epitomizes the poem's narrative format, for each stanza asks and answers a question. In the next poem of *is* 5, Cummings reverses the procedure:

> this young question mark man
>
> question mark
> who suffers from
> indigestion question
> mark

Here, the spelled out question marks call exaggerated attention to themselves not just to question whether the subject *is* young, *is* a man, etc., but, by their own waste of poetic space, to suggest the triviality of the young man's pretensions as an artist: "he's a wet dream / by Cézanne."

In "the skinny voice," punctuation composes an entire stanza. The Salvation Army captain has asked the onlookers for a quarter more to reach an even dollar.

> whereupon
>
> the Divine Average who was
>
> attracted by the inspired
> sister's howling moves
> off

will anyone tell him why he should

blow two bits for the coming of Christ Jesus

?
??
???
!

nix,kid

(*XLI Poems*, ''Portraits,'' IV)

The sequence of increasing question marks might suggest the separate, doubting listeners; more likely, it shows the *increasing* doubt of the speaker (a Whitmanesque "Divine Average") about the value of contributing a quarter—and perhaps, too, about "the coming of Christ Jesus"—until doubt hardens into the resolute refusal ("!") of the last two lines.

The working of the third "wrenched" convention, spacing and shape, is more difficult to summarize. Although, as some critics have pointed out, Cummings usually prefers to generate abstract movement rather than to represent the shape of recognizable objects in his poems, his complex of capitals, punctuation, and spacing sometimes enacts quite specific motions and concrete objects. "My eyes are fond of the east side" is a grab bag of visual tricks, kinetic and concrete.[23] In the second section, the speaker's mouth samples a potpourri of treats offered by East Side street venders; at one stop,

it(swallow   s   bun   chesofnew   grapes[. . . .]

Appropriately, the letters of "bun   chesofnew   grapes" are bunched to imitate visually what their words mean semantically; likewise, the separated "s" of "swallow   s" shows and sounds the gulp. More precisely, the space between "swallow" and "s" represents the time of the swallow in the bob of the adam's apple. The "s" is the final, sounded gulp.

In the preceding paragraph of "my eyes," Cummings twice capitalizes double *o*s: "cOOler" and "DarkcOOllonGBody." While these capitals stretch out the "ooh" sound and thus emphasize the coolness, they are also an ideograph of the narrator's eyes— a natural enough image in a paragraph devoted to seeing and one Cummings used in other poems.

Hidden shapes lurk even in well-known poems. "Stinging / gold swarms" has received much commentary, especially for the concrete shape of its last stanza.

> and a tall
>
> wind
> is dragging
> the
> sea
>
> with
>
> dream
>
> –S

(*Tulips and Chimneys*, "Impressions," V)

One critic, for example, describes this shape as "both spire-like and tall."[24] But the direction can also be seen as downward: Dragging this sea of the unconscious would require dropping a grappling hook *down* ("wind→dreams") beneath the horizontal surface ("chants→tall"). And at the bottom is the grappling hook itself: "-S"!

PLANES OVER LINES

Cummings applied his perceptual theories extensively and systematically in his poems. Not so in his paintings, where he is far less programmatic in asserting color planes over lines. For one thing, the idea was not his own. It came most immediately from the French sculptor Henri Gaudier-Brzeska, whose dicta, such as "les plans convoient la seule sensation artistique et la ligne ne [leur] sert que de cadre" found their way into Cummings's Harvard notes, via the Vorticist journal, BLAST, and Pound's memoir, *Gaudier-Brzeska*.[25] This bias for planes and against lines had a much longer thread, of course, tracing from Delacroix, through the Impressionists, to Cézanne and the Cubists. By Cummings's time, the idea was, if anything, old hat. Yet he pays it more than lip service in his painting. For it serves his aesthetic goal of appealing directly to the viewer's perception by offering color planes "feelable to the eye," rather than outlines of shapes recognizable to the mind. His immediate task in his abstractions, then, is to create planes without drawn outlines and let the contrast of colors determine boundaries.

Sound Number 2 (fig. 31), which Cummings exhibited at the Penguin gallery shortly after his success at the 1919 Independents, presents just such a clash of unbound planes. Contrasting textures, such as the checkerboard pattern, or the dot and line patterns borrowed from Synthetic Cubism, sharpen these contrasts. Although a few planes clearly form shapes and "emerge" (the dark circles for example), their "thinginess" is diminished by the intersection of differently colored planes. In the rest of the painting, particularly the jumble of planes at lower and upper left, one cannot distinguish object from background and must therefore confer tangibility to the whole. This equalizing of the parts enhances not only their perceptibility, but their free interaction, their dynamism.

Fig. 31.
Sound Number 2, 1919, oil on paper, 19 × 24 in. Memorial Art Gallery of the University of Rochester. Given in Memory of Hildegarde Lasell Watson.

Perceiving the Whole

At the same time Cummings made his poems and painting more "feelable to the eye," he made them less directly familiar to the mind. "Perception," he writes, "is related to 'Un-familiarity.' "[26] Conversely, recognition of a single object or theme usurps one's sense of the totality. To preserve the integrity of the whole, Cummings found several ways to make individual objects and themes "Unfamiliar": omit them altogether (abstraction), conceal them in a perceptually ambiguous design, or balance them against a perceptually powerful background.

ABSTRACTION

Of course, the easiest way to keep a viewer from recognizing a subject is simply to omit it and present an abstract design instead. But Cummings's attitude towards abstraction was neither simple nor absolute; and the degrees to which he employed it vary considerably among his paintings, poems, and notes. As we have seen, in his early notes on painting (up to 1925), he favored it wholeheartedly over representational art. But his early paintings ranged across the spectrum of abstraction to representation, with only the *Sound* and *Noise* series at the abstract pole. Moreover, his feelings about abstraction changed in the midtwenties, as he found new ways of reconciling nature, technique, and personality. Cummings was simply not comfortable, even during his Modernist years, in denying nature altogether, just as in his later art he resisted the temptation merely to copy nature: "your stupid wiseguy doing his worst to deny Nature equals your clever fool who did his best to possess her."[27] A better solution was to confront nature—and tame it.

In his poetry, too, Cummings rejected the idea of pure abstraction and never followed what he took to be Gertrude Stein's example of it in *Tender Buttons*. Indeed, as his published and unpublished comments on that work for his 1915 commencement address, "The New Art," indicate, he felt that the medium of language was too "familiar" to be used solely for "esthetic effect."[28] His aim, then, was not to jettison meaning but to expand it visually and aurally. A poetic picture of a grappling hook dragging a verbal sea, or a syncopated imitation of ragtime could communicate as powerfully as a conventionally "thematic" poem. But Cummings never forces a choice between sense and sensation: even the purest of his "poempictures" possesses thematic meaning. Far from wanting to divorce the visual and aural from the thematic, he seeks to join them to make his poems mean at all levels simultaneously.

Thus, nowhere in his early volumes is there an entire poem so abstract as to be nonsensical. There are *lines* in many poems where disconnected syntax and visual gestures resist thematic interpretation. But as they slow one's recognition of a central theme, these devices direct one's perception to the composite parts. Take, for example, one of the most difficult early poems, "windows go orange in the slowly."[29]

```
windows go orange in the slowly.
town,      night
featherly swifts
the
       Dark on us
all;
     stories told returned
     gather
     the
Again:who
danc    ing
goes utter    ly
churning
witty,twitters
              upon Our
(ta-te-ta
in a parenthesis!said the moon
```

It contains not one thought expressed as a conventionally punctuated sentence. The few groupings that approximate syntactical completion lack the usual signals of capitalization and punctuation:

```
windows go orange in the slowly.
town,      night
stories told returned
Dark / stories / gather / the / Again
in a parenthesis!said the moon
```

The poem's fragments are mostly visual images (windows, swifts, night, dark, moon) and actions (windows go orange, the Dark on us all, something dancing goes utterly churning). These images call to mind the title of the section of the book containing this poem, "Post Impressions," which suggests both the Impressionists' sense of a scene's fleeting visual appearance—the quick sensations of color, light, and movement received in a momentary perception—and the Post-Impressionists' (especially Cézanne's) restructuring of form to correspond to these visual sensations. Cummings's restructuring, too, is visual: the lines and sense move in many directions and thus offer several readings simultaneously. The first lines can variously be read:

```
windows [slowly] go orange in the night
   ''           ''     ''  ''   ''  '' town
   ''                  ''  ''   '' slowly [moving] town
   ''                  ''  ''   '' slowly [coming] night
```

The widely spaced middle section moves vertically and diagonally as well as horizontally—an example of what Cummings called "composition by angles and planes." Four related motifs emerge:

```
the / Dark on us / all
stories told returned [dreams?]
Dark / stories / gather / the / Again
Dark / returned / Again
```

Connected by lines, they might be represented as the diagram shown here.

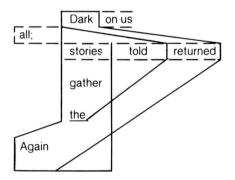

Fragmentation intensifies below "Again." The detached suffixes "ing" and "ly" effect different semantic and spatial patterns as they variously adhere to "dance" and "utter."

who dancing goes[,] utterly churning witty twitters . . .
who dancingly goes[,] uttering[,] churning witty twitters . . .
who[,] dancing[,] goes utterly churning witty twitters . . .
who dancingly[,] goes uttering[,] churning witty twitters . . .

Just as the "who" of "dancing" is ambiguous (dreams dancing or swifts?), the object of "upon Our" is missing. As we continue along the diagonal "twitters / upon Our," we arrive at "moon" as the only present semantic and structural completion, even though the narrative moves linearly back to the disjunctive "(ta-te-ta." These twitters of the "featherly swifts" fall upon the crescent moon even as the moon itself greets the speaker. The conflicting actions might therefore be drawn in the planes of the diagram shown here.

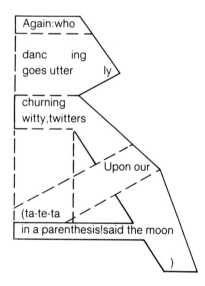

In spite of the narrative disruption, a progression emerges from these planes: sunset (orange windows)—night—dark—dreams (stories told returned)—moon (ending with a clever ideograph of a

Fig. 32.
Sound Number 5, 1920, oil on canvas,
35 × 35 in. Courtesy of SUNY College
at Brockport Foundation. Photograph
by Earl Kage, Museographics.

crescent moon). What Cummings "abstracts" is the horizontally progressive continuity of the theme "sunset to moonlight" to keep the reader from recognizing it superficially. What he presents is a multidirectional *composition* of visual and aural images to let the reader sense this progression fragment by fragment, moment by moment.

PERCEPTUAL AMBIGUITY

For an artist who thrived on the look and feel of things as much as Cummings did, it seems in retrospect inevitable that he would have let them force their way into his painting, despite his professed enthusiasm for abstraction. Of course, the material world was always part of his representational early work—the landscapes and still-lifes—but it lingers even in his abstractions, the *Sounds* and

Noises. As he explained in a letter to his mother (3 March 1922), these paintings began with "bodies scenes faces still lifes" as the "helps or raw material" of an abstract design. These "helps" were to "go under" (i.e., disappear) in the final abstraction; but some lurk stubbornly among the planes, waiting to materialize.

Sound Number 5 (plate 3, fig. 32) is a good example. Shown recently at an exhibition of Cummings's paintings and again in a scholarly article, it was displayed upside down![30] Clearly, there *is* a figure in this painting: a seated nude facing left with fair hair, one arm raised, one arm bent at the elbow with hand on hip, broad hip and thigh, and one folded leg.

One might object that in an essentially abstract design, "which side up" should not matter. Cummings, himself, supports this view when he states that he wants "every inch" of his painting to seem good.[31] But in *Sound Number 5* it does matter, because upside down, the painting is top-heavy. The broadest planes would then form the top of an unstable funnel perilously close to toppling leftward. Right side up, the weight shifts to the bottom, stabilizing the composition. Although the figure is now discernible, it does not necessarily dominate the viewer's perceptual field; for as it can emerge as a gestalt, so it can just as easily recede into an arrangement of color planes. This ability to go both ways defines its ambiguity.

Once alerted to these submerged figures, a perceptive—or paranoid—viewer may find them hiding in other abstractions. In *Noise Number 1*, Cummings sneaks in what had long since been his totem, an elephant. *Sound Number 2* (fig. 31) hints the crown and profile of a rooster, while the image of a saxophone hovers among the flowing swathes of *Noise Number 12* (fig. 22)—two concealed noisemakers.

In a more teasing ambiguity, the figures sometimes reveal themselves, but not their origins. Thus, the central spiral in *Noise Number 13* (plate 5) has provoked a variety of readings. Rushworth Kidder likens it to the circular section of the onrushing locomotive in Cummings's *train* (fig. 46). Richard Kennedy ties it to the cue-ball imagery in Cummings's poem "the surely" in *ViVa*.[32] And I see eyes in the center of the spirals which, themselves, may be ears to hear the synesthetic "Noise." That these readings are *all* plausible—and all different—confirms the essential ambiguity of the figure.

The right balance between the concealed and the recognizable sometimes eluded Cummings. *Scofield Thayer* (fig. 33), for example,

Fig. 33.
Scofield Thayer, before 1923, oil on cardboard, 18 × 14½ in. Courtesy SUNY College at Brockport Foundation.

probably began as a representational portrait which Cummings then broke into color planes in the face and curvy swathes in the torso. In superimposing Cubist techniques on an otherwise conventional portrait, he probably followed the example of the Cubist School painters (particularly of Albert Gleizes' *Man on a Balcony*, a painting he had studied early on)—and achieved the same derivative and unconvincing results. Occasional failures, however, did not diminish Cummings's fondness for perceptual ambiguity, for it suited his personality as well as his aesthetics. Its teasing, now-you-see-it-now-you-don't quality appealed to his playful humor But more important, it allowed him to work with nature without being dominated by it. So long as he held the recognizable figures in check by keeping them ambiguous, they could not usurp the viewer's sense of the work's wholeness.

In his early poems, Cummings shows the same fondness for perceptual ambiguity and with much the same intent: to raise the expressive voltage of a work by compressing several meanings into the smallest possible space and, conversely, to prevent a single meaning from overwhelming (and thereby weakening) an intricate complex of meanings. Just as concealing the subject in a painting allows for a more sensuous apprehension of the entire composition, suppressing a monothematic reading of a poem enhances one's sense of the poem's thematic richness and allusive complexity.

Cummings creates this ambiguity simply by arranging words and lines to yield two different meanings in close succession. Take the first lines of a poem already discussed for its perceptual intensity, "a blue woman . . .":

> a blue woman with sticking out breasts hanging
> clothes.
>
> (&, "Sonnets—Actualities," XVI)

Until "clothes" appears, two different readings suggest themselves: the breasts are hanging (a contradiction since they are also "sticking out"), and the *woman* is hanging, her face already blue from strangulation. The latter reading, suicide, lingers as the poem reveals the hopelessness of her life: a young mother of twelve trapped by a church (metonymized in Bishop Taylor) with rigid ideas about sex, marriage, and birth control; and stifled by deadening routines conveyed in the repetitive actions of hanging clothes, skipping rope, droning empty voices ("she says i says"), and lights going on "by schedule." In this context of futility, "blue" acquires its colloquial meaning of "depressed."

The poem's thematic climax, "(It is the consummation / of day,the hour)" is therefore triply ironic, as it alludes to the fruits of the mother's sexual consummation, twelve children, to the *un*fulfillment of a life that consumes her and makes her "blue," and to the possibility of her ending it—consuming it—by suicide. The original ambiguity governs the entire poem, concealing the woman's grim future—hanging—within her hopeless present—hanging clothes.

Technically, the ambiguity of "a blue woman" results from the intermingling of two meanings on two consecutive lines without intervening punctuation. The same arrangement appears in "i am a beggar always," only here the ambiguity is more evenly divided between the two readings and twists the poem's thematic direction from the middle of the narrative. In this bitter apostrophe, the speaker portrays himself as a blind beggar panhandling from his love "just enough dreams to live on" and "a little love preferably."

> then he will maybe(hearing something
> fall into his hat)go wandering
> after it with fingers; till having
>
> found
> what was thrown away
>   himself
> taptaptaps out of your brain,hopes,life
>
> to(carefully turning a
> corner)never bother you any more.
>
>   *(is 5,* "Four," XV)

Perceptually and thematically, "himself" is the crux of the poem. Seen as a subject ("himself / taptaptaps out of your brain"), it continues the established theme. But seen as the appositive to "what" ("what was thrown away / himself "), it provides the missing fact that explains the poem: the speaker has been jilted by his lover, metaphorically blinded, reduced to begging from her some scrap of their former love. What he finds in his hat is "himself," a self-discovery born of pain but strong enough to let him "turn . . . a corner" and put the blighted affair behind him. Lacking punctuation to clarify its grammatical function, "himself " pivots both ways and imparts two separate meanings simultaneously.

"ITEM" offers a slightly different method of creating ambiguity:

> her mouth opens too far
> and:she attacks her Lobster without
> feet mingle under the
> mercy.

(*is* 5, "One," XIV)

By spacing this complex over four lines and around one puny colon, Cummings humorously fuses three motifs: "attacks her Lobster without / feet," "feet mingle under the [table]," and "attacks her Lobster without / . . . mercy." This fusion echoes the one in Cummings's note: "he gave me a hit in the I never woke up until Wednesday was Washington's birthdays are bores." Like "himself" in "i am a beggar always," one word ("feet") serves ambiguously as the object of a preposition ("without / feet") and as the subject of a new idea ("feet mingle . . ."). But here Cummings sacrifices the syntactic continuity of the former poem by leaving the new motif unfinished and completing instead the original idea: "attacks her Lobster without / . . . mercy." The discontinuity is jarring and reflects the same clash of sensation, objective perception, and subjective narrative that begins the poem:

> this man is o so
> Waiter
> this;woman is
>
> please shut that
> the pout And affectionate leer
> interminable pyramidal,napkins

Finally, an entire poem can turn on how an ambiguity is perceived. The conclusion of "lis / -ten" offers the homonym, "no," in place of the expected "know."

> lis
> -ten
>
> you know what i mean when
> the first guy drops you know
> everybody feels sick or
> when they throw in a few gas
> and the oh baby shrapnel

or my feet getting dim freezing or
up to your you know what in water or
with the bugs crawling right all up
all everywhere over you all me everyone
that's been there knows what
i mean a god damned lot of
people don't and never
never
will know,
they don't want

to

no

(is 5, "Two," VII)

The ambiguous "no" suggests two related but distinct meanings at once. First, those who were not in the trenches cannot, and do not want to, "know" how terrible it was. And consequently, they refuse to say "no" to the political machinery that makes wars: the draft, the patriotic appeals, the national chauvinism and xenophobia. Concluding the poem, the unexpected "no" gives a shock akin to a surprise ending in fiction that forces the reader's attention to this thematic ambiguity.[33]

While all of these ambiguities can be described as structural,[34] it is important to recognize that they are also perceptual: they control the speed and manner in which a line is perceived. Typically, the reader perceives a thematic motif and expects its progression, only to have an ambiguous swing word lead to quite a different meaning. Momentarily thrown off by the unexpected turn, the reader must accommodate the new idea, either by reconciling it with the original, or by maintaining both in suspension. The result is often a balanced tension, as the competing themes struggle for dominance in the reader's eye and mind, with first one reading, and then the other, ascendant. Such a tension precludes a comfortable monothematic reading and requires, instead, an unstable and shifting perception of a thematic complex.

PERCEPTUAL BALANCE

As Cummings changed his painting styles in the mid-1920s, he faced a new perceptual challenge. In the major painting of the early period, he typically suppressed or concealed nature to prevent its dominating the canvas. But when he chose to confront it directly in his later period, how was he to prevent this domination? His solution was to strengthen the "negative" space surrounding the figure—the ground—to offset, or at least diminish, the perceptual pull of the figure.

> —in pa[inting]
> the Invisibilizing of "the object" (subject)
> thru the visibilizing of invisibles-all-around-it
> for X to be seeable, W & Y must be unseeable)
> (Houghton notes, I[55] no. 109)

"Invisibilizing" the object—diminishing its perceptual pull—required "visibilizing" the negative space all around it.

Cummings was long accustomed to seeing vacancy as something tangible. In notes on the dominance of planes over lines, he writes: "if i look where 2 trees are, what i see is the space between, the trees being its edges[.] if i look where 3 trees are, what i see is the middle tree."[35] And in notes on the "Intervening Space" between two tables, he reasons: "The space between THESE TWO TABLES EQUALS IN IMPORTANCE THE AMOUNT OF SPACE (two amounts) WHICH ARE 'TABLES'" (I[39] no. 26).

Likewise, his ear heard silences as well as sounds. In Harvard notes for an unfinished essay on poetry, he writes: "Two strokes are struck on a bell: this may be described as two weights, pulling against two other weights (silences), or as advancing, and receding [sic], intervals (of sound, and silence) . . . IN ANY CASE SILENCE IS A PERFECT PROTAGONIST.[. . .] The significance of Rhyme is as much the *interval* between its occurrence as the $\left\{\begin{array}{l}\text{extent}\\\text{nature}\end{array}\right\}$ of the repetition [. . .] to regard the interval as coherent with the repetition [. . . .]" (Houghton notes, 1892.6[29] nos. 9, 13). Many of Cummings's early poems describe empty space as something tangible.

> in the oblong air, from which a singular ribbon
> of common sunset is hanging,
>
> ofpieces ofof sunligh tof fa l l in gof throughof treesOf,
>
> my ears bend to the little silent handorgan prop-
> ping the curve of the tiny motheaten old man[36]

Conversely, some lines simply remove vacancy, compressing foreground with distant background.

the trees stand. The trees,
suddenly wait against the moon's face.
(Tulips and Chimneys, "Sonnets-Unrealities," V)

The deep space between the trees and moon vanishes with "against" —a juxtaposition reinforced by the connecting assonance of "wait" and "face." These trees seem to be touching the moon. Clearly, a painter's eye is at work in these lines, solidifying vacancy as the Cubists did, or flattening a view into the two-dimensionality of Matisse's *Harmony in Red*, and in both cases balancing figure with ground.

While these lines *describe* negative space, a vast number of poems *use* it. Indeed, the importance of white space to Cummings's poetry can hardly be overemphasized; for it acts not as passive background, a nonentity, but as an active protagonist, complementing the black print thematically and structurally. Where the print becomes silent, the white space grows eloquent. And it speaks in many ways. In "between nose red gross," it represents movement, the time and space taken by the first jounce of a rising curtain:

stage whose jouncing curtain.   , rises
(Tulips and Chimneys, "Portraits," III)

In "raise the shade," it spans the time between the end of a prostitute's sympathetic monologue on "working girls" and the beginning of her own work.

i'm

sorry for awl the
poor girls that
gets up god
knows when every
day of their
lives
aint you,

        oo-oo.   dearie

not so
hard dear

(&, "Portraits," V)

The white space in "my love is building a building" helps construct a "hanging" poetic line.

> where the surrounded smile
>
> hangs
>
> breathless
>
> (*Tulips and Chimneys*, "Sonnets-Actualities," II)

Here, as in other poems where Cummings moves lines in unusual directions, the white space is necessary to group related words and to isolate thematic lines. Recall that in "windows go orange," it made the vertical motif "Dark / stories / gather / the / Again" stand out from the surrounding horizontal and vertical movements.

Finally, by putting space around motifs and slowing their pulse, vacancy can convey pictorial equivalents of hesitation, detachment, ennui, even despair, that reinforce the meaning of these motifs. The sonnet "nearer," like so many of the early poems about sex, contrasts the speaker's lusty eagerness during the night with his self-disgust (projected to his partner) in the morning. The first eleven lines describe a night in which strands of sex, madness, evil, and fearful dreams all intertwine, as the speaker begs his lover to "take not thy tingling limbs from me." Appropriately, the single-spaced lines rush along breathlessly, as the internal punctuation, colons, pushes one motif into the next. But as the dawn breaks, the lines abruptly slow to double-spaced, widely separated fragments.

> Querying greys between mouthed houses curl
>
> thirstily.   Dead stars stink.   dawn.   Inane,
>
> the poetic carcass of a girl
>
> (&, "Sonnets-Realities," X)

Just as the ugly diction ("stink," "inane," "carcass") conveys the speaker's revulsion, the wide spacing suggests his physical and emotional detachment from his partner, who now seems to him as little more than picked over meat.

In his painting during the mid- and late twenties (the beginning of his later period), Cummings found several ways to invest background space with perceptual weight. These methods can be grouped into two basic approaches: counterbalancing the subject with a dynamic background and unifying the subject and background with a single, dominant technique.

Fig. 34.
portrait—hair, c. 1926–30, oil on cardboard, 10½ × 11½ in. Collection of R. W. Davidson.

A good example of the first approach is *Flowers in a vase* (plate 9). Here, the still life subject and surrounding space struggle for dominance. The vertically arranged flowers are nearly swamped by large, jagged swathes of blue, green, grey, and ochre that fall diagonally from upper right to center, and by a brown fissure at left. Picking up a red patch for good measure, these lines and swathes continue down through the tablecloth to the lower left. By extending the background motif this way, Cummings brings it up to the picture plane, just as his poem brings the moon "against" the trees. Once again, Matisse's *Harmony in Red* comes to mind in the way it flattens deep space by continuing a motif on objects of differing depths, e.g., the color and curving branch pattern on the wall and tablecloth.

Certainly, Matisse inspired another technique Cummings uses to emphasize background. Matisse's *Woman with Green Stripe* opposes conflicting colors both behind the head of Madame Matisse and in her face. Although Cummings does not violate the unity of the face in his portrait, *Anne in a blue hat at table* (plate 6), he does play off background colors against each other and against the subject and, like Matisse, echoes a figurative color (the light green shadow under Anne's chin) in the background (the green table). These contrasts upstage the figure somewhat and come forward, while Anne's squarish, unmodeled neck and shoulders recede as they align with the ground. Both perceptual motions moderate the figure's dominance and make an otherwise conventional portrait more subtle and complex.

Cummings's other approach to perceptual balance, unifying the figure and ground through a single technique, was probably the one he came to favor most. In painting after painting of *CIOPW*, background and subject are unified in the swift brushwork and textures of the later period.[37] In *portrait—hair* (fig. 34), for example, broad patches of negative space are as tangible as the figure itself. And the brushwork within the figure is as rough as the background textures. The result is a clearly recognizable subject that seems all of a piece with its surroundings: it shares, but does not usurp, the perceptual space of the canvas.

As with textures, so with lines and planes: these, too, can unify figure with ground. In *portrait—M. R. Werner* (fig. 35), the lines outside the pensive pipe-smoker imitate his body curves and continue their generally downward vertical-diagonal direction. While

Fig. 35.
portrait—M. R. Werner, c. 1926–30, oil. From *CIOPW*. Copyright 1931, 1959 by E. E. Cummings.

they, themselves, may describe a tangible object (an overstuffed chair or pillow?), their repetition of Werner's lines becomes the unifying motif.

Through the remainder of his career, Cummings returned to these methods of perceptual balance, letting his subjective response to each subject determine whether counterbalance or unification (or both) should become the method, and whether lines, colors, planes, or textures (or a combination of these) should become the medium of balance. *Posed woman: eyes half-closed* (plate 7), a stunning piece of Expressionism, blends the techniques of counterbalance and unification. The red-green clash in the lower-left ground is as daring as the weird red and blue eyelids. And the background red and yellow are certainly as powerful as red and gold in the face. The result is a coloristic standoff that leaves the ground as prominent and proximate as the figure.

Cummings unifies figure and ground here in a strange way. Besides repeating colors and the diagonal shoulder line in the figure's outline, he "bleeds" the two boldest facial colors into the background. The creamy pink of one eyelid runs, like smeared mascara, alongside the face. And the gold, squiggly line above the forehead merges with both the pink-white below it and the intense yellow above and behind it. Both bleedings lead one's eye from figure to ground. For all her shocking intensity of color and brushwork, the sultry woman must share the viewer's attention with an equally potent background.

The techniques Cummings devised to heighten the perceptual appeal of his early paintings and poems proved surprisingly durable. The *Self-portrait in blue tie* of 1958 (plate 11), painted only four years before his death, employs the same methods to balance and unify figure and ground that inform paintings of thirty years earlier. The later poems continue to respect white space as the visual, and often thematic, complement of black ink, while they achieve more intricate structures to make a thematic line perceptually—and richly—ambiguous.

l(a

le
af
fa

ll

s)
one
l

iness

(95 Poems, 1)

Oneliness? Loneliness? Why not both?

    Finally, the typographical innovations that Cummings generated as "gestures" prevailed as the most distinctive and characteristic features of his poetic style: the exquisite "l(a" above, published in 1958, is a spiritual and aesthetic soul mate to the *Self-Portrait* of the same year. Cummings held to these techniques simply because he remained devoted to their aesthetic purpose: to intensify our immediate, felt sense of a work's elements and of its wholeness, while inhibiting our natural tendency to turn perceptions into recognitions, concepts, abstractions. The poems and paintings, first and last, demand to be *looked* at.

"Seeing Around" Form

4

Seeing the Whole Object

▄▄▄▄ The techniques Cummings devised to intensify the perceptual appeal of his painting and poetry had one major shortcoming: they were essentially two-dimensional. The unity they strove for was a unity of surface, comprised of parts both heightened and balanced so that all could shine and none prevail. What the perceptual devices did not address, however, was the problem of depth, of structure, of the object as it occupies—or intimates—three-dimensional space. Cummings was fully aware of the problem, however, and pondered it extensively in his early notes. He was bothered, for example, by the perceptual disparity between an object's three-dimensional whole-ness and the eye's ability to see only "a little more than $\begin{array}{c}\text{1/2 cylinder,}\\\text{a hemisphere}\end{array}$ cone" rather than all the way around it (fig. 36).

    A) between "me" and "yonder wall" stands "a stove"
       i do not see
       1) part of the stove
       2) the space between the stove and the wall
       3) part of the wall
       4) part of me which does not see 1,2,3
       5)   "   "   expresses what it sees   by A
                            (does not see)
                         (Houghton notes, I[27] no. 23)

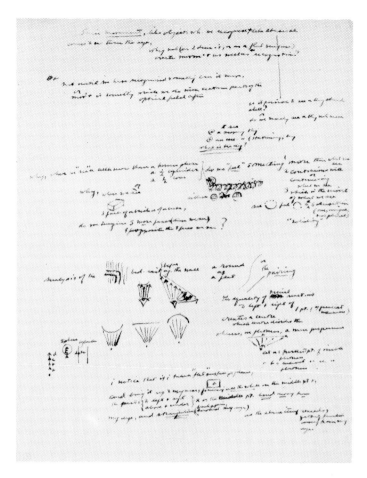

Fig. 36.
Note on "seeing around," c. 1921-23. The E. E. Cummings papers, the Houghton Library, Harvard University. By permission of the Houghton Library. Copyright 1982, The E. E. Cummings Trust.

What made this perceptual problem tantalizing for Cummings was that he could still feel what he could not see—the back, or "behind" of a structure:

> the behind is something of which we can become conscious. We can never experience it, find it. If we turn around, we merely include a new field in the Before, what is in front of us; [and create] a new Behind [. . . .] Yet we can 'have a feeling that someone has come into the room', 'someone is looking over my shoulder'—whom i cannot possibly see. Also [the feeling that] 'if i turn around quickly enough i'll catch objects as form'. (Houghton notes, I[25] no. 79)

This last feeling is provocative: to "catch objects as form." Bordering on the intuitive, this apprehension fuses perception with subjective feeling.

see ⌒   feel ⌣ = a sensation (one, unique, not plural)
"solidity"

(Houghton notes, I[25] no. 153)

Merely recognizing an object's two-dimensional shape will not elicit this sensation.

Form (seeing all of a vase, the Behind) [. . . .]
Except in D[ream] we suppress our desire to see (the around things),
    Form, in favor of merely objects.
        all of

(Houghton notes, I[25] no. 136ᵛ)

Here, then, is the three-dimensional version of the premise guiding the preceding chapter: mentally recognizing shapes as objects keeps one from perceptually apprehending the complete configuration of a work, its wholeness. Now, in three dimensions, this wholeness requires a union of the visible front and the apprehensible "Behind." A work so unified conveys "a sensation [. . . of] solidity"—the volume of three-dimensional form—just as it gives the viewer the perceptual illusion that she can apprehend that form by "seeing around" the object. "Seeing around" thus became Cummings's shorthand for sensing three-dimensional form on a two-dimensional surface.

For Cummings, the "Behind" was not merely an extension of the visible "front"—an illusion painters had conveyed since the Renaissance through chiaroscuro modeling. Nor, for that matter, was it limited to the visual art of painting: "front," "back," and wholeness were structural qualities he attributed to all of his arts, however metaphorically. To understand his sense of "behind," we must return to the seminal note of chapter 2: "(pure form) is natural to everybody in a dream state.[. . .] Meaning=a poise, 2 factors are the heard or Seen word (eg Bad) & the Unseen Unheard (Good) ie, language based on ANTITHESES (good-bad) on Syntax (position) & on Grammar" (Houghton notes, I[25] no. 136). The "behind" thus involves the idea of opposites, contraries, antitheses, negatives that are present—albeit "unseen" and "unheard"—when the "front" appears. If the positive front and negative behind can be yoked together in sudden forceful juxtapositions, the explosive composite would flash, if only for an instant, a glimpse of solidity.

That images and words may secretly convey their opposites, and that juxtaposing incongruous elements creates disturbingly new and potent structures, were scarcely original ideas in Cummings's time. As Roger Shattuck observes, they were signal features of Modernism in nearly all the arts of the later nineteenth and early twentieth centuries:

> A forceful modern style of juxtaposition broke out like a rash around 1910 in the writings of unamists and futurists, and of simultanists like Apollinaire, Cendrars and Reverdy. They recorded the world in the still-scrambled order of sensation and the style soon affected the work of Ezra Pound, Wyndham Lewis, Virginia Woolf, James Joyce, and Valery Larbaud . . . [and also] Ernest Hemingway.[1]

Indeed, Shattuck's description of the "logic of simultanism" glosses Cummings's aesthetic perfectly: "It requires that our minds entertain concurrently and without synthesis two or more contradictory propositions."[2] What is significant about Cummings's aesthetics, therefore, is not its originality but its very derivativeness, its sensitivity to widely diverse sources all espousing aspects of the same idea—a diversity that suggests not only the catholicity of Cummings's interests but also his power to integrate such unlikely aesthetic bedfellows as Cézanne, burlesque, and Freud into a cohesive aesthetics with multiple possibilities for his arts.

Sources

The immediate source of the phrase and meaning of "seeing around" was Willard Huntington Wright's *Modern Painting: Its Tendency and Meaning* (1915), a pioneering study on the Modernist movements that virtually became Cummings's bible in the teens and early twenties, and from which he typed out long paragraphs verbatim in his notes.[3] As chief apologist for the short-lived style Synchromism (and brother to its cofounder, Stanton MacDonald-Wright), Willard Wright construed art history according to the color-form aesthetics of Synchromism, an evolution that Leonardo began and Cézanne accelerated:

> Leonardo . . . in his Trattato della Pittura recorded the fact that our vision encompasses to a slight degree everything that passes before it; that we *see around* all objects; and that this encircling sight gives us the sensation of rotundity. But neither he, nor any artist up to Cézanne, was able to make aesthetic use of the fact. . . . Cézanne saw the impossibility of producing a double [stereoscopic] vision by geometric rules, and approached the problem [differently]. . . . By understanding the functioning elements of color in their relation to texture and space, he was able to paint forms in such a way that each color he applied took its relative position in space and held each part of the object stationary at any required distance from the eye. As a result of this method we can judge the depth and the solidity of his pictures the same as we do in nature. (p. 148, my emphasis)

In an otherwise skewed survey, Wright's chapter on Cézanne was brilliant and provided Cummings a thorough exegesis of the master's structural innovations. Equally important to Cummings's ideas, Wright quoted extensively Cézanne's explanations and opinions to Emile Bernard on color, form, and perception from Bernard's *Souvenirs sur Paul Cézanne*. These brilliant, though flawed sources—along with Cézanne's paintings themselves—provided Cummings an excellent grounding in Cézanne's innovations.[4]

What most impressed him was Cézanne's ability to convey three-dimensional "solidity," not by resorting to chiaroscuro modeling, but by carefully "modulating" pure colors according to their propensities to emerge or recede.[5] Typically, Cézanne placed his warmest colors at the "culminating point" of a figure—that point apparently closest to the viewer—and worked towards the edges with progressively cooler colors.[6] The result was that an otherwise flat plane appears to bulge at the culminating point, recede at the edges, and thus possess a rounded solidity. Cummings noted a similar optical curve when he focused exclusively on the "middle point" of a plane.

> i notice that if i take a "flat" surface, or plane and bring
> $\boxed{X}$
> it up to my nose, focusing <u>all the while</u> on the middle pt. X,
> the parts $\left\{\begin{array}{l}\text{to left \& right}\\ \text{above and under}\end{array}\right\}$ X or the middle pt. <u>bend away from</u>
> my eye, and <u>straighten</u> $\left\{\begin{array}{l}\text{back again}\\ \text{(towards my eye)}\end{array}\right.$ as the plane itself
> recedes, getting further away from my eye.
>
> (Houghton notes, I[25] no. 153)

By carefully arranging his colors according to their potential movement, Cézanne could make his forms "advance, recede, swell and shrink," as Wright put it. He balanced these movements against each other "by a plastic distribution of volumes over and beside spatial vacancies. He mastered this basic principle of *the hollow and the bump*" (p. 151, my emphasis). Unless Rebecca Cummings had read this passage in Wright, she would scarcely have understood what her son meant when he wrote in 1922, "speaking of chasms, I am painting that—and bumps. Or what is commonly (obscurely may I add?) called 'getting form by colour.' "[7]

If Cézanne arranged his colors in graduated sequences, the Neo-Impressionists and particularly Seurat favored more abrupt clashes of complementaries, albeit in smaller, more regular dot patterns. A student of such color theorists as Michel Chevreul and Ogden Rood, Seurat knew that an intense color leaves a faint afterimage of its complement on the retina.[8] Cummings also knew this idea (probably through Signac's *From Delacroix to Neo-Impressionism*), for in notes listing the initial stages of perception he writes:

> 1. Sensation
> 2. After-image: negative, comp[lementary] in color and brightness
>   to the c. & b. of preceding stimulus[.]
>   (Houghton notes, I[59] no. 109)

He also knew Chevreul's axiom that complementary colors, when juxtaposed, intensified each other: "Any colour in contact with its complementary is at its maximum hue."

In Picasso's Cubism, Cummings found a logical successor to Cézanne's new vision: "Picasso has given me more solidity than I have yet to feel from nature, life [. . . .] He has done this on [a] flat surface with colour, outline etc.—planes and lines."[9] Fittingly, Cummings's poetic homage to Picasso praises the Spaniard's formal solidity in the language of "seeing around."

> Picasso
> you give us Things
> which
> bulge
>
>   (*XLI Poems*, "Portraits," III)

Yet, although Cummings admired Picasso, to identify Cubism as the exclusive source of his interest in structural juxtaposition, as some critics have done, is too narrow.[10] Cubism surely influenced this aesthetics; but so did Cézanne, Neo-Impressionism, and a host of other "isms" that employed juxtaposition prominently (not to mention Schoenberg, Pound, Stein, and Apollinaire). So sensitive were Cummings's antennae to these new signals that they locked into sources quite removed from the arts—burlesque and Freud—both of which influenced his art directly and help explain some of its recondite features.

Long a fan of burlesque, Cummings paid it homage in an article he wrote for *Vanity Fair* in 1925, "You Aren't Mad, Am I?"[11] Burlesque, he writes, can convey "solidity" more naturally and accurately than painting or sculpture because it makes " 'opposites' occur together." To illustrate this, Cummings narrates a scene of "knowing around" (the conceptual equivalent to "seeing around"). A burlesque comedian, Jack Shargel, is handed a rose. He receives it with elaborate seriousness and "rapturously" inhales its fragrance,

> then (with a delicacy which Chaplin might envy) tosses the red rose exquisitely, lightly, from him. The flower describes a parabola— weightlessly floats downward—and just as it touches the stage there is a terrific, soul-shaking, earthquake-like crash: as if all the glass and masonry on earth, all the most brittle and most ponderous things of this world, were broken to smithereens.
>
> Nothing in "the arts," indeed, not even Paul Cézanne's greatest painting of Mont Sainte-Victoire, has moved me more, or has proved to be a more completely inextinguishable source of "aesthetic emotion," than this *knowing around* of the Shargel rose; this releasing of all un-roselike and non-flowerish elements which—where "rose" and "flower" are ordinarily concerned—secretly or unconsciously modify and enhance those rose—and flower—qualities to which (in terms of consciousness only) they are "opposed." (Cummings's emphasis)

This provocative anecdote generates several important aesthetic ideas. First, "knowing around" the rose involves a clash, a juxtaposition of opposites: the rose's qualities and their antitheses. The "un-roselike" and "non-flowerish elements" are, conceptually, the rose's back. By defining what the rose is not, is furthest from, these antitheses secretly "modify and enhance" what it is. Moreover, they appear simultaneously with the rose's qualities: "back" and "front" thus join into one conceptual whole.[12] But most important, these unroselike qualities are opposite only "in terms of consciousness." On another level—the unconscious—they can coexist without what the conscious mind calls "opposition." The language here is Freudian, and Cummings leaves no doubt of his source when he discusses the same aesthetics of opposition in words themselves: "language was not always blest with 'opposites.' Quite the contrary. A certain very wise man has pointed out (in connection with the meaning of dreams) that what "weak" means and what "strong" means were once upon a time meant by one word." Now it becomes clear why Cummings felt that only "in a dream state" was a sense of complete form "natural to everybody."

Freud's influence on Cummings's aesthetics was profound, as we shall see presently.[13] Here, we should briefly note Freud's import in Cummings's life. In the years during and after World War I, Freud was virtually a cause célèbre in Greenwich Village, and Cummings was one of his most ardent disciples and advocates.[14] Three of his closest friends, Scofield Thayer, Sibley Watson, and Edward Nagel, had all undergone psychoanalysis in the early 1920s (Thayer with Freud himself) and had lauded the results.[15] Unlike many of his contemporaries who merely bandied Freudian ideas about, however, Cummings read Freud extensively and carefully and pondered the relevance of Freudian theories to his writing and painting.[16] These theories, indeed, marked a watershed in Cummings's intellectual development, as he wrote in 1940: "I wonder if, from my Keats period, I wasn't opened into reality via Freud (per Thayer) and Wittels [. . . .]"[17] "Reality" in this case means the importance Freud ascribed to sex—or rather, the importance Cummings and his contemporaries believed he did in their efforts to fashion a life free of "puritanical" repression.[18]

Cummings had more than a puritanical legacy to overcome, however. As Richard Kennedy has shown, his upbringing under the aegis of the Reverend Edward Cummings was prudish, and Cummings developed a hostility, mingled with awe, towards his domineering father that could easily be construed as Oedipal.[19] Little wonder, then, that the son later saw Freud as a sexual liberator whose theories could explain and thereby remove Cummings's childhood inhibitions. Such a belief led Cummings not only to read *The Interpretation of Dreams* and *Wit and its Relation to the Unconscious* by the late teens, but to attempt a thorough self-analysis in late 1923.[20] Like any good disciple of a new religion, he sought to spread the word. Letters to his family in the early 1920s, such as this one to his sister in 1922, proffer Freud as a cure-all:

> SEX IS EVERYTHING (as Freud says): You either know this or you don't. If you don't you don't. It's not what can be taught! J'espére, in your connection! By the way, when I see you I shall expect you to be conversant with two books: The Interpretation of Dreams and WIT and the Unconscious. Both are by FREUD. ----!! GET WISE TO YOUR-SELF!!! ----[21]

Secondhand Freudianism, moreover, informs several of the essays Cummings wrote for *Vanity Fair* in the mid-1920s, suggesting that he intensified his interest as the decade progressed.[22]

He had reason to, for the teens and twenties witnessed a series of emotional crises for Cummings: his unhappy affair with Elaine Orr Thayer beginning in 1918 and resulting in the birth of a daughter whom Cummings barely acknowledged (though her paternity was an open secret), the breakup of his brief marriage to Elaine in 1924 and the painful divorce proceedings that followed, the sudden death of his father in 1926, and his turbulent relationship with Anne Barton through the latter half of the 1920s. Ricocheting between extremes of depression and ebullience, dependence and self-confidence, Cummings turned increasingly to Freud as an anchor and finally underwent a complete—and, he felt, successful—psychoanalysis by Dr. Fritz Wittels in 1928–29.[23]

Freud's influence, however, transcended Cummings's personal life to shape important aspects of his "seeing around" aesthetics. To see its contribution, we must return to the burlesque essay. The "very wise man" who pointed out that some antonymous words originally had one root was, of course, Freud in *The Interpretation of Dreams*.

> I was astonished to learn from a pamphlet by K. Abel, *The Antithetical Meaning of Primal Words* (1884) (cf. my review of it . . .)—and the fact has been confirmed by other philologists—that the most ancient languages behave exactly like dreams in this respect [i.e., combining opposites]. In the first instance they have only a single word to describe the two contraries at the extreme ends of a series of qualities or activities (e.g., "strong-weak," "old-young," "far-near," "bind-sever"); they only form distinct terms for the two contraries by a secondary process of making small modifications in the common word.[24]

Freud appended this footnote to a passage especially relevant to Cummings's aesthetics:

The way in which dreams treat the category of contraries or contra-dictories is highly remarkable. It is simply disregarded. "No" seems not to exist so far as dreams are concerned. *They show a particular preference for combining contraries into a unity* or for representing them as one and the same thing. Dreams feel themselves at liberty, moreover, *to represent any element by its wishful contrary,* so that there is no way of deciding at a first glance whether any element that admits of a contrary is present in dream-thoughts as a positive or as a negative.[25]

In a quite remarkable congruence, Freud's description of these unconscious processes of joining "contraries" involves precisely the same technique—juxtaposing opposites—that Cummings had observed in Modernist painting, poetry, and burlesque. Three-dimensional "seeing around," therefore, could be as relevant to the geography of the psyche as to the structure of a picture or poem.

Cézanne and W. H. Wright, Seurat and Picasso, Jack Shargel and Sigmund Freud—such were the diverse sources of Cummings's aesthetics of form. From their examples of apparent contradictions, secret affinities, and heightened intensities, Cummings synthesized and shaped his idea that to achieve the wholeness of three-dimensional form and to create the greatest possible aesthetic intensity requires a bringing to the "surface"—in the viewer's perception of a canvas or a poem—of juxtapositions that occur naturally in the unconscious, in color theory, and even in the words of ancient languages and the play of children. But as he had done with visual poetry, Cummings pushes these ideas far beyond their visual, psychological, and linguistic origins in fashioning a unified aesthetics.

"Seeing Around" Colors and Words

It is convenient to study Cummings's aesthetics of form by beginning with basic elements—colors and words—and then building to broader applications in themes and structures. Not surprisingly, the most derivative of these areas is color, for the young Cummings was less sure of himself as a painter and thus more likely to follow the lead of painters he admired. His notes on color quote literally from Wright or Bernard and revolve around two Modernist principles. Cézanne contributed the first. Pure colors, arranged by their apparent propensity to advance or recede, can convey three-dimensional form:

solidity = nearness-farness
Thus, no-one can "give the 3rd dimension" on a flat surface
unless: suites of color equaling progressive degrees of distance [are
    employed.][26]
(Houghton notes, I[25] no. 154)

Within these "suites of color," Cummings compares the most extreme in their sensations of depth:

Y[ellow]	and	V[iolet] extremes in
Advancing		Receeding
BulgE		Shrink
push		pull
eject, expell, emit		absorb, Suck, insert
OUTwardly		INWARDLY
bump-against the eye		Yank

Note: the Bulge is both Outwardly and BigLY—so the Shrink is both
      Inwardly and LittLY   EXPANSION
                         CONTRACTION
(Houghton notes, I[59] no. 73)

Seurat, the Neo-Impressionists, and the color theorists they studied inspired the second principle: juxtaposing complementary colors of sufficient size intensifies each color, or, as Cummings puts it, "Freshness of color through juxtaposition [of] the pure elementaries[.] [T]o avoid the dullness, we keep [?] from mixing them on the palette. Eye = the mixer" (Houghton notes, bMS Am. 1892.7[68]). More playfully, he toys with aphorisms that express the interplay of complementaries.

Green means, a kind of absence of white
         a Presence (surrounding, touching without mixing) of red
the least intensity of red is the greatest absence of green
RED IS THE PRESENCE OF THE ABSENCE OF GREEN
(Houghton notes, I[25] no. 162)

Cummings had still to reconcile, however, the disparity between arranging colors in "suites" (à la Cézanne) and in more abrupt clashes of complementaries (following the Neo-Impressionists). His early painting appears to have explored both approaches but favors the latter. While *Sound Number I* (plate 1) offers several modulations of green, many other abstractions put complementaries side by side, for example, the orange-blue and red-green juxtapositions of *Noise Number 1*.

One excellent example of how Cummings juxtaposed colors to convey three-dimensional form is the early oil, *Seated red-headed nude* (plate 4). This is one of Cummings's most successful portraits, a clever and complex balancing of formal tensions and sexual suggestiveness. The clashes between colors and planes are as bold as the nude's saucy smile and knowing eyes. Indeed, the primary purpose of these clashes is to embolden the nude visually, to bring her forward to the picture plane—to the viewer.

To this end, Cummings carefully arranges the colors to reach four bumps, or culminating points, along the nude's vertical axis: at her hair, knee, right calf, and slippers. In the top half, the dark background easily thrusts forward the white body (modulated somewhat by the ochre wrapper) and, still more, the startling red hair and mouth. In the third horizontal quadrant (the bed), the modulation is more complex. One can see "contrasts of colors submitted to a cadence" on both sides of the legs. This cadence is a rhythmical alternation of bumps and hollows, culminating in the biggest bumps: the knees, calf, and slippers. On the left, the rhythm is graduated. The muted but irregular gray-white emerges somewhat from the medium-intensity yellow which, in turn, precedes the dark gold. This regression reverses itself abruptly, however, where the recessive gold pushes the white legs forward into greater relief. Finally, the bright orange slippers, intensely white right calf, and white knees (the last at the exact center) dominate the legs. On the right, the contrasts are abrupt: the dark green recedes sharply from the legs, creating a hollow as it pushes the legs forward, while the adjoining red-orange is the near complementary of the green and creates a lesser bump.

These push and pull colors in the painting's lower half diminish some of the nude's perceptual dominance, as do the large flat planes of the floor. Cummings here not only balances flatness against depth, and abstraction against representation, but also the two-dimensional wholeness of seeing the entire surface against the three-dimensional wholeness of "seeing around" a figure. Ultimately, however, the figure dominates the ground. At each point of conflict, the elements weigh in her favor. The sharply diagonal lines in the bottom quarter lead back to the orange slippers, which, because of their intense color and position before the apex of these lines, master the large, but cool, green and violet planes beneath them. Similarly, at the muted red-orange, the hand leads one's eye back along the arm to the nude's face and hair.

Perhaps this is why *Seated red-headed nude* works so well. The technique of seeing around—color juxtapositions and sequences creating bumps and hollows—projects the nude in perceptual ways quite apart from her representational rendering. At the same time, the two-dimensional handling of the lower planes turns vacancy into volumes that keep the figure from overwhelming the rest of the canvas. If indebted to Cézanne and the Neo-Impressionists, these techniques are at least distinctively and confidently handled. And when Cummings applies analogous techniques of "seeing around" to his poems, he breaks new ground.

One of Cummings's most daring translations of his "seeing around" aesthetics was to apply the visual dynamics of complementary colors to the psychological dynamics of antithetical words. In retrospect, it seems perhaps a small step to assume that if complementary colors are optically related and mutually enhancing, the same could be true of contradictory words, emotions, even ideas. But it is a small step that only a genius could take. Cummings's technique is to design unusual oxymorons: phrases of contradictory words that secretly enhance each other.

The technique has puzzled his critics. Norman Friedman, for example, observes:

> He used it with much greater frequency in his first volume [*Tulips and Chimneys*] than ever again, and it seems there a sign of youthful exuberance resulting in a kind of ambiguity which is puzzling to evaluate. What are we to say about "the noise of petals falling silently," "peaceful terrors," "evident invisibles," "large minute hips," "precise clumsy," "grim ecstasy," "the dusty newness of her obsolete gaze," "obscure and obvious hands," or "obscene shy breasts"? . . . One gets a sense of verbal excess, of a sometimes arbitrary creative flamboyance.[27]

Most critics politely ignore the technique altogether; and one who has perceptively identified its aesthetic origins and parallels, Rushworth Kidder, does not analyze how the oxymorons themselves work.[28] Yet the technique cannot simply be put aside, for, as Friedman shows, it occurs often in Cummings's early poems. Here are some more examples, followed by their page numbers in *Complete Poems: 1913–1962*:

a skilful uncouth/prison   (66)
the serene nervous light   (85)
the whirlingPeaceful furious street   (100)
an impenetrable transparency   (137)
whose careless movements carefully scatter   (150)
taste the accurate demure / ferocious rhythm of precise
    laziness   (162)
a personal radiance sits hideously   (168)
with twists spontaneously methodical   (170)
fiercely shy and gently brutal   (214)
frail firm asinine life   (160)
the sharp days slobber   (220)
whispering fists of hail   (299)
a wise / and puerile moving of your arm   (302)

To examine one jarring example in detail, consider the closing two lines of the poem "the bed is not very big":

the bed is not very big

a sufficient pillow shoveling
her small manure-shaped head

one sheet on which distinctly wags

at times the weary twig
of a neckless nudity
(very occasionally budding

a flabby algebraic odour

jigs
      et tout en face
always wiggles the perfectly dead
finger of thitherhithering gas.

clothed with a luminous fur

poilu

      a Jesus sags
in frolicsome wooden agony).

(&, "Sonnets-Realities," V)

"Frolicsome"? What could be further from "agony," less appropriate to the spiritual gravity of the Crucifixion? True, this verbal contradiction expresses the incongruous image preceding it that depicts the gaslight illuminating the crucifix as "clothing" it in a sensuous, nappy fur ("poilu"). But the shock of the verbal contradictions between "frolicsome" and "agony" surpasses this visual incongruity, and Cummings heightens the verbal shock by isolating the final lines containing it. Yet, for all its startling incongruity, the phrase somehow works. "Frolicsome" 's anamolous presence intensifies the agony that "sags" begins and "wooden" continues; grossly inappropriate, it points ironically back to the suffering.

But how do we know that the oxymoron should work this way? To answer this, we must consider Cummings's sources. Certainly, as a literary device, the oxymoron has a long tradition of which Cummings was doubtless aware. He would not have failed to note its use by the English Metaphysical poets, by his beloved Keats, or (particularly apt here) by Petrarchan sonnets to express "love's contradictions."[29] But his primary sources were extraliterary, to be found in the interactions of colors and the combinations of the unconscious. The parallel actions of verbal oxymorons and complementary colors are unmistakable. Both couplings juxtapose opposites in jarring discords that may intensify each component. But opposition alone does not explain why contradictories such as "frolicsome wooden agony" are really congruent in affirming "agony." Recall that in Jack Shargel's crashing rose, Cummings found a model of "knowing around" not only because "opposites occur together," but because they were opposite "in terms of consciousness only." On another level—the unconscious—the "unroselike and nonflowerish" elements *secretly or unconsciously modify and enhance*" those "rose" and "flower" qualities (my emphasis).

Freud's descriptions of how contradictories work in the unconscious glosses Cummings's exegesis perfectly. Dreams "show a particular preference for combining contraries into a unity . . ."; they are free "to represent any element by its wishful contrary." Significantly for Cummings's aesthetics, "words are treated in dreams as though they were concrete things and for that reason they are apt to be combined in just the same way as presentations of concrete objects."[30] Thus, words too can signify the opposite of their meanings or can form contradictory pairings. Freud's review of Abel's pamphlet not only surveys the various ways ancient languages combined opposite meanings into a single word, but also attributes the same wordplay to children. All three sources of word play—ancient languages, children, and the unconscious—were integral to Cummings's aesthetics.[31]

In *Wit and Its Relation to the Unconscious*, Freud describes this verbal process in more detail as an example of "representation through the opposite" or "outdoing wit." The latter occurs when the opposite of the appropriate response, "owing to its context, is equivalent to a still stronger version of the appropriate response. *The contradiction takes the place of an exaggerated confirmation.*"[32] Here, in a sentence, is the psychoanalytic rationale of "frolicsome wooden agony." As in wit-technique, one side of the opposition can be made, by context, to "secretly enhance" (Cummings) or act as "an exaggerated confirmation" (Freud) of the other side. The contexts of our associations regarding the rose (delicacy), or the Crucifixion (suffering), are so firmly established that the antitheses of these contexts (the crashing rose, "frolicsome" agony) stand out glaringly enough to point back to—and "secretly enhance"—the original contextual qualities.

Of course, there are significant differences between Freud's model and Cummings's application. In Freudian theory, the juxtaposition between context and contradiction originates in the unconscious and manifests itself in the witticism or dream. Cummings reverses the process. The juxtaposition originates as a conscious artistic technique, but it appeals to the reader's memory of, and unconscious associations with, a particular context. Then too, not all of Cummings's verbal oppositions are as imbalanced as "frolicsome wooden agony." Some, for example "obscene shy breasts," seem more balanced—either adjective could control the image—and thus fail to resolve the tension of their opposition. Here, we must consider the *thematic* context of these poised tensions to discover both their origin and function. Often, the themes are sexual and divided—torn between the speaker's attraction to and repulsion from his lover. Once again, Cummings's sources help explain his puzzling dichotomies.

"Seeing Around" Themes and Motifs

The oppositions that Cummings felt were the key to seeing around form appear in his motifs and themes as well as in his colors and words. Indeed, Freud himself suggested this ambivalence of experience in his review of Abel's pamphlet: "The essential relativity of all knowledge, thought, or consciousness cannot but show itself in language. If everything that we know is viewed as a transition from something else, every experience must have two sides; and either every name must have a double meaning, or else for every meaning there must be two names."[33] For Cummings, such equivocality embodied the secret of whole form when the contradictory sides of an experience were yoked together.

Cummings's early paintings often juxtapose contrasting motifs. The abstractions play off lines against planes and frequently oppose swirling, circular forms to piercing diagonals. Both *Sound Number 2* and *Noise Number 13* (fig. 31, plate 5) derive their tension and nervous energy from these clashes. As he struggled to come to terms with the phenomenal world in his later painting, Cummings attempted several striking juxtapositions of concrete and abstract. *New York, 1927* (fig. 23), for example, presents a double juxtaposition. Anne Barton's larger than life features tower over a stylized background that is itself a conflict between Marinesque smokestacks and organic, pod shapes—a pictorial rendering of "Tulips and Chimneys." Subsequent paintings, such as *Sky over Paris* (fig. 25) often contrast naturalistic landscape with an expressionistic sky, for this painter was as unwilling merely to copy nature as he was to deny her. Self-expression transcended both extremes.

The early poetry explores thematic clashes even more than does the painting. The title of Cummings's first book of poems, *Tulips and Chimneys*, opposes the natural and man-made worlds and reflects the strident clashes within; the grimy, red-light world of "Sonnets-Realities" jostles such ethereal apostrophes as "Epithalamion," and earnest hymns to nature and childhood stand next to cynical satires of war and bourgeois America. Undoubtedly, however, the most abrupt oppositions occur *within* certain poems, particularly the "Sonnets-Realities" of the first three volumes. Most of these poems describe sex explicitly and imaginatively—but it is sex that is "enjoyed no sooner, but despisèd straight." For these poems reveal, in varying degrees of balance, a disturbing tension between the speaker's lust for his partner (often a prostitute) and his aversion to her. Significantly, both the speaker's delight in her body *and* his attendant or subsequent disgust are conveyed in incisive—and often shockingly repugnant—metaphors.

The balance between attraction and repulsion varies with each poem. If we reexamine "the bed is not very big," we find almost no balance at all: the portrait of this prostitute is unrelentingly sordid. Her manure-shaped head, neckless nudity, odorous body, and bad breath lack even the integration of belonging to a complete person: they "jig" and "wag" in spasmodic isolation. Conversely, "i like my body when it is with your / body" is all delight.

> i like my body when it is with your
> body. It is so quite new a thing.
> Muscles better and nerves more.
> i like your body. i like what it does,
> i like its hows. i like to feel the spine
> of your body and its bones, and the trembling
> -firm-smooth ness and which i will
> again and again and again
> kiss, i like kissing this and that of you,
> i like,slowly stroking the,shocking fuzz
> of your electric fur,and what-is-it comes
> over parting flesh . . . . And eyes big love-crumbs,
>
> and possibly i like the thrill
>
> of under me you so quite new
>
> (&, "Sonnets-Actualities," XXIV)

Most often, however, the sex poems bring attraction and repulsion into head-on conflict.

> the dirty colours of her kiss have just
> throttled
>   my seeing blood,her heart's chatter
>
> riveted a weeping skyscraper
>
> in me
>
>   i bite on the eyes' brittle crust
> (only feeling the belly's merry thrust
> Boost my huge passion like a business
>
> and the Y her legs panting as they press
> proffers its omelet of fluffy lust)

        at six exactly
                the alarm tore

two slits in her cheeks. A brain peered at the dawn.
she got up

                with a gashing yellow yawn
and tottered to a glass bumping things.
she picked wearily something from the floor

Her hair was mussed,and she coughed while tying strings
                (&, "Sonnets-Realities," III)

The octet is all lust. The speaker delights in describing the sensations that his lover—or rather, the parts of his lover—arouse in him. But at the same time, he degrades her humanness: the colors of her kiss are "dirty"; her heart can only "chatter"; her eyes have a "brittle crust"; her thrusting, if merry, is also "a business."

The sestet presents "the morning after" and transfers the night's sexual energy into violent, slashing images of morning. His lust only a memory, the speaker watches his lover with the aesthetic detachment and acuity of a painter. While he conveys a trace of sympathy for her fatigue, she remains, as during the night before, only an agglomeration of parts: a "yellow yawn," a "brain," "mussed" hair, undone strings.

These sexual polarities derive from the same sources as the verbal and color complementaries and address the same aesthetic goal of "seeing around." The sources—Modernist painting, the Petrarchan sonnet, and Freudian theory—are difficult to quantify separately in their respective contributions. Modernist painting, as practiced by such premier formalists as Cézanne and Picasso, put considerable distance between the painter and his human subject. The *Madame Cézanne* of 1893 and the Fernande portraits of 1909–11 resemble still lifes more than they do breathing, feeling people; the subjects concern the painter as problems in form. By treating his prostitutes as things, Cummings achieves a similar detachment that permits him to render their features with an imaginative clarity purged of sentimentality.[34]

That most of these sexual polarities (and verbal oppositions) occur in sonnets is no accident. As a lover of the sonnet form, Cummings had mastered Petrarch's and Shakespeare's models idealizing the qualities of the beloved. By turning love into sex and the idealized lady into a squalid whore, Cummings pays homage to the Petrarchan tradition by inverting it, much as Shakespeare did in "My Mistress' Eyes Are Nothing Like the Sun." Like a complementary afterimage left on the retina by an intense color, Petrarch's idealized lady hovers in the mind as a kind of ghostly afterimage of Cummings's repulsive prostitute in "the bed is not very big." The Petrarchan lady is the unmentioned standard against which the whore is measured. By simply being everything the prostitute is not, she mockingly reinforces the tawdriness of the real experience. Thus, the literary context functions here precisely as it does in Cummings's imbalanced verbal oppositions, such as "frolicsome wooden agony" of this same poem: "the contradiction takes the place of an exaggerated confirmation."

Both these explanations assume a purely aesthetic intent, removed from any sexual conflicts within the poet himself. But given what we know already of Cummings's fascination with Freud as sexual liberator, and of Cummings's rebellion against his prudish upbringing, we should look more closely at the poet's life vis-á-vis Freudian theory—just as Cummings himself did—to explain these sexual tensions more fully.

In his introduction to the 1922 manuscript edition of *Tulips & Chimneys*, Richard Kennedy writes: "Some of these poems reveal the tensions and uncertainties about sex which were common among the middle-class young men of the early 1920's, who, like Estlin Cummings, the minister's son, were just breaking free of the puritanical attitudes of earlier decades. A combination of fascination and repulsion wobbles through most of [the sex poems]" (p. xiii). Kennedy groups these poems in a style he calls the "Satyric," which "frequently treats [sex] as a dirty but necessary function" (p. xii).

Sex as "dirty but necessary" does not account for the unvarnished lust in these poems—the "attraction" side of Cummings's ambivalence. And it overlooks other expressions of Cummings's sexual interest, such as the scores of erotic drawings he made in these years. Yet, Kennedy's thesis that the sexual polarities reflect Cummings's own "tensions and uncertainties" makes good sense. In fact, the thesis finds independent support in Freud's 1912 essay, "On the Universal Tendency to Debasement in the Sphere of Love" (*Standard Edition,* vol. 11, pp. 179-90). Freud describes how a neurotic male becomes fully potent only with a "debased" woman, never with a "virtuous" one. The latter resembles too closely a mother or sister to whom he has formed an "incestuous fixation" in his youth. Conversely, the debased woman is sexually attractive because she appears aesthetically and "ethically" inferior to the male and can thus function solely as a "sexual object."

Several details of Cummings's early life fit this neurotic pattern. As Kennedy notes in *Dreams in the Mirror* (p. 103), Cummings was closely attached to his mother and sister and underwent an "Oedipal crisis" with his father. In one "primal scene," Cummings overheard his mother crying out his father's name during intercourse; Cummings thereupon resolved never "to take any more of my F[ather]'s hypocrisy." Another time, overhearing his father berating his mother, Cummings recalls his response: "I REVOLT ag[ainst] my F[ather]: would like to KILL HIM." Taking his mother's side in parental quarrels was only one expression of Cummings's Oedipal aggression. Another was his investigation of the low life that his father, a pillar of Unitarian propriety, must have abhorred. And paralleling Freud's profile of the neurotic male, Cummings's sexual initiation occurred relatively late: at twenty-three, according to Kennedy (p. 157).

Cummings's unresolved Oedipal conflicts, then, would seem to have disposed him to be both sexually attracted to and aesthetically repelled by the prostitutes in his sex poems. This aesthetic-erotic dichotomy perhaps explains why the adjectives and metaphors describing the lover's ugliness are as intensely vivid as those describing the speaker's pleasurable sensations of intercourse. Certainly, Cummings was not oblivious to these conflicts. His enthusiasm for Freud and for psychoanalysis derived, as noted above, from a desire to discover and thereby free himself of them. Thus, the ambivalence in his sex poems does not seem merely an unconscious expression of sexual conflict. Rather, the balanced tensions of lust and disgust, the clinical dissections of the repellent lovers show aesthetic distance, as if Cummings is presenting the competing sides of his sexual ambivalence, shaping and ordering their tangled relation, and thereby gaining aesthetic control of them. At the same time, he achieves a purely structural end by juxtaposing them. For as the attraction-repulsion pairings face, Janus-like, in opposite directions, they metaphorically possess a "back" as well as a "front": the rounded form of three-dimensional meaning.

"Seeing Around" Poetic Structure

Typically, Cummings's ideas of three-dimensional structure proved more inventive in his poetry than in his painting. While still at Harvard, he had abandoned the traditional concept of a poem as a "spoken lyric" that unfolds linearly for an architectural vision of it as a construction that "builds itself three-dimensionally, gradually, subtly in the consciousness of the experiencer."[35] Seeing around to a poem's "third" dimension, therefore, meant giving a spatial dimension to a temporal art form. Of course, Cummings pursued this spatiality in numerous ways. But underlying all of his spatial devices was a subversion of the poem's essential linearity, its sequential progression in which meaning builds cumulatively. By manipulating the order of his motifs, by taking them out of linear sequence and into various juxtapositions he could give them the effect of occurring almost simultaneously—side by side, as it were—much as music acquires spatiality when it presents separate themes simultaneously.

These manipulations of sequence took several forms in the early poems. One is the joining of separate strands of discourse.

> (Do you think?) the
> i do, world
> is probably made
> of roses&hello:
>
> (of solongs and,ashes)
>
>   ("into the strenuous briefness,"
>   *Tulips and Chimneys*, "Post Impressions," III)

If this passage is read linearly as a question, the parentheses and words "i do" intrude. "i do" answers the question before it is finished, while the parentheses slow the line and create a new perceptual twist: "(Do *you* think? . . . I do." The parenthetical question and immediate answer thus form a separate, but unseparated, inquiry juxtaposed to the statement "the world is probably made of . . . ." By arranging the two side by side (inquiry along the left margin, statement along the right), Cummings presents both *simultaneously* in a spatial, rather than linear, construction.

Parentheses effect an entirely different sort of juxtaposition, one revealing the discontinuous fragments of a stream-of-consciousness monologue, in the poem "it really must."

it really must
be Nice,never to

have no imagination)or never
never to wonder about guys you used to(and them
slim hot queens with dam next to nothing

on)tangoing
(while a feller tries
to hold down the fifty bucks per
job with one foot and rock a

cradle with the other)

(*is 5*, ''One,'' XIII)

As the speaker's mind jumps nervously from one thought to the next
(he suffers from insomnia as well as anxiety), his fragmented
thoughts move in and out of parentheses. This visual separator
brings the thoughts closer to each other, in time as well as space,
than complete syntax and periods would. Inspired by the stream-of-
consciousness passages of *Ulysses*, Cummings's structure expresses
the nervous twitches of consciousness ''moving in all directions''
rather than the logical, linear progression that is true to the conventions of language, but false to the workings of the mind.[36]

Just as assertion against question, and thought against
thought, may be juxtaposed, so may speech against narration and description.

this man is o so
Waiter
this;woman is

please shut that
the pout And affectionate leer
interminable pyramidal,napkins
(this man is oh so tired of this

(''ITEM,'' *is 5*, ''One,'' XIV)

Three modes of discourse, reflecting three actions of consciousness,
occur simultaneously: the speaker narrates his thought (''this man is
o so''), presents what he sees (''interminable pyramidal napkins''),
and quotes what he hears (''Waiter . . . please shut that''). Rather
than give them an artificial clarity by separating and completing

each, Cummings presents all three in the jumbled, fragmentary way they reach the speaker's consciousness. Looked at another way, the narrative comes from within the speaker's mind (thought and perception) and from outside it (external speech) simultaneously. Only gradually does the narrative resume a linear progression to reveal the object of the speaker's attention: a bored couple dining in a restaurant.

In even bolder juxtapositions, Cummings works fragments of an unrelated idea into a narrative. In between the large verse paragraphs of "my eyes are fond of the east side," a seeing, hearing, and tasting tour of New York's Lower East Side, appear these separate words set off in capitals:

TUMTITUMTIDDLE
THE BLACK CAT WITH
THE YELLOW EYES AND
THE
VIOLIN

(&, "Post Impressions," XI)

As description, they add little to the poem's huge stock of images. Their real purpose is to provide spatial contrast and visual relief by breaking up the large blocks of print surrounding them, much as fragments of the real world (whether as imitation chair caning and wood graining or as real pasted newspaper columns) break up painted surfaces in Synthetic Cubism.

Nor does the Cubist parallel end there; for just as Picasso often juxtaposed the newspaper fragments in his collages to form bawdy puns, Cummings (as John Peale Bishop has noted) fashions equally lewd juxtapositions from extraneous material.[37] In the poem, "O It's Nice to Get Up In . . ." for example, the capitalized lines that intersperse the poem come from a music hall song:

Oh, it's nice to get up in the morning
When the sun begins to shine,
And it's three or four or five o'clock
In the good old summer time.
But when the sky is murky
And it's cloudy overhead,
Oh, it's nice to get up in the morning,
But it's nicer to stay in bed.[38]

But in Cummings's hands, this innocent song of sloth acquires a leer:

O It's Nice To Get Up In, the slipshod mucous kiss
of her riant belly's fooling bore

(&, "Sonnets-Realities," I)

The most experimental and abstract of Cummings's linear manipulations are those that interject a word or letter into a line seemingly at random, such as *of* in this line:

the

ofpieces ofof sunligh tof fa l   l in gof throughof treesOf.

("inthe,exquisite;" &, "Post Impressions," XIV)

On closer inspection, however, the intrusive *of*'s suggest the pieces of sunlight themselves, filtering irregularly through the trees, while the rise and fall of each curving *f* may convey the kinaesthetic sense of falling, the central action of the line. If *of* has a semantic function, however, it escapes me, as does the semantic function of *A* in the poem "SNO."

from!the:A wending putrescence. a.of,loosely

;voices

(&, "Post Impressions," X)

That both of these poems, and "my eyes are fond of the east side," appear in a grouping called "Post Impressions" is no coincidence. The parallels between their semantic disjunctions and the discontinuous lines and planes of "Post-Impressionist" painting, particularly Cézanne's and Picasso's, are self-evident.[39] The playfulness of these juxtapositions also recalls Gertrude Stein's *Tender Buttons* in the latter's sophisticated wordplay that flirts with literary abstraction when it sometimes treats words as material equivalencies (aural, visual, or textural) of titled objects. In fact, the closing lines of Cummings's "inthe,exquisite;"

her sureLyeye s sit-ex actly her sitsat a surely!little,
roundtable amongother;littleexactly round. tables,

resemble one of the *Tender Buttons* he quoted in his Harvard commencement address, "The New Art":

Suppose a collapse is rubbed purr, is rubbed purr get.
Little sales ladies little sales ladies little saddles of mutton.
Little sales of leather . . . .[40]

And following the lead of both Stein (who concealed in *Tender Buttons* references to her lover, Alice Toklas) and Picasso (who painted into some Cubist canvases the words "Ma Jolie" as a loving reference to his new mistress), Cummings playfully hides an abbreviation of his lover's name, *Elaine Orr*, in verse from a book he dedicated to her:

> her:hands
>
>> will play on,mE as
> dea d tunes OR s-cra p-y leaVes flut te rin g
>>> ("i will be," &, "Seven Poems," I)

Cummings's "buttons," however, are more tender—at least more malleable—than Stein's. They require us only to rearrange a phrase here, a line there, to grasp the narrative progression. But to do so wreaks havoc on the contrived structures, on the sense of several things happening at once—Cummings's temporal analogy to the many-sidedness of three-dimensional form.

"Seeing Around" in Film, Theater, and *Him*

Cummings considered the possibilities of seeing around in arts other than painting and poetry, particularly those that already convey a third dimension such as film and theater. In September 1924, he visited the Astoria Film Studios on Long Island, considering a possible job as a scriptwriter. His observations over the next month produced a spate of sketches, a few articles for *Vanity Fair* (whose editor, Frank Crowinshield, got him the assignment), and several pages of notes on "seeing around" in the movies.

As a medium based on the continuous motion of successive images, film might seem congenial to Cummings's aesthetics of motion; but what interested Cummings was not simply the representation of moving subjects by a static device, but the *creation* of motion itself in the act of filming (i.e., of seeing): "the camera was not merely a passive instrument for recording an image but actually became the 'protagonist' of every picture through its manner of shooting the 'set.' Whereas, hitherto, 'moving' (pictures) has been used pictorially, to describe what things do (i.e. they move), I wish to employ 'moving' in a new sense—as revealing the essential data of phenomena, the truth of thing" (Houghton notes, I[39] nos. 250, 257).

To this end, Cummings devised a number of imaginative filming techniques for seeing around based on what he termed "concentric values." Among these techniques were: (1) having the camera revolve around a stationary subject, a subject revolve around a stationary camera, or both revolve around each other in opposite directions; (2) altering the speed of these revolutions to "convey the emotional content"; (3) using vertical perspectives—the camera "shooting straight down from the summit"; (4) breaking a scenario into "measures" by alternately speeding up and slowing down the film; (5) reversing the film to suggest the impossible; and (6) using "trick" lenses (concave-convex mirrors, etc.). The goal of these techniques was a "mobile revelation" of the object using "concentric x vertical" techniques. "This," Cummings concludes, "is my idea of 'aesthetic' significance of the moving picture."

Apparently, it was not his employers' idea, for he was not hired and was happy to leave when his assignment expired. One wonders whether Cummings—had he continued in that medium—might have created the kind of avant-garde techniques in film that he did in his poetry and that a fellow artist, Jean Cocteau, did achieve in film.

One three-dimensional medium in which Cummings did leave his mark was theater. Besides *Him* (1927) and the allegory *Santa Claus* (1946), he wrote the choreography of a ballet based on *Uncle Tom's Cabin, Tom* (1935), a brief allegorical drama of an artist amid "infrahuman creatures" entitled *Anthropos: The Future of Art* (1930, 1944), and several articles on theatrical events in Paris and New York during the twenties for *Vanity Fair* and the *Dial*.

The articles are particularly interesting in the way they apply the "seeing around" aesthetic to theater (which Cummings considered, with a largesse reminiscent of Gilbert Seldes' *The Seven Lively Arts*, to include the popular entertainments of burlesque, the circus, Coney Island, the French revue, and boxing). Published between October 1925 and September 1926, these articles lay the perceptual and structural groundwork for *Him*.[41] What is common to all of them is Cummings's interest in innovative stagings that create a "homogeneous" relationship between audience and performers and his corresponding distaste for the traditional arrangements that inhibit such homogeneity: "the conventional 'theatre' is a box of negligible tricks. The existing relationships between actor and audience and theatre have been discovered to be rotten to their very cores."[42]

The "discoverer" of this rottenness was Friedrich Kiesler, whose designs of open structure in architecture, sculpture, and theater were known for their spatial continuity. Large chunks of his program notes for the 1926 International Theatre Exposition are quoted verbatim in one of Cummings's theater pieces.[43] In these notes, Kiesler excoriates the "peep-show-stage" for flattening its internal space (from the audience's perspective) and thus for destroying the organic relation between the actors and their environment. The solution, Kiesler concludes, is a "space-stage," "a kind of four-sided funnel, opening towards the audience" that will foster "elastic space" (versus "rigid space"), "space by whose relative tensions the action of a word is created and completed"—all of which Cummings calls "a noble ideal." "Elastic space"—space that can be manipulated to express thematic tensions and to bring audience, actors and stage into an organic whole—thus becomes a means of achieving three-dimensionality, of "seeing around" the drama.

The subject was not merely theoretical, for Cummings was grappling with these problems in his own play, *Him*, at the time. The title character, Him, who is also a playwright, thus speaks for Cummings when he declares: "Damn everything but the circus! (To himself) And here am I, patiently squeezing fourdimensional ideas into a twodimensional stage, when all of me that's anyone or anything is in the top of a circustent" (I, ii).

Understanding the handling of space in *Him*, moreover, is crucial to grasping the play's manifold meanings, for its spatial construction visually expresses its social and psychological complexities. Not only does one see "around" a three-dimensional stage, but also "around" the characters of Him and Me in their evolving relationship with each other and in the psychoanalytic dimensions of their personalities.[44] This occurs most obviously in the circuitous way the audience sees the scenes between Him and Me. In each successive scene, the room has revolved ninety degrees, making a formerly tangible wall into the now-invisible fourth wall (the window wall), and vice versa. Since the characters remain oriented to the original room arrangement, the audience literally sees *around* the characters and scene from all four sides.

This spatial seeing around serves as a perceptual metaphor for the social and psychological seeing around of Him and Me. Each of their scenes successively reveals (literally and figuratively) a new fragment of their disintegrating relationship. In act 1, for example, the tensions between Him and Me are repressed largely through Him's dominant personality. But in act 3 (scene 1), these tensions emerge, as Me "begins to distinguish things" and recognizes her emotional and intellectual incompatibility to Him. The scene concludes with Me's sending Him away. When they meet again (scene 5), they confront the deeper source of their division, the dream-wish of having a child, and they realize finally that the dream cannot be made real, nor bring them "into the light" again. Thus, as their self-knowledge and understanding of their relationship grow, their union withers—a fact that Him, now the unsteadier of the two, cannot bring himself to accept: "I cannot feel that everything has been a mistake—that I have inhabited an illusion with you merely to escape from reality and the knowledge of ourselves" (III, v).

If self-knowledge is the ironical consequence of the social seeing around, self-fragmentation and integration is the theme of the psychological seeing around. The text on which this psychology is based is clearly Freudian, with some Jungian overtones. Often, in fact, the play seems a rather crude dramatization of Freudian concepts—a burlesque slapstick recalling the burlesque-Freudian connection in "You Aren't Mad, Am I?" The examples are legion: the Englishman in Him's play (II, vi) struggles with a heavy trunk on his back labeled "the unconscious"; Him meets his alter-ego, or libido, in the park (III, v); Me makes an obviously Freudian slip of saying "hump" when she means "pocket" (I, ii); "Will" and "Bill" play musical chairs with their identities in Him's play (II, iv); one of the Three Weirds refers to "the gospel according to Saint Freud"; and so forth.[45]

In a kind of psychoanalytic striptease, the play reveals progressively deeper levels of Him's personality, chiefly through mono-

logues in which he breaks down his psyche into Freudian components, using mirrors as both the means and symbol of his psychoanalysis. In the mirror, he confronts his artistic persona, "Mr. O.
Him, the man in the Mirror" (I, iv). Later, he meets his libidinal alter-ego (III, v). In both encounters, he wants to kill his other self (or
rather, see it kill itself) but cannot. Finally, in "a still deeper mirror,"
beneath "the windows of sleep," Him glimpses an image from the
nethermost region of his psyche, his unconscious, in the form of the
child he "wishes—and fears—to have."[46] While the child as dream-
wish exerts a profound and enigmatic force at the play's deepest psychological and social strata, Cummings goes to considerable lengths
to make Him's wish "foreign to conscious thinking" and yet still
present in veiled allusions, dreamlike gestures, and images.[47] Not until Him actually recounts the dream itself (III, v), and again at the
denouement of the midway scene (III, vi), does the child emerge into
full view.

Even when visible, however, the child's significance is
shrouded. Some critics take it literally as the baby Me actually has.
But there is as much reason to suppose that it is no more than the
unrealized dream-wish of Him and Me.[48] First, as noted above, it
never appears directly, but always in allusions, symbols, images, and
dream references, until the two climactic scenes of act 3. In the first
of these scenes (III, v), Him recounts to Me in loving detail a dream
in which he beholds their child. But when he sees Me's response is "a
different nothing"—and she tells him outright that the dream "was
made of nothing"[49]—Him's response is to "throw it away" "into the
mirror." And in the mirror, that is, in Him's unconscious, is exactly
where the dream resides in the next scene, where it emerges as his
nightmare. The setting is a carnival freakshow whose last attraction
(introduced by a barker, alias the doctor, named "nascitur") is Me
disguised as a princess of necessity ("anankay"). Him, as dreamer,
watches "from the outskirts"; when he sees Me holding up a baby
and "proudly" revealing her identity, he "utters a cry of terror,"
while the scene plunges into "total darkness" and "confused ejacula-
tions of rage dwindle swirlingly to entire silence."

Both scenes suggest that each character wants—and at the
same time fears—to have the child. Perhaps their failure to realize

the dream results from their inability to reconcile the divergent sides of themselves. Certainly, Him cannot reconcile the demands of his artistic persona, which creates beauty, with this still deeper longing for love, union, and wholeness that can create new life:

> Me: Now you want—truth?
> Him: With all my life: yes!
> Me: You wanted beauty once.
> Him (Brokenly): I believed that they were the same.
> Me: You don't think so any longer?
> Him: I shall never believe that again.
> Me: What will you believe?
> Him (Bitterly): That beauty has shut me from truth. . . .
>
> (III, v)[50]

Little wonder, then, that Him recoils in horror when confronted with the image of his failure: the baby itself.

One point seems clear: the baby represents the possibility of unification, or in Jungian terms, of the "transcendent function" that integrates the opposing sides of personality. It can reunite Him and Me, as it can reintegrate the fragmented selves of Him's personality by putting Him in touch with his deepest longings and most submerged wishes. More, the baby stands for a self-transcendence, an extension of the union between Him and Me, a new oneness growing out of their oneness. But the possibility ends in the stillborn images of "total darkness" and "entire silence." Thus, the psychological action, like the social, moves toward fragmentation rather than reintegration: the "seeing around" reveals selves rather than self.

In sum, the staging of the scenes between Him and Me works in tandem with the play's psychoanalytic imagery to create three-dimensional "seeing around": perceptual, social, and psychological. As the revolving room parses the personalities of Him and Me horizontally to reveal evolving *sides* of their relationship, the imagery and symbols parse Him's personality vertically to disclose progressively deeper *levels* of his psyche. Both movements compose a cube that one can see only part way around at any one time. In his notes, Cummings compares the seen and unseen sides of a character to the "conscious" and unconscious.

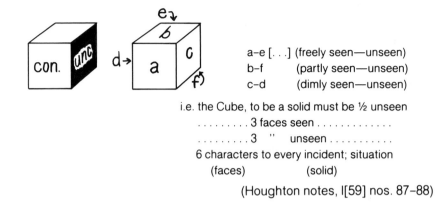

a–e [. . .] (freely seen—unseen)
b–f (partly seen—unseen)
c–d (dimly seen—unseen)

i.e. the Cube, to be a solid must be ½ unseen
. . . . 3 faces seen . . . .
. . . . 3 " unseen . . . .
6 characters to every incident; situation
(faces)   (solid)

(Houghton notes, I[59] nos. 87–88)

Here, in short, is psychoanalytical Cubism.

The audience's relation to the characters is both intimate and dynamic, as its perceptual, social, and psychological vantage points keep shifting. A similar shifting occurs in the play's scenic structure, only here the shifts are juxtaposed rather than progressive or continuous. In act 1, the play alternates the lengthy, "realistic," serious, deep-space scenes between Him and Me with brief, surreal, nonsensical, flat-space scenes in which the Three Weirds speak in chorus. Both contrast sharply to the medium-length, comic skits of Him's play in act 2 and to the lengthy restaurant and midway scenes of act 3. In this juxtaposition of durations, depths, moods, and contents, the successive scenes scrape against each other just as do the colors and words, themes and structures of Cummings's other juxtapositions. A note, probably written well after *Him*, indicates that juxtaposition remained an essential part of Cummings's dramatic aesthetics:

line = plot ("sense")
not / to write play via a plot [which] = melodic line
but   to let a play create itself by counterpoint:
opposites (contrasts)
i.e. that the succeeding of tableaux or incidents
     "les plans"; the "touches" of Cézanne
     modelling a volume)→ Motion

(Houghton notes, I[55] no. 22)

One final form of seeing around in *Him* aims directly at destroying the conventional relationship between the drama and its audience by intentionally obscuring the distinctions between reality and illusion, truth and fact, art and life. Actually, nearly every device in the play does this: the continuous masking and unmasking, the mirror reflections that own their owners, the painted bodies with talking heads of the backdrop, the play-within-the-play created by a persona of a character. The concluding scene is most significant, however. It attacks the most fundamental of all dramatic illusions: the fourth wall. Cummings had already called attention to it by revolving it in the scenes between Him and Me. Now, Me (always alert to the physical world) merely announces the absence of the wall and the presence of the audience behind it. In so doing, she acknowledges that she and Him are illusions—the audience only pretends that they are real—but that "this" (their illusion) is "true" rather than real. Thus, while the audience creates an illusory reality, the playwright—if successful—creates a true illusion: art.

If, as Simon Lessor argues, an audience must maintain a psychological balance between participation (by pretending the illusion on stage is real) and detachment (realizing that it is not), then Me's revelation upsets the illusory side of that balance.[51] But the play assaults the detachment side of the balance as well, as it brings the audience over the divisive barriers of the proscenium stage through the structural and psychological devices of seeing around. These disruptions keep the audience perpetually edgy and prevent it from discerning too easily between reality and illusion. Indeed, the tangled skeins of illusion in *Him* suggest that "real" and "illusory" are, metaphorically, only two dimensions of a three-dimensional play; the third and overriding dimension is, as Me states, the "true": the imaginative truth of art. That both the theme and structure of *Him* ultimately impel the audience to "see around" to this dimension demonstrates on how many levels—perceptual, structural, psychological, and now philosophical—Cummings has developed his aesthetics of three-dimensional seeing around.

Motion

5

I am abnormally fond of that precision which creates movement.

— E. E. Cummings, foreword to *is 5*

The Aesthetics of Motion

████ Of all the sensuous qualities that inform Cummings's poetry and painting, motion is probably the most prominent. The contentious color planes of his abstractions and the exploded lines, sprung syntax, liberated capitals and punctuation of his poems, besides serving his aesthetics of wholeness and perception, are the means to motion. For, like the fission of the atom (still a provocative theory in the late teens), the disruption of each orderly convention liberates energy that can be converted to motion on the page or canvas. Thus, it was aesthetics, and not mischief, that led Cummings to declare: "TO DESTROY IS ALWAYS THE FIRST STEP IN ANY CREATION."

That Cummings prized motion is evident not only in his poems and paintings, but also in his few published exegeses of his work and in his unpublished notes. This artist rarely talked shop in public but in one of the few places he did, the foreword to *is 5* (which he later quoted at length in his *Nonlectures*), he gives prominence to motion: "At least my theory of technique, if I have one, is very far from original; nor is it complicated. I can express it in fifteen words, by quoting The Eternal Question and Immortal Answer of Burlesk, viz. 'Would you hit a woman with a child?—No, I'd hit her with a brick.' Like the burlesk comedian, I am abnormally fond of that precision which creates movement."

The "precision" of this gag actually results from an imprecision: "with" can mean both "having" and "using." Suddenly shifting from the expected meaning ("having") to the unexpected ("using") creates not only precision—specificity—but also surprise, humor, and motion.[1] The ambiguity and sudden shift in meaning, moreover, connect motion to the intentional ambiguity Cummings devised to expand the viewer's perception. But most important, the motion he describes in his foreword recalls his central aesthetics of wholeness: "Ineluctable preoccupation with The Verb gives a poet one priceless advantage: whereas nonmakers must content themselves with the merely undeniable fact that two times two is four, he rejoices in a purely irresistible truth (to be found, in abbreviated costume, upon the title page of the present volume)."

If the verb (linguistic motion) makes two times two equal five, then it makes the whole greater than the product of its parts. Significantly, Cummings identifies the whole (five) as "a purely irresistible *truth*," as opposed to the product (four) which is a "merely undeniable *fact*." His connections, too, are revealing: verb→motion→whole (truth) greater than parts. This formula simply extends the one stated in chapter 2: feeling = "IS"→motion. Indeed, motion underlies and connects the various sides of Cummings's aesthetic interests. Cognitively, it fuses symbol and referent, subject and object, even objects and space for those who feel intuitively rather than think analytically: the child and the "primitive." For the child, Cummings imagines, "the amount between two objects (nouns) is homogeneous with the nouns and they with it, the whole constituting a verb, and being apprehended by the child in terms of mobility or by the apparatus (mechanism, subjective) of motion" (Houghton notes, I[39] no. 26).[2] Motion is also vital to perceiving entire surfaces, which occurs when "the eye-mind remains in *motion*, does not stop; [conversely,] recognition opposes motion."[3] Two-dimensionally this motion is circuitous; three-dimensionally, it involves a simultaneous push and pull of contradictory colors, words, themes, and structures that move the mind—if not the eye—to "seeing around" form. And beneath the levels of cognition and perception, in the dream-world of the unconscious, Cummings found "an enriched all-moving universe" whose "fused space-time concept" permitted combinations of opposites impossible in the waking world of "linear time/separate space."[4]

Motion, then, runs all through Cummings's aesthetics: as causes, as effects, often as both; at the most abstract and philosophical extreme and at the most physical. And little wonder, for it is central to Cummings's speculations on time, space, and matter.

Motion, Time, and Space

The one premise underlying Cummings's various ideas of time, space, and matter is that stasis is only an appearance; everything is really in motion. Although the *kind* of motion—its pattern or randomness—varies according to the subject and its context, the *fact* of motion does not. One note expresses this so well that Cummings put it into *Him*, with only minor changes, as a sample of the playwright's aesthetic scribblings.

> These solidities and silences which we call "things" are not separate units of experience, but are poises, self-organising collections. There are no entities, no isolations, no abstractions; but there are departures, voyages, arrivals, contagions. I have seen an instant of consciousness as a heap of jackstraws. This heap is not inert; it is a *kinesis* fatally composed of countless mutually dependent stresses, a product-and-quotient of innumerable perfectly interrelated tensions. Tensions (by which any portion flowing through every portion becomes the whole) are the technique and essence of Being . . . . (I, iv [my emphasis])[5]

Tensions, stresses, strains—all interrelated, all pulling against each other in a fragile balance, a "poise," all in constant motion. As with the universal, so with the particular: Cummings applies the same paradigm to the problem of balance in a painting or poem.

> a painting, a poem should be like a pile of jackstraws: a heap of strains, of stresses, enormous and minute, each necessarily and incredibly through its neighbor related to and responsible for an [. . .] entirety fortunately existing through the impossibility of a single dislocation or subtraction, whose niceness easily defeats the merest tool of thought, so that down comes the bungled breathless whole. (Houghton notes, I[27] no. 2)

What kind of motion governs these stresses and strains, these silences and solidities in a poem, a painting, a moment of consciousness? No single one, to be sure. Cummings's ideas encompass both the orderly, cyclical rhythms of nature and the random, almost entropic confusion of events in human life.

From his very earliest poems to his last, Cummings celebrated nature's cyclical renewals in all living things and in the seasons. And with the language of these rhythms he identified his own growth as an artist: "We can never be born enough. We are human beings; for whom birth is a supremely welcome mystery, the mystery of growing: the mystery which happens only and whenever we are faithful to ourselves. . . . [N]ever to rest and never to have: only to grow" (introduction to *Collected Poems* [1938]).

What mattered for Cummings was not the separate stages of life, but the continuous rhythm uniting them, a rhythm even death cannot stop ("And death i think is no parenthesis") because death, too, is part of that rhythm: "the verb is inherent in life [. . . .] it is not birth with which we are concerned, but a *MOTION*, a *MOVEMENT*, going all through our life—starting with the actual occurrence of *being born*, which is only one aspect of Movement, and transpiercing any number of things (which are not really things at all, but 'being born's') [. . .]; until 'death' (being born)" (Houghton notes, I[39] no. 41).

One can see precisely this motion of continuous, cyclical rebirth, both thematically and structurally, in the poem "O sweet spontaneous."

O sweet spontaneous
earth how often have
the
doting

    fingers of
prurient philosophers pinched
and
poked

thee
,has the naughty thumb
of science prodded
thy

   beauty   .how
often have religions taken
thee upon their scraggy knees
squeezing and

buffeting thee that thou mightest conceive
gods

```
        (but
true

to the incomparable
couch of death thy
rhythmic
lover

        thou answerest

them only with

                spring)
```

Corresponding to the rhythmic mating of death and earth to recreate spring is the rhythmic movement of the lines, out and in, to suggest the mating itself (note that the line going furthest out ends on "conceive," then shrinks back disappointedly with "gods") and the perennial cycle of seasons ("spring," as the rightful object of "conceive," is also far to the right).[6]

If the rhythms of nature represent a meaningful, and ultimately spiritual, motion, the hubbub of human affairs signifies the opposite: a confused motion of events ordered arbitrarily by chance. In one fragmentary series of notes entitled "Life and the Artist" (synthesized here), Cummings describes this tumult.

> The idea of Life is a multiplication of successive Incidents. It is a confusion of these. [. . .] granting that my life is a succession of incidents[,] at any one instant my conception of Life will not be the arithmetic sum of these incidents in their logical order, but a CONFUSION of them taken arbitrarily, it would seem at random, [. . .] an instantaneous [and simultaneous] quilt-of-sensation composed of various moments taken [. . .] arbitrarily, without regard to their original sequence or importance, not only arbitrarily juxtaposed but relative in the temporal sequence and confused into a whole wherein an arbitrary emphasis works a design [. . . .] the spatial and temporal perspective [of this quilt produces] sometimes overlapping and mutually penetrating incidents [. . . .] (Houghton notes, bMS Am. 1892.7[82] no. 3)

Here is the ontology that underlies the aesthetics of simultaneous meanings (chap. 3) and simultaneous structures (chap. 4) in Cummings's poems. And "quilt" is the same word Cummings uses to describe his early abstractions ("crazy quilts"), those organizations of "spinning jerking and generally petulant chromatic planes."

Given such a sense of simultaneous phenomena, what schemata of time and space best express it? One that Cummings rejects is cause and effect: "If the logical (time & space) world were built on hard and fast principles and stuck to these, o.k. But whereas the 'fact' that A preceeds [sic] B (in time) generally establishes a $\longleftrightarrow$ relation ('cause & effect' A *makes* [?], is *responsible* [?] for B), this active and passive [illeg.] does not always hold. Out of it slips the silverfish 'Coincidence' (Houghton notes, I[39] no. 46)."[7]

In place of cause and effect, Cummings sees a reflexive relationship between A and B where the causal direction of A→B can be reversed to read B→A. Ultimately, this reflexive interaction produces "A CIRCLE. (Circuit, in the electrical sense)." Circularity, reflexivity, lines moving in "directions other than the horizontal"[8] were among the aesthetic motions Cummings devised to express a cosmology in which time and space become intersecting coordinates.

> Art is something which reads backwards & forwards
> exists simultaneous on various
> levels { picture
> { fugue
> (Houghton notes, I[55] no. 57)

This chafing against linearity was common enough in Cummings's time.[9] What is surprising is how pervasive he felt motion to be in nature, even to appearances of stasis, and how such motion could be liberated. Like the child and the primitive, whose intuitive feeling permits them to conceive of time as having "no divisions, value or object,"[10] Cummings required that his analytical powers be numbed—if only by liquor—before he could realize the motion inherent in all things.

> suppose that everything in this room is mobile:that things which appear to be still are really in terrific motion, are turning (revolving on their own axis) so fast that we cannot see them move—as a sphere, or a cylinder, or a cone, may revolve with terrific velocity and still the motion may be invisible. Well, then, when I am rightly drunk I succeed in speeding-down the invisible, utterly-fast moving things, so that they turn slowly or perceptibly—hence I get a resultant dislocation of various parts of objectivity. (Houghton notes, I[39] no. 26^v)

Quite apart from their validity as physics, Cummings's conclusions are aesthetically interesting: disrupting normal perception ("speeding-down" things) releases hidden motion that, in turn, "dislocates" the "various parts of objectivity." Dislocations thus replicate themselves. Like the fissure of atoms, disruption is necessary to release motion: "Force itself is manifested in a change, dislocation."[11] These "disruptions," "dislocations," and "destructions" of the normal order are the birth labors by which any new style of art liberates aesthetic energy and motion. And Cummings realized as early as 1916 that disruption is all the more essential when the new art—abstraction—utterly overturns the old.

> The symbol of all Art is the Prism. The goal is unreality. The method is destructive. To break up the white light of objective realism into the secret glories it contains [. . . .] (Houghton notes, 1892.7 [149] no. 1)

> Poetry is then a disruption of the easiest order, I mean of conversation [. . . .] unrest is the very virtue [. . .] of the new poem. (Houghton notes, 1892.6 [29] no. 7)

His own poetics becomes clearer in light of this idea, not only because he thought of art as something mobile, but also because he felt that only disruption of the normal order would release that intrinsic energy of motion.

Sources

Cummings's interest in motion owed something to other artists and styles, but far less than was the case with "seeing around." More accurately, he was drawn to artists and styles that shared this interest: Futurism (including Joseph Stella and John Marin), Vorticism, Eliot, and Joyce. Futurists, Cummings noted, paint "the fact of motion" and thus provide a lively antedote to the "cold and frozen grammar" of Cubism.[12]

> Futurism—seeks the authentic holler   dynamism
>   seeks the spry and edible
>   vs. the chomp slobber wobble [of Cubism]
>   worship of speed...vs. worship of the big
>   (Houghton notes, I[39])

What particularly appealed to Cummings in his reading of the Futurists' manifestoes was their concept of reality as complex and simultaneous interactions of inner and outer space, of states of mind, and of moments of past and present: "The translation of this Idea [that life is a multiplication and confusion of successive incidents], through a space-medium on canvas [. . .] has been designated by the Italian Futurists, as the addition or multiplication of overlapping mutually penetrating planes, each plane standing for a moment of time" (Houghton notes, bMS Am. 1892.7 [82] no. 4).

Of the numerous techniques the Futurists fashioned to express their Modernist sense of space and time, the one most relevant to Cummings's aesthetics was "force lines": "Every object reveals by its force lines how it would resolve itself were it to follow the tendencies of its forces. . . . Furthermore, every object influences its neighbor, not by reflections of light . . . but by a real competition of lines and by real conflicts of planes, following the emotional law which governs the picture."[13] Force lines "must encircle and involve the spectator"—precisely what Cummings's "seeing around" staging attempted. That the concept addresses *planar* structures in conflict, moreover, permitted him to reconcile his planar sense of solidity with his striving for dynamism.

Yet, for all their appeal to Cummings's proclivities, Futurist techniques of motion exert relatively little influence on his *Sounds* and *Noises*, which are more abstract, generally flatter, and less prone to repeating lines and planes in close succession than are Futurist paintings. About the closest single resemblance is between *Noise Number 13* and Balla's *Mercury Passing Before Sun as Seen Through a Telescope*. For one thing, Cummings distrusted the Futurists' posturing, their collectivist identity, and their categorical repudiation of the past.[14] Nor did he find kinetic models worth emulating in Futurism's English cousin, Vorticism. Of course, he avidly read the two issues of their short-lived magazine, *BLAST*, and observed in an unfinished review that their "creed is devoted to the interpretation of Energy" symbolized by the vortex, that point of maximum energy.[15] But the group was only a loose collection of English Modernists with neither a shared style nor a common technique. Futurist painting most influenced Cummings through the mediation of two American painters, John Marin and Joseph Stella, who captured the vibrating dynamism of the New York landmarks that Cummings would also celebrate in words and colors: the Woolworth Building, the Brooklyn Bridge, and Coney Island.

Futurist poetics, on the other hand, offered Cummings both aesthetics *and* techniques of dynamism worth studying. To capture on the page, "the great mechanical, noisy, dynamic world" in all of its fragmented, overlapping and simultaneous impressions, the Futurists wanted to abolish such aids to coherence as traditional syntax, meter, and punctuation. Marinetti, the chief theorist, explains:

> The man who has witnessed an explosion does not stop to connect his sentences grammatically. He hurls at his listeners shrieks and substantives. Let us imitate his example! This release from grammatical subserviency will also enable the artist to do what no one, so far, has succeeded in doing: to communicate by words the sensations of weight and the power of diffusion by which he can express odours. It is a new field which is opened to asyntactical writers.[16]

What must replace conventional grammar, Marinetti declared, was "free expressive orthography . . . freely deforming, remodeling the words by cutting or lengthening them . . . enlarging or diminishing the number of vowels and consonants."[17] Parts of speech received special attention: verbs were reduced to infinitives (which, Marinetti asserted, would make syntactical halts impossible and thus provide style with speed); adjectives and adverbs were usually dropped; nouns, stripped of their modifiers, were juxtaposed to suggest condensed metaphors that Marinetti termed "analogies."[18] The sounds of language were to be enhanced through an extensive use of onomatopoeia, and, most important, the appearance of language would reinforce jumbled syntax through a juxtaposition of different kinds, sizes, and colors of typefaces and by words and phrases slanted at conflicting angles to each other. "My reformed typesetting" Marinetti boasted, "allows me to treat words like torpedoes and to hurl them forth at all speeds: at the velocity of stars, clouds, aeroplanes, trains, waves, explosives, molecules, atoms."[19]

That Cummings knew of Futurist poetics is certain: as he did for Futurist aesthetics of painting, he made copious notes from excerpts of these theories in A. J. Eddy's *Cubists and Post-Impressionism*. One note reads:

Futurism
1. same propositions as to literature [as in painting]
    a) use only infinite form of verb giving sense of continuity of life
    b) abolish adjectives
    c)   ''   adverbs
    d)   ''   punctuation (use certain accentuating & directing signs).
    e)   ''   ''I'', replace it by the *matter*.
    f) [illeg.], ornaments, fancy initials—use 3–4 dif. inks. Use italics for rapid sentences, capitals for violent—*Graphic* printed page.
           (Houghton notes, bMS Am.1892.7[150] no. 9)

If a careful student, however, Cummings was still his own artist and parted company with Futurist techniques on several points. The Italians conceived of the poem as a "free word composition," a verbal collage meant to be *seen* and heard more than read. Like Apollinaire's *ideogrammes*, Futurist "compositions" such as Marinetti's cover for the 1915 "Parole in Liberta" (fig. 37) escape the gravitational pull of traditional poetic progression: their phrases and phonemes skitter all over the page. Exclamatory nouns ("GUERRE") and snippets of onomatopoeia fall helter-skelter, further disrupting syntactic continuity. By contrast, Cummings conceived of the poem as a unified text to be read *and* seen, unfolding sequentially (at least in its essential narrative thread) even as it encompasses a multitude of spatial movements. Disconnected words and onomatopoeia would thus interrupt this continuity of thought. Yet the Futurists' philosophy, if not their precise techniques, permeates Cummings's thinking in the desire to explode poetic structure, syntax, and typography so as to liberate maximum force and motion—goals for which he could fashion his own techniques.

Closer to home, Eliot and Joyce also inspired Cummings with their formal innovations—but in ways Cummings himself could not easily articulate.[20] In 1918, he sketched notes for a possible essay on Joyce in which he asserts that the revolution in free verse and fiction is primarily "plastic and graphic," not musical; that it derives directly from modern painting, from the "new way of seeing things" achieved by Cézanne et al.; that the "old forms" of rhyme and meter have "ceased to be plastic."[21] Both Joyce and Eliot exemplify the graphic revolution: "with Joyce prose [. . .] takes its place as one of the graphic arts In E[liot one] realizes devel[opments] in poetry stem from painting and are not [of] musical but graphic sig[nificance]"

the
    sky
          was
can dy lu
minous
          edible
spry
      pinks shy
lemons
greens coo l choc
olate
s.

    un der,
    a lo
co
mo
    tive s pout
              ing
                  vi
                    o
                      lets

        e m u
      f
    i
    u q
      é m u
        l l
          l
          UN CIGARE a

Fig. 37.
Cummings, "the / sky / was," *XLI Poems,* "Songs," I. Apollinaire, "Calligramme." Marinetti, "Parole in Liberta."

(Houghton notes, [59] nos. 67, 63). But precisely *how* each artist achieves graphic plasticity Cummings never explains, save for a revealing note showing how ideas in Molly Bloom's soliloquy "follow in associative sequence, not simply logically." Association moves "with the logic of the UN conscious" "IN ALL DIRECTIONS," for it lacks the conventional punctuation that would "artificially" order ideas into the linear logic of the "thinking" mind. "Association" thus bears a suggestive resemblance to Marinetti's "analogies" in that both processes bend the rules of syntax and punctuation to achieve a freer and faster flow of ideas, unexpected juxtapositions, condensed metaphors, hidden connections. These lessons would not be lost on Cummings.

Techniques of Motion: Painting

"Motion is the painter. NOT it is a painting of motion."
(Houghton notes, I[59] no. 2)

That Cummings considered motion essential to his painting is obvious from his letters home describing his work, letters depicting his striving for "colour and motion," for a "binding rhythm" to "integrate" his painting and make it "a single moving ThingInItself," letters portraying the contents of his abstractions as "circles going on a bat" or "spinning" and "jerking" chromatic planes that are "mating." Typically, he personifies the motion in his painting, makes it as playful and mischievous as he himself was. "[It] tips furniture about gaily, upsets a ceiling, collides with infinity, and enjoys itself immensely."[22] In his later painting, Cummings also prized motion. Only now, he pursued it directly through his technique.

Just did (March 10 '45) a really *gay* flower picture [. . . .] Haven't the intensity of the hues (especially of deep red gladioli) but have a spontaneity & a motion which is Alive . . . thru painting direct on naked canvas & carrying out the whorls of my models in pure white—instead of washing a canvas with a tone, & either depicting flowers upon, or modelling them out of, it. (Houghton notes, I[55] no. 70)

In the early painting, however, Cummings's motion was more calculated, less spontaneous. It flowed not from his immediate feelings about this subject, conveyed through fast brushwork and impastoed color, but from his analyses of how the primary elements (color, line, shape, etc.), singly and combined, could express dynamism. Of these elements, color and line receive the most attention in Cummings's notes.

COLOR

Color is important enough to be equated with the act of seeing itself.

> By color I mean anything and everything which I see
> [. . . . .]
> the eye is the organ of colour [not sight]
> Color is: to see
> (Houghton notes, I[25] no. 159)

It is especially vital to seeing *around* form—to sensing the third dimension of depth.

> It's not.that color implies movement
> (color is one kind of movement [. . . being] the
> dimension of inward-outward [. . . .]
> without color (accurately, with black and white).
> movement—up & down. left & right on the canvas[.]
> (Houghton notes, I[39] no. 300ᵛ)

This dimensional function led Cummings to classify colors by how much—and how fast—they appeared to emerge or recede.

> Every hue bears a relation to every other hue, Purple IS BEHIND Yellow [. . .] moreoever, Yellow is only a degree of Forwardness in relation to purple. YELLOW PUSHES the Eye. MADDER PULLS.
>   (resulting in Subjective Depth)
>   (Houghton notes, 1[39] no. 300)

> A painting is a unique Velocity comprising the interaction of various
>   speeds
> a hue range[s] from.   heavy & slow—V[iolet]
>   [to] swift & light-Y[ellow]
>   grey is standing still
>   (Houghton notes, I[59] no. 13)

Juxtaposing these advancing and receding colors, of course, would intensify their distinctness.

> does a 'hue' have edges increasingly as it "emerges" from a cooler hue[?]
> If so, the sharpest chrome would be [that] which "surrounded" is by violet & grey
>
> (Houghton notes, I[39]11)

Noise Number 1 (plate 2) shows these theories at work, as Cummings pushes the bright oranges forward by juxtaposing them to their recessive complementary, dark blue, and to the recessive greens.

LINES

Cummings's early notes belittle the importance of line in order to emphasize color planes, but only those lines that delimit a shape and hence make it more recognizable. For he also realized that "line = direction (implies movement."[23] Accordingly, he exploited the kinetic potential of this element.

Although he used all sorts of lines in his early work, Cummings's notes favor lines that create motion, tension, and direction, similar to the "force lines" of the Futurists, though without their associations with "states of mind."

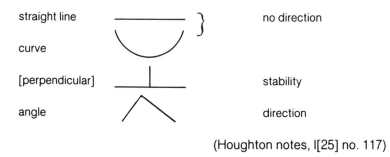

straight line		no direction
curve		
[perpendicular]		stability
angle		direction

(Houghton notes, I[25] no. 117)

In notes probably influenced by W. H. Wright's *Modern Painting*,[24] he continues:

The angle considered as "made up of" X & Y [i.e., as *separate* lines] equals a pure noun. IN ACTION or FUNCTIONING, it is a verb!
(direction, Where)
[. . . . .]

dead   lively

If we adopt the nom. of Angle.——motion is always into the angle; its speed is proportional to the acuteness of the angle[.]

(Houghton notes, I[39] no. 304)

Elsewhere, he diagrams this angle-speed relationship.

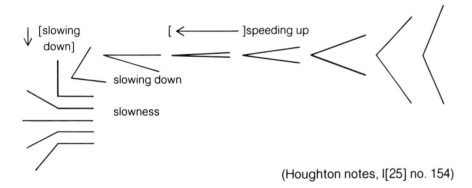

↓ [slowing down]   [←]speeding up

slowing down

slowness

(Houghton notes, I[25] no. 154)

If acute angles are dynamic, "PARALLEL LINES DO NOT MOVE."[25] True to his penchant for finding analogies among the arts, Cummings equates stodgy "parallelism" in representational art to the simple octave harmonies of diatonic music: "Parallels are octaves. As long as units of design have a parallel in nature, that is experience, the artist is hampered to the same degree, if not in the same way as a musician who works always in octaves is hampered" (Houghton notes, I[39] no. 324).

A number of early drawings and paintings evince Cummings's preference for diagonals and acute angles. In figure 38, jagged lines crash into each other like lightning bolts and dominate the drawing so thoroughly that the few curves are scarcely visible.

Fig. 38.
Jagged angles, c. 1921–23, pencil drawing. The E. E. Cummings papers, the Houghton Library, Harvard University. By permission of the Houghton Library. Copyright 1982, The E. E. Cummings Trust.

The same angular assault occurs in one of the dozens of skillful drawings Cummings made in the twenties of dancers of the Irene and Vernon Castle ilk (fig. 39). Here, design and subject neatly reinforce each other: the powerful thrusts outwards in the dancers' joined arms, in the woman's bent elbow, and in the paired legs create tension by pulling the viewer's gaze in opposite directions. The lines and angles heighten this tension. The strong diagonals of the legs and acute angles of the arms, particularly the woman's bent arm, seem to be a working out of Cummings's theory that acute angles accelerate motion. Some relief comes from the elegant curve that fuses the woman's upper torso to the man's and from the curve of her left shoulder. But these curves receive scant help from other parts: straight, segmented lines turn the buttocks and small of the woman's back into choppy planes rather than sinuous curves, and even the man's facial features are mostly angular.

To see how much tension these angles evoke, compare this drawing to another Dancers of the same series (fig. 40). Note the latter's curves in the buttocks, arms, shoulders, and heads. Here, the dancers do not thrust, they glide.

In practice, Cummings was not doctrinaire about applying his theories of angles and diagonals. Many of the early works, in fact, employ curves either as the dominant motif or in conjunction with straight lines. Figure 41 is a splendid example: a finger-snapping, "red-hot momma" from the twenties glides to music, her body a flowing euphony of curves. From the pit of her upraised arm to the toe of her pump is one undulating line, dynamic in its daring slant from upper left to lower right. Every other line is perfectly harmonized to this one, and only in the slinky, upraised arm is there a hint of a straight line and angle.

Both curves and angles foster motion, then, but markedly different kinds of motion. The curves generally undulate in a relaxed fluency, while the angles collide and rebound in tense intersections. To be sure, there are exceptions. The humped curve connecting the boxer's head to his legs in figure 42 is a coiled spring of compressed energy ready to drive the pistonlike arms and jabbing gloves. While Cummings's early notes and letters typically dwell on angles, he probably felt that without some contrast and visual relief offered by curves, sharp angles and diagonals would simply overwhelm the eye and offer no relief from the tension, no "poise." Acknowledging the

Fig. 39.
Dancers in angles, early 1920s, pencil drawing. The E. E. Cummings papers, the Houghton Library, Harvard University. By permission of the Houghton Library. Copyright 1982, The E. E. Cummings Trust.

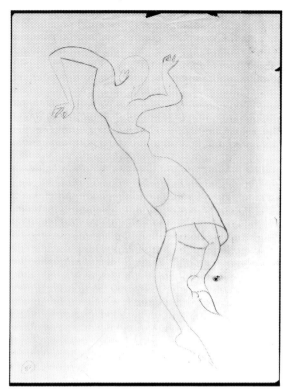

Fig. 40.
Dancers in curves, early 1920s, pencil drawing. The E. E. Cummings papers, the Houghton Library, Harvard University. By permission of the Houghton Library. Copyright 1982, The E. E. Cummings Trust.

Fig. 41.
Dancer, c. 1921–23, pencil drawing. The E. E. Cummings papers, the Houghton Library, Harvard University. By permission of the Houghton Library. Copyright 1982, The E. E. Cummings Trust.

Fig. 42.
Boxer, early 1920s, pencil drawing. The E. E. Cummings papers, the Houghton Library, Harvard University. By permission of the Houghton Library. Copyright 1982, The E. E. Cummings Trust.

need for both types, he writes: "The units of line seem to be the $<$ and the $\subset$."[26]

The combination of curves and angles that Cummings most favored, to judge from his early abstractions, is a polar contrast of curves that develop into spirals and spheres and angles that form razor-edged planes or acute shafts piercing these spheres from all sides. *Noise Number 13* (plate 5, fig. 43) typifies this contrast.

On first glance, the large, spiral shapes seem to stabilize the design, while the narrow tubes and jagged cones that cut into the spirals diagonally generate dynamic tension. But the spirals are themselves dynamic. As they turn inward, they suggest three-dimensional depth; as they sweep outward toward the edges, they counterbalance the inward thrusts of the tubes and cones. To complicate the perspective still more, Cummings puts edges on some spirals and turns one into a cylinder with a severely foreshortened vanishing point. Just as the shafts create breadth and the spirals depth, these edges and foreshortenings convey a dimension of height by taking the viewer's eye *down* into the painting. The conflicting lines effect not only opposing forces but also contrasting and ambiguous dimensions—all to keep the painting's components (and the viewer's eye) in restless motion.

PUTTING IT ALL TOGETHER: COLORS, LINES, AND SHAPES

In his painting after 1927, Cummings came to prefer curves to angles, the former symbolizing the transcendent spirit, the latter the mechanistic world.[27] One early objective that did not change, however, was matching the right color to the right line and shape to get the correct degree and kind of motion. "The important thing," he observes in notes about line, "is to establish a relation between (a) colour [and] (b) line e.g. [to determine] if yellow curves."[28]

Some of the early notes grope for laws governing these combinations.

1) given any 2 hues and a constant angle
the direction of the hues will be the same
the velocity   "   "   "   "   "   different
[. . . . .]

red   yellow

Fig. 43.
Noise Number 13, 1925, oil on canvas, 59½ × 43 in. Private collection, New York.

2) given any 2 angles and a constant hue.
   the velocity will be different
   '' direction '' '' different

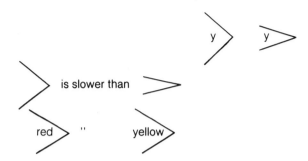

(Houghton notes, I[59] no. 13)

The trick, then, is to match the "fast" color to the "fast" angle and slow to slow. Cummings humorously likens it to shifting gears on a car to build up speed.

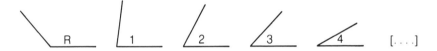

if clutch be put in 4th [at a stand still] it will stall [=] violet
the proper proceedure [sic] for obtaining speed is to pass through

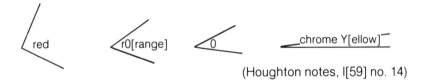

(Houghton notes, I[59] no. 14)

Taking his analogies a step further, Cummings wondered if colors and shape are intrinsically related.

1) is there a shape by which a Hue completely expresses itself
   i.e. is green most stable when a disk?
      (and when next to, say, Red?)

(Houghton notes, I[39])

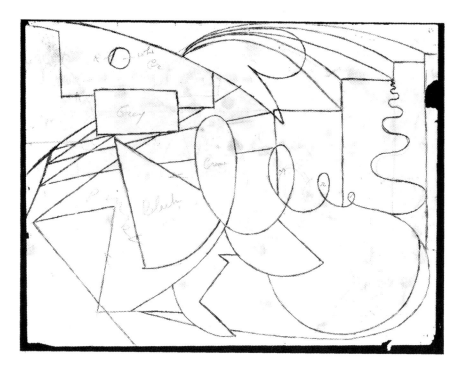

Fig. 44.
Shapes with color notation, early 1920s, pencil drawing. The E. E. Cummings papers, the Houghton Library, Harvard University. By permission of the Houghton Library. Copyright 1982, The E. E. Cummings Trust.

Does the circle most express (full-fill) the color Green
  cf. green——go, all right   circle...satisfaction
      red———stop, danger
      —green - indicative (rest, peace, quiet)
                                    complementaries
      red - imperative (STOP!)

                              (Houghton notes, I[39])

2) Is one hue firmer than another?
   Square grey is rigid
   [square] lemon is fragile
      ''   crimson is solid
      ''   green is stable
      ''   violet is frail
Has every hue a shape intrinsically which expresses its percussive value or is the percussive value of any hue due to its shape and is the percussive value the same for all hues of a given shape [?]
                              (Houghton notes, I[39])[29]

As one might suppose from the tentativeness of these queries, Cummings did not transform these speculations into systematic practice. Yet many of his drawings (e.g., fig. 44), reveal a careful matching of colors and shapes. And a survey of his abstractions confirms some marked similarities between his theory and practice.

The theory suggests that recessive colors (e.g., green, blue, crimson, purple, and brown) should combine with curving lines, obtuse angles, and stable shapes (circles and elipses), while emergent colors (red, orange, and yellow) should go with diagonal lines, acute angles, and dynamic shapes (triangles). In *Noise Number 5* (fig. 16), the stable shapes are mostly oblongs and all recessive colors: blues, pea greens, and crimsons. Conversely, many of the dynamic lines combine yellow, orange, and white. In *Sound Number 5* (plate 3), the central circle is, appropriately, green; the blue pod beneath it, while livelier than the circle, is far less dynamic than the jagged red-orange funnel.

Noise Number 1 (plate 2) applies the theory more shakily. The most dynamic shapes here are sweeping crescents that form an implied diagonal across the left center, and these crescents also possess the liveliest colors: orange, red, and yellow. Conversely, the most stable plane, an almost horizontal backdrop (a table?) to the lower crescent, is a recessive green. But one might argue that the dark blue crescent and brown arrow violate the theory: their shapes are too dynamic for their colors.

Without doubt, gaps exist between theory and practice. Perhaps Cummings felt too constrained by these one-to-one associations. Working out these ideas, moreover, may have opened up other approaches to his goals (e.g., using crescents instead of acute angles in *Noise Number 1*). In any case, pragmatism had to prevail for an artist still finding his way: it was the end, motion, rather than the means to it, that mattered.

DISTORTED PROPORTIONS

Just how intensely Cummings pursued motion appears in the grotesque distortions he gave some early representational figures—a technique he gleaned from Lachaise's overbearing nudes.[30] Their inflated features bulging forward, their diminished ones receding, these figures display startling, almost surreal, dynamism. The nude in figure 45 bounds toward the viewer with one elephantine leg (folded at the knee), accentuated by a ballooning stomach and upcurved hip. Conversely, the stationary leg seems to recede as it narrows to normal proportions, while the tiny neck and head shrink to vestigial appendages.

Perhaps the central principle of these distortions is that as the features expand and become more planar, they appear to approach the picture plane; as they contract to a point, they seem to recede. Cummings's notes show his awareness of these principles.

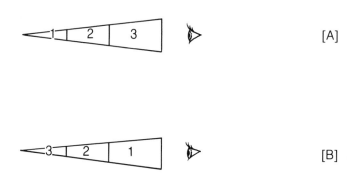

if line of motion of hurrying train=line of looking eye, we have
A) Approaching from a point to a plane—train approaches a plane
B) Receding from a plane to a point—train approaches a point

(Houghton notes, I[59] no. 34)

The ink drawing *train* (fig. 46), applies this principle, as the enlarged frontal plane of the engine narrows to an abruptly foreshortened point to express onrushing motion.

When the point of view is from above or below the subject, the distortion is even greater. Seen from above, the muscle-bound athlete (or tightrope walker) in figure 47 is nearly all arms, shoulders, and neck; one narrowing leg descends far below to the ground (or highwire). Seen from below (but curiously, from above the heads of the groundlings—as if from a theater loge), the stripper in figure 48 is all bumping stomach, grinding hips, and curving legs. Her head, least important from the spectator's point of view, is least visible.

Fig. 45.
Nude with distorted proportions, n.d., pencil drawing. The E. E. Cummings papers, the Houghton Library, Harvard University. By permission of the Houghton Library. Copyright 1982, The E. E. Cummings Trust.

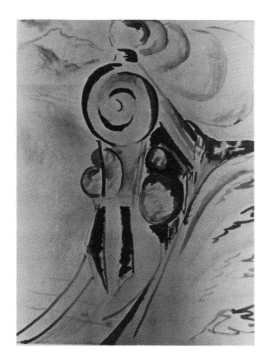

Fig. 46.
train, c. 1926–30, ink drawing, 28 × 32 in. From *CIOPW.* Copyright 1931, 1959 by E. E. Cummings.

Fig. 47.
Tightrope walker, c. 1921–23, pencil drawing. The E. E. Cummings papers, the Houghton Library, Harvard University. By permission of the Houghton Library. Copyright 1982, The E. E. Cummings Trust.

Fig. 48.
Stripper, n.d., pencil drawing. The E. E. Cummings papers, the Houghton Library, Harvard University. By permission of the Houghton Library. Copyright 1982, The E. E. Cummings Trust.

A far more sophisticated handling of figurative motion appears in a 1920s watercolor appropriately entitled *shimmy* (fig. 49). The distorted proportions noted in the drawings are evident here in the exaggerated left leg, left buttock, and left shoulder blade: all appear to move toward the left edges of the picture plane (1). But as the enlarged shoulder leans far back, the right hip is thrust up and forward, the elongated right arm swings around, and the right foot pivots inward. Countering the backward lean of the left side, these right-side features combine into a powerful forward swivel from foreground left around to the right and continuing, by implication, around to the dancer's front (2). At the same time, the dipping left arm wriggles off to the left side (3). Together, the three separate motions (see diagram) all flow into one beautifully coordinated shimmy.

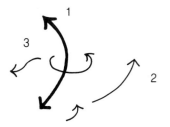

POISE

One final feature of Cummings's aesthetics of motion should be noted. What he works for in his painting and poetry is not unrestrained, erratic motion, but a careful balance of conflicting forces "each necessarily and incredibly related to and responsible for an entirety. . . ."[31] He called this balance of stresses a "poise," and his work shows the pains he took to balance motion with counter-motion, stress with strain, by gauging and counterposing the strengths of various colors, lines, and shapes.

In *Noise Number 1*, for example, the powerful sweep of one orange crescent, aims almost head-on at the upthrust of another. *Anne in cloche and gray dress* (fig. 50), translates these tensions into representational painting. What at first seems a conventional portrait conceals a subtle interplay of kinetic forces. The primary tension, of course, is caused by Anne, herself, leaning far into the picture's center from the right front. This leftward motion is furthered

Fig. 49.
shimmy, c. 1926–30, watercolor on paper, 11 × 13½ in. From *CIOPW*. Copyright 1931, 1959 by E. E. Cummings.

somewhat by the baseboard lines. But the left side of the painting offers several counterforces that partially offset this imbalance. The curtain rod points toward (and the white curtain bulges toward) Anne as if to prop her up; the left baseboard counterposes the force of the right one. Even in Anne, herself, several features intersect the lower-right to upper-left lean: the folded arms, the shoulders, even the large eyes. These features do not remove the imbalance; they only help counter it with diagonal tensions of their own (see diagram below). The right angle of the door frame, meanwhile, stabilizes these opposing stresses somewhat. While the painting does not achieve perfect poise, it is less imbalanced than it first appears.

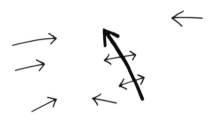

poise of tensions in *Anne*

Techniques of Motion: Poetry

"Life is a series of Verbs."

(Houghton notes, bMS Am 1892.7 [82])

Poetry, like painting, was always a dynamic art for Cummings. In Harvard notes for an unfinished essay, he writes: "this completion [of the 'new poem'] is itself dynamic, no mere balance, deadness, cessation, but poise, perfection, a 4th dimension. To only the vulgar is finality synonymous with rest: unrest is the very virtue (as of all art which combines a high development with a superior vitality) of the new poem" (Houghton notes, bMS Am. 1892.6[29]). The experimental poems that Cummings composed soon after this note (see chap. 6) search for ways of exploiting this unrest. Many bear important technical notes the young poet wrote to himself, such as this one (marking perhaps the precise moment his mature style

Fig. 50.
Anne in cloche and gray dress, c. 1926–30, oil on cardboard, 29½ × 20 in. Memorial Art Gallery of the University of Rochester. Gift of Friends of the Gallery.

began): "how about getting movement by dividing words i.e. arranging[?] by syllables."

Cummings's success at "getting movement" in the early published poems far exceeded this tentative query, as motion was indeed to become an essential, and unmistakable, feature of his mature style. The techniques he devised to convey motion, moreover, are so numerous and varied as to defy any simple summary and to require, instead, an extensive survey, if one would encompass them.

THEMATIC MOTION

The first category is fairly self-evident and requires little comment. Throughout his career, Cummings loved to aim his poems at moving targets: birds wheeling overhead, a mouse scampering across a floor, a grasshopper doing flips, a cat suddenly leaping, even mountains dancing. The slower, cyclical motions of nature also caught his eye: winter melting into spring, evening yielding to twilight, twilight fading into night. Typically, his method is imagistic, rendering the most subtle changes of a twilight sky, for example, in precise, painterly notation.

> spiral acres of bloated rose
> coiled within cobalt miles of sky
> yield to and heed
> the mauve
>   of twilight
>
> ("Paris, this April sunset completely utters,"
> & "Post Impressions," V)

When several such poems are chronologically ordered, like photographs superimposed, they form larger quasi-cinematic progressions. Thus, the "Impressions" in *Tulips and Chimneys* comprise five segments of a diurnal cycle: in "the sky a silver," the disappearing late-afternoon sky reveals the first stars and low-lying moon of evening; "writhe and" presents the fragmented colors and perspectives of sunset dissolving into "dimensionless" night; "i was considering how" begins with night stars and ends with the "stale shriek" of an alarm clock; the next poem, "the hours rise up . . . ," spans an entire day, from morning to night, while "stinging" overlaps the nightfall of "the hours" by moving from the late-afternoon gold on church spires, through the sunset rose of the bells, to the "dream / S" of night.

Cummings does not merely describe motion, however; he discovers and releases it—just as his note on "speeding down invisible" motion suggests. "At the ferocious phenomenon of 5 o'clock . . . ," for example, describes the speaker's stroll into the "mouth" of downtown Manhattan, his elevator ride up to the top of the Woolworth Building, and his view down to the street far below at rush hour as snow begins to fall.[32] The motion thus alternates from horizontal (walking), to vertical (riding up, looking down), to horizontal (the hubbub in the streets), to vertical (a "ribbon" of sunset hanging and snow falling).

These perpendiculars convey not only motion but shape: a rectangular plane or cube. Indeed, the poem's genius is to fuse the two: to find motion in matter, describe matter in motion. Thus, for all its towering verticality and perpendicular solidity, the Woolworth Building is a "swooping," "squirming" "kinesis." Focusing on the Cubist imagery of the matter—and perhaps on the poem's planar look—one might agree with Richard Kennedy that Cubism is the poem's rightful source.[33] But as these images (and the speaker with them) swoop, rise, and squirm, they surge with a dynamism closer to Marin's vibrant *Woolworth Building* watercolors than to Picasso's static *Houses at Horta*. Whether in a skyscraper or a leaf, rhythmic or convulsive, motion was intrinsic to Cummings's cosmic vision.

Poems about motion, however, could not sufficiently express this cosmic kinesis. The poems themselves had to move. And as he had done with his perceptual techniques, Cummings looked to the structural elements of language to generate this motion: to parts of speech, capital letters, punctuation, rhythm and tempo, context, narrative line, and textual shape.

THE TRIUMPH OF THE VERB

Of all these linguistic elements, parts of speech receive the most attention in Cummings's notes. His assumptions are simple: verbs create motion, nouns stasis. Any particle resembling a verb thus approaches motion; approximating a noun, it approximates stasis. One note explains this with particular clarity:

not to completely Feel is Thinking, Reality, A Noun
Sentience = The Verb

a plough standing still in a field and the field itself are Two Nouns. a plough in motion against the field=One Verb, to plough. As soon as The Verb disappears the Nouns reappear. The difference between the two cases is that in the second Energy is applied to the plough to force it through the earth, in the first it is not. In the first case we have A SITUATION, in the second A PROCESS or Single Verb. Nouns have separateness. Verbs are Single. Nouns have differences, Verbs are Identities. (Houghton notes, I[39])

As identities, verbs join subject and object and foster the wholeness underlying Cummings's aesthetics. More accurately, verbal motion is the condition in which wholeness occurs: "A child feels what it is taught to call 'horse' i.e. 'horse' = verb. horse means (is felt by child to Be the verb, to ride, a degree of Is or motion[)]" (Houghton notes, I[59] no. 70). Verbs symbolize primal motion in Cummings's cosmology.

the earth spins eastward on its own axis (morning & night) & drawing ellipses around the sun (spring and winter)[.] beyond what we recognise, *behind the nouns of morning & night* [is a] verb which creates these particle nouns & of this particle we make further nouns—we call it "rotation of the earth[."] But this particle comes from a largest verb: this rotation itself describes a more essential curve, binding the sun with the ellipses, providing "spring, summer, autumn, winter." (Houghton notes, I[27] no. 100)

At the microcosmic extreme, the essential verb "IS" embodies his conjugation of individuality and motion.

IS = the cold singular, the unique strict sexless sensual adventure of
        conscious unconsciousness.
    Kinesis; or the spatial movement [. . . .]
        Sensation—Is,[. . .]
                    succeeded by emotions
    A Force Art=IS
[. . . . .]
Are = the warm plural, derivative [. . . .]
[Being =] from the warm vertical steals the tall,

insipid participle and civilization—[. . .] warm, orderly vertical putrescence, the enormous product & sum of countless decomposing units identical in participial pitch.

(Houghton notes, I[39] nos. 344–45)

Other parts of speech suffer by comparison with verbs. Nouns, of course, oppose all of Cummings's values, they represent things, "differences," and stasis—all the consequences of analytical thinking that separates felt identities into *a* and *b*: "the verb . . . is just as inherently intense as, from the plastic standpoint, declensions and nouns are inherently flabby."[34]

"Adjectives," Cummings writes in 1921, "conduct the motion of thinking into a noun—As a path leads you [. . .] into a house (rest)." One epigram captures this relationship perfectly: "Nouns are stuffed birds; adjectives are the lice." As modifiers of verbs, adverbs do better. "Adverbs lead Thinking into a verb.—Like various [?] springboards which [. . .] precipitate moving." If verbs equal light, Cummings writes elsewhere, then adverbs equal reflected light.[35]

Cummings's concern with verbs produced some concrete results in his poetry. He distinguishes in his notes, for example, between vivid, "pure" verbs that are self-sufficient, such as "Jerk, Dash, Spurt, Lumber" and more general, impure verbs that require adverbial support for clarity, e.g., "fly" or "run."[36] Pure verbs radiate the same energy as angular lines in a painting: "the highest form of Composition is the Squirm, it is made of Creeping, Stretching, Gliding, Shrinking, Gripping. As emphasis tends towards angularities, the composition Wags, Hops, Bounds, Fiddles, Sprints, Fumbles, Trembles and Struts."[37] Accordingly, his notes contain lists of "pure" verbs such as the onomatopoeic noises written in his 1921 travelogue (alongside of notes on the tone colors of various musical instruments):

grunt	squeal	giggle	tinkle	squeak
click	squeak	gurgle	tickle	croak
cluck	scream		trickle	grunt
clack	shriek			cluck
croak	screetch			click
				bang bung bing boom

(Houghton notes, I[98])

The second column ("squeal," etc.) almost duplicates the variety of harsh verbs and verbals in the poem "Picasso" written three years earlier.[38] The latter's verbal cacophony aurally enacts Picasso's Cubist fracturing of the figure and develops the tribute of the last line, "you hew form truly." The dissonance carries over into the adjectives ("shrill," "sharp"), the participial adverbs ("shrieking"), and especially into the verbal nouns ("screech," "squeak," "squeals," "screams"). Sounding the crash of planes, these former verbs infuse the deadest part of speech, nouns, with intense action and protect it from the same "prettiness" that Picasso "lopped" from his canvases. Equally important, the verbal energy of these elements frees the verb of each statement to convey new actions, such as the "chops"-"lopped"-"hew" or the "bulge"-"pump"-"gush" series—all pure verbs. The remarkably distinct sound painting of these verbs and verbals stands in flat contradiction to the common (and in some ways justified) accusation that Cummings used words imprecisely.[39]

Besides looking for "pure" verbs, Cummings also sought ways to infuse the rest of his syntax with verbal motion. One way was to use verbs as nouns, as he did in "Picasso." Another was to use the "reflected light" of near-verbs—participles and adverbs—in place of shadowy adjectives. An "adverb cannot modify a noun," he notes, "but I make it—'a wonderfully arm.' "[40] In the sonnet "when i have thought of you somewhat too" the speaker can "feel your suddenly body reach / for me" to show the whole body, and not just the reaching, as spontaneous. Further on, he refers to a "swiftlyenormous light," merging the implied speed of "swiftly" with the overpowering size of "enormous."[41]

The sonnet "a fragrant sag of fruit distinctly grouped" combines both techniques. On the streets of the Lower East Side,

> A new curve of children gladly cricks
> where a hurdy-gurdy accurately pants.
>
> and pompous ancient jews obscurely twitch
> through the bumping teem of Grand. a nudging froth
> of faces clogs Second . . . .
>
> (*XLI Poems*, "Sonnets," XV)

This passage fairly bursts with the verbal energy of pure verbs ("cricks," "pants," "twitch"), verbs as nouns ("curve," and "sag" in the title), and participles as adjectives (a "bumping" teem, "a nudging froth"). On the page, as they did in life for Cummings, these side streets surge with vitality. In sum, Cummings's verbal transformations set him apart from both the Futurists, who emphasized noun pairings and infinitives, and Gertrude Stein, whose participles slow time and change into a glacial gradualism. Cummings's verbals strive for maximum energy and motion.

CAPITALIZATION, PUNCTUATION AND SPACING

After verbs, the two grammatical elements that could best effect motion, as they did visual gestures, were capitalization and punctuation. Since capitals emphasize importance, moving them in a pattern shifts the emphasis and thus intimates motion. The poem "candles and"[42] exploits this technique brilliantly.

candles and

Here Comes a glass box
which the exhumed
hand of Saint Ignatz miraculously
inhabits.   (people tumble
down.   people crumble to their
knees.   people
begin crossing people)and

hErE cOmEs a glass box:
surrounded by priests
moving in fifty colours
,sensuously

(the crowd
howls faintly
blubbering pointing

see
yes)
It
here
comes

A Glass
Box and incense with

and oh sunlight—
the crash of the
colours(of the oh
silently
striding)priests-and-
slowly,al,ways;procession:and

Enters

this
    church.

toward which The
Expectant stutter(upon artificial limbs,
with faces like defunct geraniums)

The speaker's curbside vantage amid the crowd is important in the immediate, but limited view that it affords of the religious procession. He sees the center of the procession—a glass box holding the relic of St. Ignatz's exhumed hand—at first from a distance with only the box's front visible; as the box draws nearer, its front and side offer him a three-quarter view; and as it draws abreast of him, only its side is visible. To capture this shifting perspective of the box, Cummings moves the capital letters in the "box" sentence progressively from front to rear with each repetition of the phrase:

Here Comes a glass box [. . . .]

hErE cOmEs a glass box [. . .]

here

comes

A Glass
Box

The view thus moves from anticipation and distance (capitals for the words announcing the box) to realization and immediacy (capitals for "A Glass Box" itself). Reinforcing this immediacy, the horizontal lines suddenly shift to vertical ("see . . . Glass"). This shift not only slows down the description, and hence, our perception of the box; it also converts the temporal procession into a spatial and timeless experience where (not when) the glass box draws abreast of the speaker.

Working in tandem with capitalization, the punctuation in the next section also imparts a processional motion, albeit a jerky one.

> striding)priests-and-
> slowly,al,ways;procession:and
>
> Enters
>
> this
>
> church.

Each mark signals motion according to its traditional function. The hyphens following "priests" connect them to the box (above, they "surrounded" it); the commas, reinforcing "slowly," provide pauses in the procession, the semicolon brings it to a brief halt; but both the semantic meaning of "procession" *and* the grammatical function of the colon following it resume the motion, until it has been closed off from the speaker's sight by the church (as the period closes the sentence).

Cummings, then, sought to join semantic and punctuational meaning as tightly as possible. "Every 'word' purely considered," he writes in 1918, "implies its proper punctuation."[43] While he does not elaborate on what "purely" means, how "implies" works, or what "proper" constitutes, we might reasonably infer that at least one factor in determining "proper" punctuation was the motion literally denoted or structurally required by each word in the poem.

The varieties of motion Cummings achieves with punctuation are remarkable, and analyzing them would fill many pages. The example above, however, is sufficiently representative for us to draw some conclusions about his treatment of capitals and punctuation.

First, Cummings did not choose these features arbitrarily. He selected each on the basis of its visual and kinetic potential and respected its traditional function. His periods halt; his commas pause; his colons merge and move; his dashes separate and interject. What he changes, in both his capitalization and punctuation, is placement, so that each element can immediately act out changes in the semantic motion of each word, in thematic motion of each line.

Second, he does not use punctuation indiscriminately and only to slow the tempo of a line, as S. V. Baum asserts: "One cannot predict what punctuation marks Cummings will use to retard the tempo of a poem, for in this respect all are employed with undifferentiated effect."[44] As "candles and" shows, the punctuation marks slow or speed the line's movement by degrees, according to the grammatical function of each mark. With a watchmaker's precision, Cummings inserts these marks like gears to turn the rhythms of his lines in perfect synchrony with their meanings.

Finally, both punctuation and capitalization rarely work alone or apart from spacing. All three form a "complex," as Cummings called it,[45] to create immediately perceptible action, to reinforce semantic meanings, to speed or slow those meanings, and to move lines vertically and diagonally as well as horizontally.

RHYTHM AND TEMPO

One particularly well-concealed side of Cummings's artistry is his musical interests: he understood the fundamentals of musical notation and composition, played the piano ("like fireworks," according to Dos Passos),[46] pondered musical analogues to his painterly and poetic aesthetics (see chap. 6), and composed several songs, many of which still exist in his notes. While Cummings's biographers have generally overlooked this unrealized facet of his creativity, composers from David Diamond to Luciano Berio have long recognized the musicality of many of his poems and have set them to music. What is particularly interesting about these song poems is the way Cummings creates rhythmic and metrical movement through his complex of capitalization, punctuation, and spacing. These visual devices shape the twists of his aural rhythms. "Jimmie's got a goil" is a fine example.

```
When you see her shake
                    shake
                          shake
                                when
you see her shake a
shimmie how you wish that you was Jimmie.
```

                                                    (*is 5*, "One," VI)

The three descending "shake"'s visually evoke a shimmie dancer giving her hips and bottom three hefty shakes. It can also suggest her gyrating body itself: snaking diagonally downward from head to hips with increasing vigor (just as in the dancer of fig. 41), snapping the hips over to "you," then bouncing rightward again to "Jimmie." The aural repetition and metrical interruption of "shake," breaking the strict trochee, further emphasize the word. This, and its visual force (spatially separated and descending in a forceful diagonal), give it the "oomph" of a shimmie.

"Ta" offers the more syncopated rhythm of ragtime to capture the music, as well as the features, of a fat piano player.

tà
 p̀pĭn
g
tòe

hip̀
p̀ŏpot̀
ămŭs Bàck

gĕn
teèl-l̆y
lŭgù-
b̀ri ŏus

                    èyes
                                        (&, "Portraits," III)

Although the meter changes from double in the lines "ta . . . popot" to triple subsequently, all three sections quoted above syncopate the accents by carrying them over into the next line or word. Thus, part of the stress of "tap"—the "pp"—carries over into the unstressed "in," which, in turn, spills over to the next line, "g." Likewise, the divided "hip / p" also divides its stress, while hyphens in the third section extend the stresses of "teel" ("gĕnteèl-") into the adverbial "ly," and of "gu" ("lŭgù-") into the next unstressed syllable, "bri." The flowing movement created by these syncopated carryovers is in exact opposition to the crisp tempo and emphatic beats of "Jimmie's got a goil."

One of the trickier rhythms Cummings devised grew out of an irregular patterning of letters, spaces, and capitals in the poem "I remark this beach":

w h e e saysthesea-brE aking-b Re   akin g(brea)K
ing
                                        (&, "Post Impressions," VI)

The shifting pattern of capitals in "breaking" combines with the varied clumps of letters to evoke the irregular aural and visual pattern of waves breaking on a beach in a constantly shifting rhythm. A *single* wave may break cleanly, as each appearance of "breaking" is set off from the others by hyphens or a parenthesis. But waves breaking in the context of other waves never strike at precisely the same interval, as the shifting capitals and letter groupings demonstrate.

CONTEXT

This difference between movement in isolation and movement in context was important to Cummings because he saw how a context could not only change the meaning of a single word, but also generate a new motion with it. In one early note, he asserts that, "ideally speaking," a word has two kinds of meanings:

1) its own permanent individual "meaning," e.g. "dog," "god," in common with all other words considered purely as elements of a Vocabulary.

2) its momentary or transient meanings, whenever modified by its fellow chameleons of a context: whenever it combines with another word or words to constitute a going-somewhere, an en-routeness, a self-directing entirety.

Still ideally in the case of

1) a word has a recognizable silhouette, it has edges.

2) a word is one or more of a number of ideas which thru mutual interpenetration (modifying more or less one another) create a direction, an impetus: of ideas which simultaneously abandon their individual silhouettes, edges . . . and fuse or melt into a movement. (Houghton notes, I[25] no. 182ᵛ)

"Context," Cummings concludes, "is movement."[47]

This idea underlies the burlesque joke Cummings used to illustrate "precision that creates movement" in his foreword to *is 5*: "Would you hit a lady with a child? No, I'd use a brick." The ambiguous "with" offers two different contexts: maternity in the question (woman as defenseless and vulnerable), and misogyny in the answer (woman as target for attack). The movement from one context to the other sets up the surprise of the answer.

Unquestionably, Cummings's most dramatic device for achieving motion is his dynamic spacing and shaping of lines. As the analysis of "windows go orange" has shown, narrative lines move in several directions within the context of the conventional left to right, top to bottom progression. In one seminal note (fig. 51), written beneath an early experimental poem of 1916–17, Cummings spells out clearly what he hoped to achieve:

> for great fluidity:
> sense may move in other directions than horizontal, and in latter from
>   right to left as well as v.v.; and may change its direction at suitable
>   times (e.g.-perpendicular down to up, zigzag, right angle (90°) etc.)
>   *Composition by Angles, & Planes*
> [. . . . .]
> as to method—*blocking* into cubes=*plotting* curves and angles
>
> thus it is seen that several motives will run side by side, or offshoot,
>   fuse into each other, emerge, or what not; while harmonically
>   speaking, a complicated colour-counterpoint occurs in *directions*
>   *other than those chosen by the sense-motives* as well as in the lat-
>   ter, if desired.
>
> (Houghton notes, I[21] no. 149)

Three different effects result from redirecting these "sense" lines: (1) "greater fluidity," (2) new shapes analogous to those of Modernist painting, such as "planes" and "cubes," and (3) a "complicated colour-counterpoint" of sounds moving harmonically against, rather than melodically with, the progression of the narrative line. The latter two of these effects (shape and harmonics) will be discussed in chapter 6; "greater fluidity" is what concerns us here.

In listing the possible directions the "sense motive" may follow—i.e., right to left, perpendicular, down to up, zigzag, right angle, curves and angles—Cummings offers a blueprint against which the linear motion of his poems can be measured. His list also invites comparison with the way his early painting used lines. In practice, Cummings rejected some of these motions, such as horizontal right to left, as unworkable. But others worked well, and three are particularly important: perpendicular, "explosive," and diagonal.

While some of Cummings's experimental poems toyed with thematic lines that move "perpendicularly from down to up," only one made it to publication, a portrait of a twelve year old prostitute. It ends:

tiny

add

death

what

shall?

("being," & "Portraits," I)

Unscrambled, the last stanza reads: "what shall tiny death add?"[48] At first, the vertical jumbling seems just a nuisance, a cheap trick. But as it forces the eye to move down ("what shall"), then up to "tiny," then down to "death," then back up to "add," the scrambling compels a kinesthetic participation in the poem's theme and appearance. If the poem's shape suggests a silhouette of the girl, then this last vertical section, below the skirt-wide middle section, represents her legs, over which the reader's glance moves carefully down and up. The participation thus transforms the reader into a prospective "john"!

The down-to-up vertical, so contrary to the traditional movement of Western languages, is obviously awkward and unwieldly. Probably for this reason, Cummings preferred to move his verticals downwards, following the larger top-to-bottom progression of his poem. When these verticals meet a horizontal line above or below it, the resulting perpendicular presents new possibilities for motion.

In "somebody knew Lincoln somebody Xerxes," the setting is a park where

pigeons circle

around and around and around the

irresponsible toys

```
circle wildly in the slow-ly-in creasing fragility
—  Dogs
bark
children
play
-ing
        Are

in the beautiful nonsense of twilight
```
                            (*Tulips and Chimneys*, ''Portraits,'' X)

The lines describing the circling pigeons stretch out horizontally to
show not only the circling motion, but the breadth of sky that encompasses it. The children (''irresponsible toys'') and dogs play *below*
the circling birds, shown by the downward-moving vertical column
''—. Dogs . . . Are.'' As the speaker's gaze shifts back to the twilight
sky—the pigeons' realm—the line returns to horizontal.

   Cummings also tried ''exploding'' a word or line to express its
semantic meaning in a visual gesture. One often-cited passage ends a
poem about night stars yielding to dawn:

```
              when over my head a

shooting
star
Bur      s

      (t
        into a stale shriek
like an alarm-clock)
```
                            (*Tulips and Chimneys*, ''Impressions,'' III)

The *s* and *t* of ''Burst'' burst out of the linear word and expand over
space in a falling arc: a meteor's brief, brilliant plummet. But the
spent ''(t'' falls directly ''into a stale shriek / like an alarm-clock,''
pulled in by gravity and a parenthesis. The dreamy visions of a starry
night have ''burst'' into the raucous shrieks of waking anxiety.

Diagonals are probably the direction Cummings used most frequently and with most success. He knew, of course, that of all lines, they are the most dynamic; and his early abstract painting employed them liberally for this reason. In a poem, they offered two possibilities. Used separately, they create individual motions, such as hanging or falling. But in a sequence (implied by an alternation of longer and shorter lines), they form a zigzag pattern that can parallel thematic and aural rhythms.

A graphic example of the first use, a diagonal creating a specific motion, occurs in the poem "her" (&, "Portraits," XI).

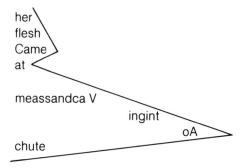

Following the graduated descent of "her . . . at," the horizontal "meassandca V" and the diagonal "V / ingint / oA" change the direction and speed of the motion. The diagonal, of course, *shows* the sand caving, but the tempo is tricky. The bunched "meassandca" hurries the sand towards the brink; at the spaced and capitalized "V" (a visual gesture of "her" crotch?), the sand hesitates, then falls rapidly down ("ingint / oA"), pausing only once more at the edge of the chute. This chute, a noun, abruptly yanks the motion away from the direction of greatest force (the falling diagonal rightward) and pulls it almost horizontally back to the left margin where it began. In short, it stops the motion cold.

After the compact central section, appropriately bunched to show the two lovers merged into "tumbling garble," the speaker's climax appears in another diagonal.

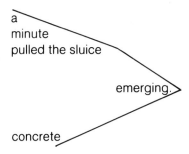

The diagonal here is somewhat less acute, and both the ample white space surrounding "emerging" and the period following it slow the action of "pulled the sluice." The still more distant "concrete," causing (like "chute") a counterdiagonal back to the left margin, solidifies the action in position as well as in semantics. But although these diagonals move noticeably slower than the "sand" diagonals, they form a point of maximum force at the exact moment of the speaker's climax: "emerging."

Zigzags implied by the alternation of long and short lines are common in Cummings's poems, but their acuteness varies with the contrast of line length. The more acute the zigzag (i.e., the greater the difference between long and short lines), the more abrupt the rhythmic changes will be.

"Babylon slim" (&, "Portraits," II) begins with a moderate rhythmic alternation.

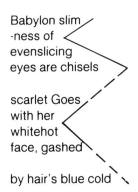

This gradual rhythm is rather at odds with the harsh imagery (slice, gash, whitehot) describing this powdered pagan, but it might suggest the fashionably concealed curves of her "slimness," a twenties style after all. As the description turns to her dancing, however, the diagonal rhythms grow more jagged.

```
jolts of      ⟨- - - - - - ⟋
lovecrazed abrupt \
                   \
flesh  split "Pretty \
Baby"
to  ⟨
numb rhythm before christ
```

Clearly, Cummings tied linear to thematic motion, and nowhere is this better shown than in the poem "i will be," a virtual compendium of these motions.[49] Thematically, it describes at least four motions: (1) love-making (using the metaphor of city travel: "i will be / M o ving in the Street of her / body") and several related actions (feeling, touching, kissing, playing); (2) actual city travel of the speaker's lover visiting him ("my [. . .] street / where / you will come"), (3) pigeons flying in circles ("whee [. . .] l- / ing"); and (4) sunlight becoming twilight and then moonlight.

Matching these kinetic subjects are a variety of kinetic lines each enacting semantic meaning. (See diagram at right.) The two lines closest to the margins (diagonals *a* and *b*) progress from "sunLight," through "twi li ght," to a visual gesture of a crescent moon: ")n". A counterdiagonal (*c*) connects "oh / ver / mYverRylitTle" to convey movement *down*, from the circling pigeons overhead to the street below. The birds themselves fly (as they did in "somebody knew Lincoln . . .") in horizontal lines (*d*) that form a dynamic arrow with the point at "sunlight." By contrast, the "street / where / you will come" receives an appropriate right angle (*e*).

Other angles pop up. "Maybe Mandolins / look" joins with the first pigeon line to form another arrow (*f*) with its point of maximum force at "l oo k-" (the act of perception so important to Cum-

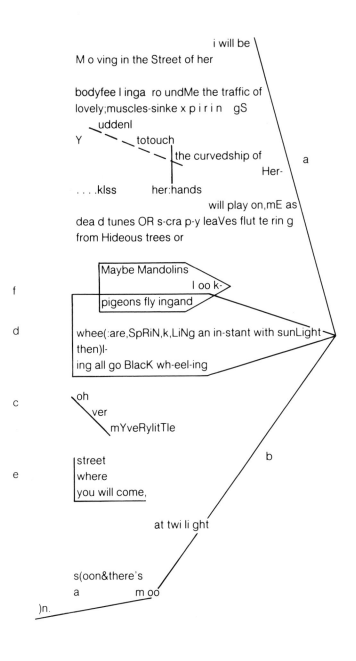

```
                              i will be          \
          M o ving in the Street of her

          bodyfee l inga  ro undMe the traffic of
          lovely;muscles-sinke x p i r i n   gS
                uddenl                                      a
          Y           totouch
                          the curvedship of
                                      Her-
          . . . .kIss        her:hands
                              will play on,mE as
          dea d tunes OR s-cra p-y leaVes flut te rin g
          from Hideous trees or

               Maybe Mandolins
f                          l oo k-
               pigeons fly ingand

d          whee(:are,SpRiN,k,LiNg an in-stant with sunLight
           then)l-
           ing all go BlacK wh-eel-ing

c            oh
               ver
                  mYveRylitTle

             street                         b
e            where
             you will come,

                    at twi li ght

          s(oon&there's
             a         m oo
      )n.
```

(&, "Seven Poems," I)

mings's aesthetics, here reinforced by ideographic eyes: *oo*). Vertical lines in the middle appear to connect identical letters of widely spaced words, e.g., "tou*ch*" and "*h*ands." As Cummings's street teems with the motions of nature, so his poem teems with the visual motions of lines.

Taken together, the many techniques by which Cummings achieves motion in his paintings and poems are predicated on the same assumptions and strategies. All reveal a pattern of destruction and reconstruction. The faithful imitation of nature in painting, the adherence to traditional spacing, mechanics, progression, and verbal functions in poetry—these conventional orderings had to be destroyed to liberate new energy on the page and canvas and to foster new perceptions of that energy ("the speeding down of space").

Conventional orders shattered, the perceptual significance of a work shifts to the broken parts: the colors and lines, the parts of speech and punctuation, the spacing and shaping and proportions. And these Cummings exploits for their greatest kinetic potential: colors that infuse a canvas with contrasting push and pull motions; verbs that loan other parts of speech their energy; lines and angles that move dynamically; spacing and proportions that group or disperse, expand or contract features; punctuation and capitals that hurry semantic meanings along or trip them up. All of these intensified parts, now kinetic, are reassembled into a *new* whole, balanced not by stasis but by the conflicting tensions of the elements.

Thus, as was noted in chapter 3, the new whole does not overwhelm or mask the parts; its tenuousness is a transparency through which the parts assert their sensuous and dynamic personalities continuously and distinctly. The paintings and poems, therefore, never cease to gratify the eye in creating an immediately felt kinesis.

Lights That Failed: Interrelating the Arts

6

Tell me, doesn't your painting interfere with your writing?
Quite the contrary: they love each other dearly.
They're very different.
Very: one is painting and one is writing.
[. . . . .]
where will you live after this war is over?
In China; as usual . . . . Where a painter is a poet.
—E. E. Cummings, Foreword to an Exhibit: II

■■■■■ The fictitious dialogue above—from Cummings's statement for a 1945 exhibition of his painting—conveys an idea that runs through the preceding five chapters: that although Cummings practiced two "different" arts, he did not consider his painting and poetry as independent of each other. And they were more than just complementary. If they "loved each other dearly," it was the love of siblings who sprang from the same parent: a unified system of aesthetics.

Cummings believed that the arts, in both their aesthetic underpinnings and in their practice, could be integrated, just as he felt that the data of the senses could be. His view, of course, reflected his times—and the century preceding them—which witnessed a steadily increasing interest in the interrelationship of the arts, from the Romantic and Symbolist artists, to the theorists of color-music analogies and inventors of color-music projectors, to such Modernist practitioners as Kandinsky, Scriabin, the Futurists, and the Synchromists.

As both painter and poet, Cummings came by his interest in aesthetic integration naturally and early on. At Harvard, he gravitated towards the most notable theorists and practitioners of integration with an almost prescient sensitivity. Their examples, in turn, stimulated his own thoughts on the interrelationship of the arts and of the senses. In his Harvard notes, for example, he wrote: "intertranslation by the senses is proved by the individual's ability to *remember* an odour."[1] Another note reveals how he imagined synesthesia to work to intensify felt experience:

if this wind
which communicates itself as a series of pressures (touch)
smelled (like seaweed)
(a) I would seem to see the wind
(b) the wind would therefore seem (bec[ause] I saw it)
more real

(Houghton notes, I[59] no. 109ᵛ)

So interested was Cummings in establishing these interrelationships, that he devoted scores of pages of his early notes to analyses and comparisons of the elements of painting, music and poetry.[2] Many of these comparisons, particularly those between painting and music, do not go much beyond theory. Others, for example those between poetry and music, produce some interesting structural experiments in poetry that Cummings ultimately abandoned. But a few "intertranslations" matured into prominent techniques in the published poems. A survey of these early efforts to yoke the arts is useful both for what it reveals about the interdisciplinary web of Cummings's ideas and for the aesthetic rationale it offers for some of his poetic devices.[3]

Historical Context and Immediate Influences

Establishing correlations among the arts has long fascinated aestheticians, artists, and even inventors and scientists. At bottom, the search probably derives from the unquenchable belief that all phenomena can be logically related in what Swedenborg called the "oneness of the universe" if man only digs deeply enough to find the common structure, the points of intersection. The search for these artistic correlations traces a long and fitful history, waxing in some periods, waning in others. In his encyclopedic study, *Coloured Light: An Art Medium*, Adrian Klein traces attempts to relate color and painting to music, for example, back to Aristotle, through such Renaissance painter-theorists as Arcimboldi and Leonardo, and into the Modern period in the writings of Newton, Goethe (who doubted the proposition), Chevreul, Rood, Ruskin, Pater, and a host of lesser-known theorists, many of whom worked out elaborate systems of analogy.[4]

In Cummings's time, particularly from 1911–13, interrelating the arts peaked in the separate efforts of Kandinsky, Scriabin, A. Wallace Rimington, the Futurists, the Synchromists, and the Imagists, culminating a century of steadily increasing interest. For if ever an idea were "in the air," the interrelatedness of the arts was in the nineteenth century. The idea was cardinal to both the Romantic and Symbolist artists. Keats's exotic synesthesia, Shelley's belief in the interpenetration of the senses, Poe's predations into music, Wagner's idea of *Gesamtkunstwerk*, even Swedenborg's mystic "oneness"—all developed within a few decades of one other and laid the groundwork for the Symbolists' more comprehensive aesthetics of interrelatedness. [5] By 1860, Baudelaire had composed "Correspondances," which asserts that "all scents and sounds and colors meet as one":

> Perfumes there are as sweet as the oboe's sound,
> Green as the prairies, fresh as a child's caress
>
> (Trans. Richard Wilbur)

Significantly for Cummings, the Symbolists felt that words, too, "would cease to be mere signs and participate in the things that they present or evoke."[6] Later Symbolist poets developed Baudelaire's correspondences either by specifying them, as Rimbaud associates particular colors and vowels in "Voyelles," or, more typically, by suggesting and yet obscuring their relationship in indirection and nuance, as Huysmans described of Mallarmé in *Á Rebours:* "Sensitive to the remotest affinities, he would often use a term that by analogy suggested at once form, scent, color, quality, and brilliance to indicate a creature or thing to which he would have had to attach a host of different epithets in order to bring out all of its various aspects and qualities, if it had merely been referred to by its technical name."[7]

Symbolist painters were equally prone to tap other arts for literary subjects and ambiguous musical metaphors. Thus Gauguin: "harmonious colors correspond to harmonies of sound" and "One does not use color to draw but always to give the musical sensations which flow from itself, from its own nature, from its mysterious and enigmatic force."[8]

Like Eliot before him, Cummings read the Symbolist poets while at Harvard and probably found their idea of correspondances as seductive as he did Keats's synesthesia.[9] But Cummings's interdisciplinary interests also drew him to the work of theorists and artists outside of literature who were not content with the hazy metaphors of Symbolism and sought, instead, to quantify precise analogies among elements of the arts: A. Wallace Rimington, Scriabin, and Kandinsky. The analogic theories of all three men appear in Cummings's early notes and themes.

Rimington was perhaps the most influential figure in the surge of interest in color-music analogies at the turn of the century.[10] A painter, theorist, and inventor, he invented in the 1890s a "colour-organ," a keyboard instrument that treated the spectrum band of colors as musical octaves and projected on a screen colors of varying intensities, values, durations, and relationships to other colors in blends and juxtapositions. His performances on this color-organ drew considerable attention to his theories, and in 1911 Rimington published *Colour-Music: The Art of Mobile Colour*, in which he argued for the viability of a new "colour art analogous to the art of music" (p. 2). While part of the book is given over to technical descriptions of the color-organ, the remainder offers a theoretical basis for Rimington's color-music analogy. Rimington analogized the octave scale and it vibrations per second to the spectral color scale and its relative wavelengths. These scales appear in toto in Cummings's college paper, "The New Art,"[11] alongside Scriabin's tone-color scale.

Key	Vibrations per second	Scriabine	Rimington	Vib. per sec. [wavelength]
C(middle)	256	Red	Deep Red	395
C(sharp)	277	Violet	Crimson	433
D	298	Yellow	Orange Cr.	466
D(sharp)	319	Steel	Orange	500
E	341	Pearl White	Yellow	533
F	362	Deep Red	Yellow Green	600[sic]
F(sharp)	383	Blue	Green	600
G	405	Orange	Bluish-Green	633
G(sharp)	426	Purple	Blue-Green	666
A	447	Green	Indigo	700
A(sharp)	469	Steel(rep'd)	Deep Blue	733
B	490	Pearl Blue	Violet	757
C		(Invisible to eye.)		

Rimington, by his own admission, was far less interested in proving an exact analogy between color and tonality than in promoting a new color art—a hope that was never to be realized, except perhaps faintly in the psychedelic light shows of the 1960s. Yet his theories of analogy must surely have informed Cummings's nearly identical correlations of hue and tone.[12]

Cummings's 1915 survey of Modernism, "The New Art," devotes considerable space to Scriabin's *Prometheus: The Poem of Fire* (1911) and quotes extensively from a review of the premiere in the *Boston Evening Transcript*. In this complex score, Scriabin wrote one staff for *tasteria per luce*, a light keyboard capable of projecting colored lights to accompany particular tonalities and to change with harmonic progressions. A review of the 1915 premiere (which Cummings may have attended) reports: "The medium of color effect was two series of gauze strips, about eight feet by ten, hung at the back of the stage ten feet from the floor, and presenting to the eye simply a white rectangle. . . . With the beginning of the orchestration this gauze rectangle became animated by flowing and blending colors. . . . These colors were 'played' by a keyboard with fifteen keys and following a written 'score.' "[13]

Scriabin's associations of color and tone derived from his Theosophical belief that all vibratory phenomena are interrelated and reveal a spiritual oneness. His pairings are thus more subjective than Rimington's, more dependent on the "feeling" of color he received from a particular tone. Not suprisingly, these "feelings" could vary. According to C. S. Myers,[14] "the successive colors corresponded to tonalities rising by a series of fifths":

Red		Orange	Yellow	Green	Blue	Violet
C	G	D	A	E	B	F#

But in Cummings's chart taken from the *Transcript* review, Scriabin's scale shifts the color-tone pairings and includes accidentals, probably to encompass the chromaticism of *Prometheus*. In any case, Scriabin's bold experiment proved a critical failure, as reviewers considered the color accompaniment weak, blurred, unrelated to the music, and therefore distracting. Although Cummings praised *The Poem of Fire* in "The New Art" as "the consummation of Scriabin's genius," he appears later to have sided with the critics. A fragment of fictitious dialogue in his Camp Devens notes of 1918 reads:

—how about music? Scriabine's Prometheus.
—I saw that. The colour part was rotten.
—I know the score only. He used steam didn't he?
—Of course it was. Nothing sharp, no collisions between planes. A mere saccharine diffusion, crescendo & diminuendo, ad infin.
—You talk like Pound. A bas les bores.

(Houghton notes, I[21] no. 186)

Wassily Kandinsky's influential treatise, *Concerning the Spiritual in Art*, appeared in 1912 and was translated into English in 1914. Cummings read lengthy excerpts from it in 1914, both in A. J. Eddy's *Cubists and Post Impressionism* and in the first issue of BLAST (July 1914). Although it contains no color-music scale, the treatise often compares particular colors to timbres: "The sound of colors is so definite that it would be hard to find anyone who would express bright yellow with bass notes, or dark lake with treble."[15] Like Scriabin, Kandinsky followed no scientific theory and guided his analogies of music and color solely by his Theosophical and aesthetic sensibilities. Once again, subjectivity proved an unreliable criterion, for his pairings are rife with contradictions: the violin is linked to "absolute green" and to "cool, light red" a few pages later; the cello is paired first with "dark blue" and then with "deepened red." About the only analogies that anticipate Cummings's pairings are trumpets with "light warm red" and white with silence.

When Kandinsky matches pitch and color value, however, he is more consistent and closer to Cummings's parallels. The lighter valued colors (light blue, light warm red, cool light red) all correspond to instruments of comparatively high pitch (flute, trumpet, and violin, respectively); lower valued colors (blue from "darker" to "darkest," deepened red) correspond to lower pitched instruments (cello, double bass, organ). Another similarity between Kandinsky's and Cummings's analogies is in the implied movement of a given color. Like Cummings, Kandinsky sees yellow as reaching out towards the spectator and finds convincing similarities between sharp colors (e.g., yellow) and sharp forms (e.g., a triangle), and between soft, deep colors (e.g. blue) and rounded forms (e.g., a circle). These parallels may indeed have informed Cummings's associations of color with shape and motion.

Beyond theorists of analogies, Cummings was drawn to fellow artists who espoused—and practiced—the interrelations of the senses. The Futurists, with typical stentorian bravado, declared that the artist should strive for the "acutest synthesis of all the senses in a unique universal." Boccioni and Marinetti even predicted the possibility of painting with colored gases, echoing Rimington's and Scriabin's contemporaneous ideas.[16] And once poetry had freed itself of conventional syntax and grammar, it could communicate "the sensation of weight" or "express odors." Pictorial or "symphonic" typography, moreover, "welded painting to poetry just as onomatopoeia has wedded lyricism to music," Marinetti declared. "The poet will hurl along parallel lines several chains of colors, sounds, odors, noises, weights, thicknesses, analogies," expressing the dominant "chain" in the largest type.[17] If short on specifics and bereft of science, the Futurists at least gave Cummings the synesthetic titles for his abstractions (noise and sound)[18] and promised a dynamic intensity from their interminglings that Cummings probably found preferable to the amorphous stasis of the Symbolists or the "saccharine diffusions" of Scriabin.

Another group whose synesthetic ideas anticipated Cummings's was the Synchromists. In their introduction to the catalog of their first American exhibition in 1914 (which Cummings almost surely read), they assert: "we have applied ourselves to a close study of the harmonious relation of these colors to one another. And, as a result of the incorporation of these colors into gamut-form, they convey the notion of "time" in painting. They give the illusion that the canvas *develops* like music, in time, while both the old and modern paintings [of others] exist strictly in space."[19] Incorporating colors into "gamut-form" (literally, "the entire series of recognized musical notes") suggests a musical system in the color arrangement. Morgan Russell provides glimpses of this system in a "Harmonic Analysis" of his painting, *Synchromy in Blue-Violet*. The most prominent color, blue-violet, serves as the "tonic" to a "dominant" of yellow and "subdominant" of orange. These tonalities combine into a "principal rhythm" and a "second theme or rhythm."[20] Russell even planned a "kinetic light machine" not unlike Rimington's. His mentor, however, was not Rimington but Percyval Tudor-Hart, his teacher in Paris, whom Klein calls "one of the most ardent supporters of the Analogy of Sound and Colour." As Cummings was later to do, Tudor-Hart equated specific components of sound and color.

Sound		Colour
Pitch	=	Luminosity [i.e., value]
Timbre or Tone	=	Hue or Color
Intensity	=	Saturation or Purity

The twelve chromatic intervals of the musical octave . . . have corresponding sensational and emotional qualities to those of the twelve chromatic colors.[21]

While these analogies do not quite match Cummings's own, Tudor-Hart's pairings of hue and tone do: "Red—C, Red-Orange—C#, Blue-Violet—A."[22] Tudor-Hart also envisaged a color-keyboard (truly, this was the age of inventors!) and although he never completed it, he did publish his analogic ideas in two articles of *Cambridge Magazine* in 1918 that Cummings may well have read.[23]

Finally, we should look to the poets closest to Cummings *himself*, the Imagists, for examples of "intertranslations" of the arts. In "The Poetry of a New Era" (pp. 37–38), he quotes the "first movement" of a poem Amy Lowell apparently wrote while listening to Stravinsky's *Three Pieces for String Quartet*. So titled, the poem imitates various sounds with onomatopeia, images, and metaphors and projects the rhythm in a stream of consciousness flow.

Sabots slapping the worn, old stones,
And a shaking and cracking of dancing bones,
Clumsy and hard they are,
And uneven,
Losing half a beat
Because the stones are slippery
Bump-e-ty-tong! Whee-e-e! Tong!
The thin Spring leaves
Shake to the banging of shoes.
Shoes beat, slap.
Shuffle, rap
And the nasal pipes squeal with their pig's voices . . . .

It is perhaps no compliment to Cummings's taste that he admired this poem; yet Lowell's example pointed the way: "To us who have heard the music which the poet is describing this is perhaps the most remarkable instance of the translation of one art into terms of another which it has ever been our happiness to encounter" (p. 38).

In "The New Art" (p. 24), similar significance is given to synesthesia in a sonnet by Donald Evans. Cummings comments, "the figure 'Her voice was fleet limbed' and the phrases 'white words' and 'dusty noises' . . . . furnish a sought-for literary parallel to the work of 'sound painters' [i.e., the Futurists]." From these modest antecedents, Cummings would expand synesthesia into a major technique in his own poems. Even his notes tend toward it, as when he figuratively praises the way "Eliot squeezes a whole tube of violet in[to] one line of the Rhapsody [on a Windy Night]."[24]

The very profusion of these ventures to interrelate the arts, and Cummings's intense interest in them, predisposed him to believe that the dynamics of one Modernist art cannot be understood apart from related processes in other arts. As he declares in 1915, "there can be no greater blunder than to isolate for inspection a particular specimen or even type of the new art without first illustrating, however imperfectly, the expression of kindred fields of that animating spirit which to be appreciated must be grasped in its entirety."[25] Yet his *own* practice of several arts, his search for their aesthetic underpinnings, and his natural curiosity would not permit Cummings merely to accept someone else's correlative theories. He had to establish his own.

Cummings's Analogies and Experiments: Painting and Music

The analogies between painting and music apparently fascinated Cummings, judging from the careful and repeated parallels he drew between the individual elements of each art. Yet these parallels remained largely theoretical and account for few practical techniques in his art. For although he improvised at the piano and briefly tried his hand at composing songs, he never developed his musical proclivities to the level of his painting or poetry. Still, his theories themselves deserve consideration if only for the obscure phrases they clarify in the early poems.

Several elements of painting and music seemed analogous to Cummings: color and timbre, color and tonality, and lines and harmony. Perhaps his most comprehensive note compares the contexts, methods, and organs of perception required of each art.

```
[hearing]                              [seeing]
                    BRAIN
"ears"                                 "eyes"
----------------
                    Range of
Audibility                             Visibility
(inaudible)                            (invisible)
11 8ves                                1 8ve
----------------
                    Mechanism
"air" becomes                          "light" becomes
a sound                                a colour
(through being                         (through being
disturbed)                             reflected-absorbed)
               VIBRATIONS common to both
                    waves
1) air holds all sounds                1) light holds all colors
2) all sounds are made                 2) all colors are made
   out of air (by disturbance)            out of light (by disturbance)
3) all sounds are heard                3) all colours are seen
   in air (vs. VACUUM)                    in light (vs. DARKNESS)
4) air has a sound of                  4) light has a color
   its own (the wind)                     ("white" or sunlight)
                                       (Houghton notes, I[39] no. 120)
```

The basic properties of each art are also compared, but in a manner that varies from Tudor-Hart's comparisons.

```
hue   ⎫                                pitch    ⎫
shade ⎬ colors                         loudness ⎬ sounds
tint  ⎭                                quality  ⎭
                                       (Houghton notes, I[59] no. 39)[26]
```

The parallels become more imaginative as Cummings narrows his comparisons to individual components of color and sound. Two notes, for example, compare hue to timbre ("quality" above) by assigning colors to orchestral instruments.

```
Timbres   flute—Y[ellow]
          trumpets—R[ed]
          harp—G[reen] (cool, water transparent)
```

DRUMS—GREY
        you can't play a tune on drums. . . .
        you can't draw with Grey: but only
        with 2 things, opposites, Black&White
        [. . . .]
        cellos—green?
        oboes—purple?
                                            (Houghton notes, I[39] no. 123)

Timbre=Colour
    (impossible,—lilac Shriek . . Scarlet Bellow
    drums.
            snare—black rattle of sparks) or, Grey rustle
            kettle—lilac thuds
            bass—purple booms
    a cello is dark [. . .]
    the highest not[e] on a violin squeaks
            (squeal of thinness
    piccolo—scarlet chirp
    flutes are Chrome,Opaque,luminous
    horn—ochre blare,snarl
                                            (Houghton notes, I[39] no. 294)

While such comparisons are commonplace—timbre in music is often referred to, synesthetically, as "tone color"—Cummings's pairings are, like Kandinsky's, quite specific. Indeed, their similarity in linking warm colors with piercing timbres, and cool colors with deeper, more recessive timbres suggests that Cummings's pairings were not entirely arbitrary and subjective. Even the common description of piercing timbres as "bright" supports Cummings's criterion. Of course, his basis allows some subjective latitude in matching *particular* piercing colors and timbres, but not in *crossing* bright colors with deep timbres: a trumpet's timbre may be red, or yellow, or orange, but not purple or violet.

These pairings of color and timbre provide useful glosses for some obscure synesthesia in Cummings's early poems. In "my eyes are fond of the east side" (&, "Post Impressions," XI), the first section matches the colors of the streets to the timbre of appropriate instruments:

> dark colours like 'cellos keen
> fiddling colours colours cOOler than harps colours
> p r i c k i n glike piccolos [. . . .]

A more obscure synesthetic mystery in the poem "my mind is"[27] may now be solved. The speaker, who has been "altered" by the chisels of his senses, concludes:

> Hereupon helpless i utter lilac shrieks and scarlet
> bellowings.

Yet in his notes, Cummings claims that these pairings are "impossible." Why impossible? First, Cummings's two notes pair "forward" colors (yellow and red) with instruments of the most piercing, or "forward," timbres: flute (yellow), piccolo (scarlet), and trumpet (red). Conversely, the receding colors belong to instruments producing timbres that are lower, deeper, blunter, and thus more "recessive": cello (green, dark), kettle drum (lilac thuds), bass drum (purple booms), and horn (ochre). For Cummings, then, a "lilac shriek" is a recessive-aggressive coupling and therefore "impossible": the terms simply do not go together. Why, then, does he pair them in the poem?

Context provides some clues. The speaker has been chiseled into "something a little different" by his senses: into his real "self" as an artist. The last line emphasizes his passivity ("Hereupon helpless"), his subservience to his senses. The "impossible" couplings that he helplessly utters, "lilac shrieks and scarlet bellowings" are also "altered" from the normal or more logical pairings for Cummings: i.e., lilac bellowings (both recessive—cf. "lilac thuds" in the notes) and scarlet shrieks (both aggressive—cf. "scarlet chirp" in the notes). Thus, as the speaker's mind is changed from a hunk of inert "nothing" to a vibrant receptor of sensory flashes—as it acquires an artist's sensibility—so, also, do the sensory responses change from the "normal" to the "impossible" that are *only* possible to the artist's sensibility. But, curiously, the speaker has no control over these changes—in fact, the "shrieks" and "bellowings," expressing "agony" in the poem, convey the pain of his involuntary metamorphosis and unconventional responses. It appears that the muse has become a sadist, the artist its helpless victim.

Besides instrumental timbre, Cummings also considered tonality and its relationship to color, following the examples of Rimington and possibly of Tudor-Hart. But Cummings compared not only individual tones to colors but also intervals, chords, and accidentals to pairs and triads of colors, noting the resulting "consonances" or "dissonances." The single hue-tone analogies show up repeatedly in the early notes, usually as color wheels and always in the same pairings:

C	D	E	F	G	A	B
Red	Orange	Yellow	Green	Blue	Violet	Indigo

(Houghton notes, I[59] no. 26)

These pairings virtually duplicate those of Rimington and Tudor-Hart (as well as those of numerous theorists before them) and are thus clearly derivative.

"Tint" (more commonly called "value" today) expands the range of a hue by denoting its degree of whiteness. Cummings likens this expansion to the repetition of the same tone in successive octaves: "any hue : its tint = C : C^{8ve}."[28] Further, he compares the variants of a single hue to the accidentals of a single tone:

[C]	C#		C$^\flat$
Red	scarlet	or	crimson

(Houghton notes, I[59] no. 46)

As the diatonic tones can be combined to form harmonic intervals and chords, so could primary colors be joined to form "intervalic" or "chordal" secondary and tertiary colors. Both color and tonal combinations could result in consonance (thirds, fifths, octaves) or dissonance (seconds, sevenths, ninths).

Melody:notes
R[ed], Y[ellow] (c,e
R[ed], Orange   (c,d
    or
Vermillion,Lake (c,csharp
red & blue   (c-g

Harmony:chords
Orange (third [Consonance]

DISSONANCE [. . .]

(fifth
(Houghton notes, I[39] no. 122, I[59] no. 42)

In sum, the primary hues equaled the tonic triad in C and were consonant: Red/C, Yellow/E (a third), Blue/G (a fifth).[29] The secondary hues, formed by these primaries, equaled the more remote intervals from Red/C: Orange/D (a second), Green/F (a fourth), Violet/A (a sixth). Finally, Cummings likened the "luminous" advancing colors (red, yellow, orange) to the major mode and the "deep" receding colors (green, blue, violet) to the minor.[30]

If colors equaled tones, then white equaled silence:

White is	1) a hue—complementary Black
	2) light, considered as a fusion of all hues
Silence is	1) an integral part of music (in *tempo*)— complementary,sound
	2) air, considered as that into which all the sound-vibrations disappear, fuse.

(Houghton notes, I[39] no. 119)

To design in black and white equaled "to sing in octaves, to magadize." To this equation, Cummings added another action: to draw in parallel lines or in circles.[31] All three were too easy, too consonant, and too tepid for Cummings: he preferred the dissonant excitement of lines that crossed, harmonies that clashed, and colors (not black and white) that opposed each other. Among the possibilities of line, for example:

circularity [equals]	octave
angle	interval
obtuse	–	major
acute	–	minor
right	–	5th

(Houghton notes, I[39])

Color combinations could be seen as metrical: "YV/RG/OB = 2/4 YgbV/RoyG/OygB = 3/4." And likewise, alternations of black and white: "white-black (2/4?), white-grey-black (3/4?)."[32]

For Cummings to entitle the major works of his early period "Sound" and "Noise" suggests how profoundly music inspired his early painting. Beholden as they were to Futurist synesthesia, these titles are neither homage nor detached metaphors, however; for they reflect several kinds of musical content in the early abstractions. The most obvious and least original of these is the guitar imagery in

Sound Number 1 (plate 1) and in *Sound Number 2* (fig. 31). Cummings is far more himself, however, when he translates music into the "binding rhythms" he felt would unify his work. *Noise Number 12* (fig. 22) is a superb example. Less contentious than its fellow *Noises and Sounds*, its lines curve and flow: the shapes move in graceful arcs as they swoop and spiral, wind around each other, expand and contract in gentle pulsations of visual rhythm. With typical ambiguity, one motif suggests the half-hidden shape of a saxophone at upper-center, while the broad concentric circles at right-center narrow and withdraw into a tight oblong to imply (besides the figures cited in chap. 1) an expanding musical note not unlike the one in Gleizes' *Igor Stravinsky.*

Just how specifically Cummings *translated* his theoretical analogies between color and tone into his painting, however, is less clear. Something he wrote in a later note (ca. 1940-45) may have been in his mind all along:

in painting the thing is to get your keys straight
establish your *triad*   white–cerulean. . . .sky
                           green–purple. . . . . .mountain
                           yellow–green. . . . . . .earth
                                   (Houghton notes, I[55] nos. 109, 115)

And the color wheel on one early worksheet indicates that he did plan his colors—in one study for an abstraction, at least—around a central triad: here, yellow-orange, green, and violet.[33] But while his colors in this triad and in the ratios discussed below show Cummings's regard for balance—in having at least two of the three colors equidistant from each other—they do not necessarily evince a musical intent. Just as likely, their source may have been in the triadic color schemes advocated by a scientist of color optics, Ogden Rood, whose *Modern Chromatics* (1879) had influenced the Neo-Impressionists. And Rood considered analogies between color and musical tonality "quite worthless."[34]

Painting and Poetry

In the broadest sense, nearly all of Cummings's "poempictures" demonstrate the analogies between painting and poetry that he thought possible. Previous chapters have explored many of these pictorial techniques in depth, including the "gestures" of pictorial capitalization, punctuation, and spacing; the balance between white space and black print; juxtaposed structures; and pictorial motion. But Cummings went still further in searching for analogues between painting and poetry: first, in finding equivalent colors for the rudimentary elements of language, and second, in composing poetic structures "by angles and planes."

COLOR AND GRAMMAR

In punctuation, for example, Cummings saw not only pictorial and kinetic possibilities, but also colors: commas were somewhere between yellow and red, periods between black and white, colons between veronese green (in one note) and blue (in another).[35] Curiously, these pairings do not quite square with the kinetic potential of each component in Cummings's other notes. Colons, which facilitate syntactic progression, should logically correspond to red or yellow; and commas, in slowing movement and separating clauses, to green or blue. The black periods, however, match nicely.

Grammatical voice, case, number, and person all find analogous colors or shapes in Cummings's early notes, just as they did in Futurist writings. A collation of Cummings's analogues would appear as follows:

[Grammar]		[Color]	[Shape]	[Comment]
Verb, voice:	active	yellow	cone	(angle, going somewhere
	middle		sphere	
	[reflexive]			
	passive	violet	cylinder	
Verb transitive			cone	point(apex)-angle-base: motion
	intransitive		cylinder	
Verb, mood:	indicative	green		
	optative			
	(wish)	orange		
		[also: white x mauve]*		
	subjunctive	blue		
		[also: white x blue]*		
	conditional			
	("if")	violet		
	infinitive	yellow		
	imperative	red		

Noun, case:	nominative	white	
	objective	black	
Noun, person:	"I"		sphere
	"you"		cone
	"he/she/ it		cylinder
	they		
Noun, number:	singular	white	
	dual	grey	
	plural	black	

(Houghton notes, I[59] no. 1, I[55] no. 86, *I[25] nos. 30–33)

Clearly, these matchings do not replicate Marinetti's notion that "moods and tenses are triangular, square or oval. The infinitive alone is circular. . . ."[36] But they adhere closely to Cummings's other theories. Dynamic constructions (active voice, transitive verbs, imperative mood) go with dynamic colors (yellow, red) and with shapes that imply structural tension (a cone narrowing to a point). Static constructions (passive voice, intransitive verbs, conditional and subjunctive moods) take recessive colors (blue, violet) and less dynamic shapes (cylinder).[37] Noun-related elements (case, number) receive colorless black-gray-white designations appropriate to their low caste in Cummings's linguistic hierarchy. Apparently, Cummings's analogues remained fairly stable, even if his preferences for certain colors and lines changed; for the I(55) notes date from the midforties, while the others were written between 1921–23.

VISUAL STRUCTURE: THE *FAIT*

Whether Cummings actually applied these analogues of color and grammar to his poetry—whether, for example, he really saw his verbs as colors and shapes—is an interesting question and a real possibility, given the proof of his efforts to apply visual motion to poetry. But to demonstrate such applications in his poetry by translating words into colors and shapes and then examining the resulting visual harmonies, balances and structures, would be a separate study in itself. What *is* certain from his poems is his distinctly painterly notion of "planar" structure. He wrote in his 1921 travel notebook:

Poetry is [the] Art of Form
    placing of ideas next to each other
      to produce impression or expression
          (inward)   (outward)

(Houghton notes, I[98])

In analogical terms, Cummings described his poetic technique as creating form by juxtaposing colors (i.e., by using verbs), *not* by modeling form from the light and dark contrasts of conventional grammar and nouns.[38] This sense of poetic structure as a juxtaposition of planes is stated explicitly in a seminal footnote (fig. 51) beneath an early experimental poem: *"Composition by Angles and Planes* [. . . .] as to method—*blocking* into cubes,-*plotting* of curves and angles" (Cummings's emphasis).

The poem bearing this crucial note was one of several Cummings composed between 1916–17 and left unpublished, to yellow in his notes.[39] He called them *faits*—constructed objects—to identify their Modernist character as things, rather than as traditional vehicles of personal expression. They were dedicated to his hero, Paul Cézanne, and their cover sheet proclaims:

I

Most significant pieces
Everything is in *arrangement*
Sounds not words
Purity for the first time

(Houghton notes, I[21] no. 134)

The poems in this sheaf are anything but "significant" in content: many are barely a sentence or phrase of utter banality. For Cummings's interest was solely in the "arrangement" of the words, syllables and letters, not in their semantics or theme. Many of the *faits* are harmonic: vertical orderings of vowel sounds. Others, however, are primarily visual: "compositions of angles and planes," cubes and curves that move the narrative line (when there is one) into shapes and directions other than the traditional left-to-right-descending pattern. And several *faits* bear important footnotes on the experimental techniques Cummings was just then inventing, notes that give one the uncanny feeling of witnessing the first stirrings of genius.

Above the most important of these footnotes is a poem beginning "dark [or "dark- / ness"] flicker / -ings" (fig. 51). Its narrative line makes little sense (a farm during a thunderstorm at night is discernible); but the spacing and shaping of the words seem to describe "planes," "angles," and "cubes," as words and syllables co-

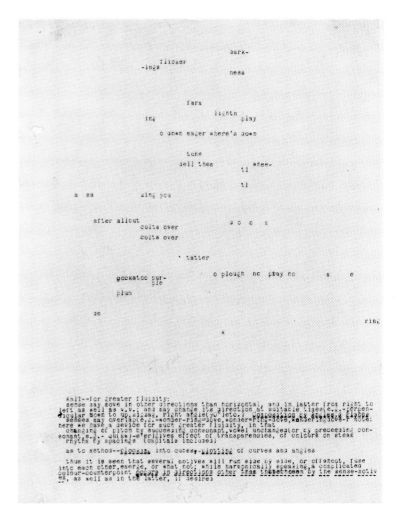

Fig. 51.
"dark / ness flicker / ings," c. 1916–17. The E. E. Cummings papers, the Houghton Library, Harvard University. By permission of the Houghton Library. Copyright 1982, The E. E. Cummings Trust.

here in vertical and diagonal patterns, partly according to aural harmonies (the vertical row of "ing" suffixes, the diagonal rhyme of "tune," "d o o m," and "home,") and partly to visual proximity. The syllable "dark-", for example, can move vertically down to "ness" or in a reverse diagonal to "flicker / -ings." Precisely where one sets the boundaries of these planes to include or exclude word-groups is decidedly arbitrary. Should the left-side cluster ("a ma zing you" to "tatter" to "plunde [ring]") form *one* arrowhead pointing right or two distinct planes? Does "tatter" belong to the left group, the right, both, or neither?

In fact, the poem would not be worth pondering at all, save that Cummings refined the "blocking" technique in such published poems, as "writhe and."[40] As Richard Kennedy notes, Cummings wrote an earlier version of this poem (below) as one of his first sorties into free verse, and the title is included in "Index 1916," a list of his best contemporary work.[41] Shortly thereafter, Cummings reworked the poem, barely changing its content but radically altering its structure.[42] This revision, then, was contemporaneous with the experimental poems and the notes on the painterly structure of poetry quoted above. A comparison of the early and revised versions of "writhe and" clearly shows the extent of this painterly influence.

First, however, the pictorial content should be noted. For unlike "dark- / flicker / -ings," "writhe and" coherently describes a scene: the disintegrating perspective of a cityscape under the shifting and darkening colors of sunset. The first half, however, (up to "collapse") barely refers to sunset and attends only to the visual havoc it causes, perhaps in the blinding glare of the red sun's rays coming from between the skyscrapers. Significantly, the skyscrapers are reduced to "planes" that collide and "collapse," "crackle and sag"; the perspective of these planes is distorted, "tortured": it "writhes." The imagery is abrasive, aurally and semantically dissonant ("rasp," "crackle," "clamors"), and almost identical to the Cubist crunches in "Picasso."

By contrast, none of these grinding images is present in the second half of "writhe and." Here, the city is personified as a blushing young woman who sheds her "dimension"—as she would her clothes, Kennedy observes[43]—in the darkening night and "enters / the becoming garden of her agony." The final allusion to Christ's agony in the garden of Gethsemane brings the poem back to the "torture" of the first half, but it is an agony the speaker finds "becoming" to this city, perhaps because the agony also suggests a sexual initiation.

Given the planar perspective and the discordant imagery, the poem's revised structure is appropriate. The original version attempts the rhythmic alternations of line length noted in "o sweet spontaneous," leaving the final line as a surprise twist:

Writhe and gape of tortured perspective,
Rasp and graze of splintered horizon,
Crackle and sag of planes,
Clamors of collision,
Collapse;
As peacefully
Lifted
Into the frightening beauty of sunset
The perfect young city,
Putting off dimension
With a blush,
Enters the becoming garden of

Her agony.

(Houghton notes, 1823.5[354])

The revision visually *constructs* the broken planes of the first half in clusters of words and *enacts* the collisions by juxtaposing these planar clusters:

writhe and
gape of tortured

  perspective
  rasp and graze of splintered

normality
        crackle and
        sag
  of planes   clamors of
  collision
  collapse   As

peacefully,
lifted
into the awful beauty
               of sunset

             the young city
putting off dimension with a blush
enters
the becoming garden of her agony

(*Tulips and Chimneys*, "Impressions," II)

Note how the indented "perspective / rasp and graze of splintered" forms one splintered plane, how "crackle and / sag / . . . clamors of" forms another:

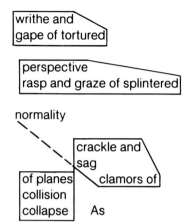

About this planar structure, Rushworth Kidder writes, "Here the pattern of indentations from the left margin suggests more than the block-like appearance of city buildings—a common enough subject for painters in the twenties. The 'tortured / perspective,' 'splintered / normality' and 'crackle and / sag / of planes' recall the Cubists' devices of reducing objects to their planes. Here Cummings lets the indentations suggest various planes out of which such a painting is constructed."[44]

Appropriately, when the scene and tone change to the "peaceful" lifting of the city into sunset, the structure also changes. The lines lengthen and flow more smoothly; while pausing at "enters" (as perhaps the shy, young woman might hesitate at the moment of penetration), they make the entry into night one smoothly continuous act.

SHAPE VS. MOVEMENT

One question that arises in considering the visual structure of Cummings's poems is: Should one perceive the narrative lines by the static shapes they form or by the dynamic movement they effect? The famous "Buffalo Bill's" points up the problem perfectly.[45]

```
Buffalo Bill's
defunct
          who used to
          ride a watersmooth-silver
                                    stallion
and break onetwothreefourfive pigeonsjustlikethat
                                              Jesus

he was a handsome man
                        and what i want to know is
how do you like your blueeyed boy
Mister Death
```

Seen as shape, its structure approximates an arrowhead triangle pointing right, with the apex at "Jesus." But the narrative line takes the eye, conventionally, back and forth, left to right. Both readings, it is true, place maximum visual importance on the lines:

```
and break onetwothreefourfive pigeonsjustlikethat
                                              Jesus
```

As the apex of the triangle and thus the point of maximum force, and as the longest and yet fastest line, it represents Buffalo Bill at his most vital, at the apex of his career. But while the poem's *shape* recedes gradually to the left margin, the point of least force that visually and literally signifies death, the *line* pulls back abruptly to "he was a handsome man," ventures out further with "and what i want to know is," and then returns again to the left margin. Should this zigzag motion of the narrative line or the stable, triangular shape take visual precedence? Both contribute to the thematic and visual meaning and both can be considered individually. But as chapter 5 has demonstrated, the dynamic lines are crucial to Cummings's aesthetics and should never be obscured by the shapes they might form.

Poetry and Music

In Cummings's most important technical footnote to his experimental poems (fig. 51) appear these comments:

changing of pitch by succeeding consonant, vowel unchanged(or by
   preceeding consonant,e.g.-qu(kw)-e'er)gives effect of transparen-
   cies, of colours on steam
rhythm by spacings (capitals included)
[. . . . .]
harmonically speaking, a complicated colour-counterpoint *occurs in*
   directions other than those chosen by the sense-motives [. . . .]

One might dismiss "complicated colour-counterpoint" as merely a careless, synesthetic metaphor, such that some critics, then as now, are given to using. But the first excerpt reveals genuine concern for the musical (cum painterly) effect of concerted vowels and consonants. The passages imply both technical interest in and knowledge of music and the musical aspects of language, and Cummings indeed had both. His fascination with modern music,[46] his extemporizing on the piano, even his efforts at composing songs suggest that he considered music an important contributor to his interdisciplinary aesthetics.

Cummings's notes on music and the musical qualities of language appear among his earliest speculations on literature and art at Harvard. His interest was probably sparked by Raymond Alden's *English Verse*, a college textbook on poetry which, as Richard Kennedy notes, "discourses on tone quality, especially tone-color . . . by means of which sounds of words can increase their expressiveness."[47] What particularly interested Cummings were the structural and kinetic effects he could achieve by manipulating vowel and consonant sounds. An unfinished Harvard essay on poetry, for example, describes these effects in musical terms:

To sum up: the length of any line [of poetry] is determined by the occurrence of "modulations"-&-"slides".[. . .] As far as line's length
goes, the slide counts as a modulation. . . . .
          progression
The horizontal *speed* of any line takes into account the slide as a
                      elevation
separate and distinctive factor [. . . .] The vertical *level* of any line depends on the vowels.[. . .] That is, not only the degree of each vowel's force or colour, but the inherent and unchanging position of any
vowel at any time with reference to all other vowels at the same time
(its pitch) determines the elevation-curve of any line. (Houghton
notes, 1892.6[29] nos. 7–8)

An example illustrates these ideas:

"Ten men love what I hate" (tĕnmĕnlŭvwhŭtāīhēt)
[. . . . .]
Now let us consider the function of the vowels here: the effect is
merely one of suspension (4 shorts) plus glissando (a-i) leading *down*
into long e ("hate").[. . .] Here the modulations are really 4, not 3:
n-m,n-l,v-wh,y-h, and between the latter two occurs the slide t–.[. . .]
here, t— by its precipitate character as a slide drags ahead the preceeding [sic] syllable with it, faster than the preceeding syllables (in
this case) [. . . .] (Houghton notes, 1892.6[29] no. 7)

Note that Cummings equates "pitch" in words (created by
vowel sounds) to pitch in music and attributes to verbal pitch the
same capacity for *vertical* structure that harmonics (i.e., simultaneous pitches) creates in music. He even specifies in his example the
relative "elevation levels" of the various vowels: "Here (short is
high)[;] it is maximum with e,e ["tenmen"]; slightly lower with u,u
["Lovewhat"]; and descends rapidly with ai,e ["Ihate"]." "Modulations" and "slides" reinforce the musical parallel. Their relative
movements—i.e., the ease or difficulty of the transitions—affect the
horizontal progression of a line, particularly its speed.

Cummings saw phonetic movement not only as vertical elevation and horizontal progression, but also in three-dimensional depth,
as advancing or receding—more grist for his theories of three-
dimensional "seeing around." Thus, one handwritten fragment in
this Harvard draft observes:

Advancing   Receding
tā en—always   shŏe—always
  [illeg.]   cf ȯf (ŏw)
    mōre
          ∴ suitable for "*accented*" position in line
i.e. there is a pre-existing fitness between the sound of a vowel
      and its normal position in line—perpendicularly speaking
i.e. just as some consonant combinations are "comfortable" so may
      be some vowels.
Thus ē = naturally suited for accent
    i (it)   "   "   "   short
    ŭ (uv, thru)"   "   "   "   (less so)
                (Houghton notes, 1892.6[29] no. 7ᵛ)

In his experimental *faits*, Cummings tinkered with musical arrangements of consonants and especially of vowels, guided by his sense of their "pre-existing fitness" for particular positions in a line. A few poems attempt to create "harmonics" by vertically ordering like vowels of different words. The most notable of these is the experimental poem "two / brass / buttons." Two drafts appear in Cummings's early notes. The first of these (fig. 52) resembles a musical score.[48] Like notes, the words rise and fall according to the pitch of their vowels along a narrow vertical span resembling a staff, while the "sense" of the line—a dialogue between two women following a spree —moves it along from left to right. The vertical hierarchy of vowel pitches in each "staff" generally conforms to Cummings's note that "short is high" and long low:

ōō "two"
ă "asked"
ŭ "buttons"
ô "off"
ĕ "let, retta"
ō "open, loretta"
ĭ "dint, it"
ă "and, have"
ā "ain't"
ē "rēmember"
e "rememb__e__r"
ī "knife"

And significantly, the twelve vowel pitches here recall the twelve tones of the octave.

But as his footnote indicates, Cummings was dissatisfied with this pitch arrangement because his pitches were not structured to convey harmonic *simultaneity* the way music could vertically combine two simultaneous pitches into an interval, or three into a chord, while the thematic line proceeds horizontally. It was this harmonic "pedal effect," constructed vertically on the page, that guided his revision of "two / brass / buttons" (fig. 53).

Here, the assonant vowels are stacked in vertical columns (abandoning the pitch progression within stanzas of the first version), while the sense moves in the traditional horizontal-downward progression. The footnote cites a "pedal effect by 'scarlet.' " That is,

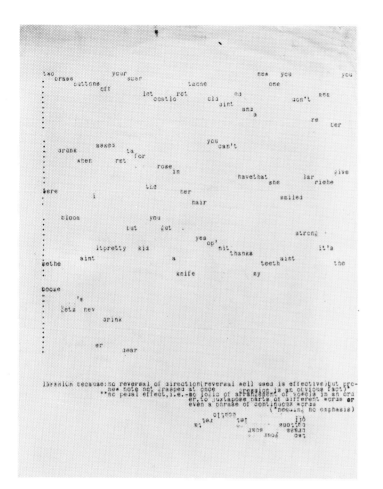

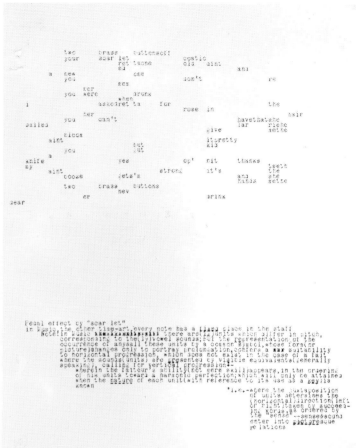

Fig. 52.
"two / brass / buttons," c. 1916–17. The E. E. Cummings papers, the Houghton Library, Harvard University. By permission of the Houghton Library. Copyright 1982, The E. E. Cummings Trust.

Fig. 53.
"two / brass / buttons" (revision), c. 1916–17. The E. E. Cummings papers, the Houghton Library, Harvard University. By permission of the Houghton Library. Copyright 1982, The E. E. Cummings Trust.

as the sense-motive progresses rightward with "scar," it suddenly expands harmonically with the vertical assonance "let / red / ed," precisely as a melodic line is filled out harmonically by a chord or "pedal effect." Significantly, the footnote claims that a *fait* whose "sound units are presented by visible equivalents [i.e., phonemes]" is *more* suited for vertical progression than is musical scoring whose symbols can denote only duration. The note concludes, "the faiteur's ability (not mere skill)appears in the ordering of his units toward a harmonic perfection; which will only be attained when the *nature* of

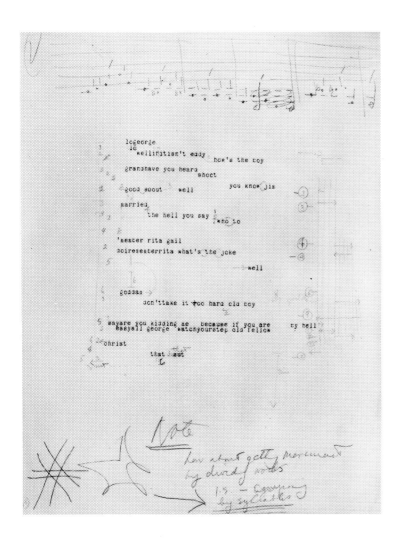

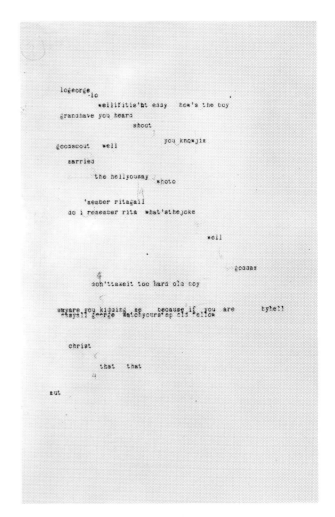

Fig. 54.
"logeorge," c. 1916–17. The E. E. Cummings papers, the Houghton Library, Harvard University. By permission of the Houghton Library. Copyright 1982, The E. E. Cummings Trust.

Fig. 55.
"logeorge" (revision), c. 1916–17. From *Etcetera: The Unpublished Poems of E. E. Cummings,* ed. George James Firmage and Richard Kennedy. New York: Liveright, 1983.

each unit(with reference to its use as a *key*) is known" (Houghton notes, I[23] no. 142).

Another experimental poem loosens this rigid horizontal-vertical structure by trying some diagonal "harmonics." Like "two / brass / buttons," the poem "logeorge" conveys a banal dialogue, this one between a jilted suitor and his friend who breaks the bad news; also like "two / brass / buttons," "logeorge" went through several drafts. The first typed version (fig. 54) is bordered by musical scoring on two sides and bears the startling footnote:

Note
#*how about getting movement by dividing words i.e.-arranging[?]
by syllables.

Harmonically, however, the revision of "logeorge" (fig. 55) is more significant. At least three harmonic rhymes are evident. First, a parallel set of diagonals—an octave?—rhyme on "el": "well" and "hell." The other two harmonic diagonals help counterbalance the first: an "ā" rhyme connects "hellyous*ay*," "ritag*ail*" (note Cummings's line connecting the two phrases), and "don'tt*a*keit"; and a rhyme on "s/t" slants from upper right ("how'*s* *t*he boy") to lower center ("what'*s*thejoke" and "watchyour*s*tep"). Certainly, Cummings's primary concern is with tempo: spacing the dialogue to mirror the speech rhythms of the speakers, in sudden accelerandos and dramatic ritards, as the big news is revealed and absorbed. But he also had an eye—and ear—on the harmonic patterns of this dialogue.

In his published poems, Cummings abandoned these harmonic structures, probably because they interfered with his many other structural techniques. But he did not give up the idea altogether. Rather, he appears to have funneled it into the established musical devices of alliteration, consonance, and especially assonance —all of which he employed extensively in his early poetry. These devices let sounds linger in the reader's ear, much as a piano pedal holds a note while new ones are sounded. Consider, for example, the subtle modulations of long vowels in "Paris; this April sunset completely utters."[49]

spiral acres of bloated rose	ī ā	ō ō
coil within cobalt miles of sky	oi	ō ī ī
yield to and heed	ē	ē
the mauve	ō	
of twilight		ī ī

If "ī" is the tonic (the first and most prominent tone), then "ō" becomes the dominant (very close to its relative position in the vowel scale above). Modulations to "ā" and "ē" precede the emphatic return to the tonic on "twīlīght." The music is lovely in its own right! What makes these modulations more fitting still is that they belong to words that denote the delicate modulations of colors in a twilight sky, as light pink within blue gradually evolves to violet.

The early poems use assonance and the other musical devices freely—so freely that one is often tempted to conclude that the tail wags the dog: that the assonance, not the sense, determines the word or line. Such poems as the Hopkinsesque "god gloats upon Her stunning flesh" and "before the fragile gradual throne of night" might be suspected of musical excess.[50] Yet we have seen elsewhere, for example, in the verbal complementaries discussed in chapter 4, that what seemed an arbitrary and meaningless device (even to Cummings's most sympathetic critics), proved to be both logical and meaningful within the context of Cummings's aesthetics. Can we be certain that the same is not also true here? And even should such a broader aesthetics be lacking, Cummings would certainly not be the first American poet to employ musical devices for the pleasure of the sound alone: witness Poe.

Fortunately, however, the musical lines and poems for which a larger aesthetics remains hidden are outnumbered by those whose brilliant fusions of music and meaning are self-evident. To cite but a few: rain as "ropes of silver gliding from sunny / thunder into freshness" (note the sibilant *s*'s that catch the hissing of the falling rain), the "acute brutal feet" of a prostitute, and a star that "sleepily, feebly, scratches the sore / of morning."[51] If he moderated his more radical ideas of poetic harmonics to incorporate conventional musical devices, Cummings certainly exploited these devices with abandon and considerable finesse.

When it came to finding poetic equivalents for musical *subjects* in his poems, Cummings could be as unconventional as he pleased and bring to bear his flexible techniques of spacing and punctuation. For example, in that marvelously sensuous tour, "my eyes are fond of the east side," section one, while ostensibly about colors, leans heavily on musical imagery.

<pre>
                                    colours
p r i c k i n glike piccolos thumPing colours like a
bangofpiano colours which,are,the,flowery plucking
of a harpsichord [. . .] colours-
like-trumpets they(writhe they, struggleinweird chords
of humorous,fury heapingandsqueezing [. . . .]
</pre>

Likewise, the line from the poem's third section, "ladies dancing / thicklyfoolish, with,the,tam,bou,rine,s[.]" At least three musical elements are discernable: staccato notes, legato notes, and chords. The chords are the most obvious; they appear in the fused words ("bang-ofpiano," "struggleinweird," "heapingandsqueezing") to be read as *one* word, as the several tones of a chord are heard as one sound. If these fusions do not capture the pure simultaneity of musical chords, they at least come close. The staccato notes appear via the opposite device of separation. Thus, the commas separating "which,are,the, flowerly" convey the staccato "pluckings" of a harpsichord (whose notes cannot be blended by pedal), in contrast to the "bangof*piano*" chord. Likewise, the repetitive, staccato clappings of the "tam, bou,rine,s" are also set off by commas. And one might even see the separated letters of the "p r i c k i n glike piccolos" as representing that instrument's distinct, piercing notes. Between these extremes of fusion and isolation, the hyphenated "colours-like-trumpets" might suggest a legato tune played on that instrument, the words connected (as legato notes are) without being fused.

Painting, Poetry, and Music

Cummings's analogic cast of mind—as well as his aesthetics of wholeness—prompted him to attempt integrating all three of the arts he studied. These efforts took at least one conventional form, synesthesia, and two experimental forms: "vowel-color" (associations of phonemes with musical and coloristic motion in a poem) and the integration of musical harmonics and visual shapes in a poem.

SYNESTHESIA

Given the extensive examples of synesthesia in Romantic, Symbolist and Imagist poetry, the synesthesia in Cummings's early poetry had ample precedent. It also found a less likely precedent in the classical literature Cummings studied at Harvard. As he wrote in a college paper on "The Greek Spirit":

> I believe that the most ultramodern, the most vitally "Futuristic" ideas, such as the translation of an image of one of the senses in terms of another of the senses, are to be found in pristine and full fledged glory in those classics which are dear to the most conventional as well as the most original men. When Dante says, "the sun is silent," he is a poet of the 21st century. Homer and Virgil are far less

poets of antiquity than of today—and in this consists their fame.''
(Houghton notes, 1892.6 no. 47)

Cummings's synesthesia, however, distinguishes itself both in its vigor—touching a vast number of early poems—and in its predominantly painterly bias. To be sure, musical, olfactory, and tactile synesthesia were not ignored. Thus we can hear the sights, feel the abstractions, and even smell the sounds in such lines as these (followed by their page numbers in *Complete Poems 1913-1962*):

> she smelled of silence   (135)
> the weak noise of her eyes easily files
>   my impatience to an edge   (147)
> snickering shop doors   (172)
> omelet of fluffy lust   (132)

But the painter's eye tended naturally towards color to make generalities sensuous. Here are a few brushstrokes from Cummings's verbal palette.

> orange inch of moon   (86)
> silver minute of evening   (86)
> bright rain   (92)
> the greenslim purse of whose
>   face
>   opens
>   on a flatgold grin   (114)
> a gashing yellow yawn   (132)
> the dirty colours of her kiss have just
>   throttled
>   my seeing blood   (132)
> hunks-of-lilac laughter   (133)
> frail azures . . . strong silent
>   greens serenely lingering   (204)

Perhaps the most interesting examples are those that merge music (or sounds) and colors.

> the sky a silver dissonance   (47)
> the
>   great bells are ringing with rose   (51)
> a thud of scarlet   (143)

lilac shrieks and scarlet bellowings   (199)
the speed of white speech   (157)
your body's whitest song   (306)
where noisy colours stroll   (220)

This profusion of sense blendings makes possible the refined synesthesia in the later poems, where we encounter such masterful condensations as "[Your] self whose eyes smell of the sound of rain" and such marvels of delicacy as the closing lines of "somewhere i have never travelled . . .":

the voice of your eyes is deeper than all roses)
nobody,not even the rain,has such small hands

"VOWEL-COLOR"

Cummings's unpublished experiments in synesthesia were less successful but perhaps more interesting in their efforts at inclusiveness. The "Painting and Music" section above shows that he imagined colors for the timbres of various musical instruments and saw these color-timbres as advancing or receding. The "Poetry and Music" section considered the kinetic potential of particular vowels. It is not surprising, then, that he tentatively explored the next logical step of joining these separate analogues into what he called "vowel-color." In imagining the colors of vowels, Cummings had at least two precedents: Scriabin and Rimbaud. In 1909, Scriabin worked on a choral composition, *Mysterium*, from which *Prometheus* was later drawn. Faubion Bowers describes his plan.

The chorus is supposed to be robed in solid white, and originally, when *Prometheus* was a section of the *Mysterium*, the audience was to be similarly dressed. It [the chorus] sings vowel sounds. Each vowel had a connoting color for Scriabin though less fixed and different from Arthur Rimbaud. . . . To Scriabin the choral hum (with which it plunges into the music's ending) is a pearly blue, the color of moonshine; E is violet; A, steel with violet in it; and O, pearly white or sometimes red.[52]

The Rimbaud poem to which Bowers refers was written in 1871 and entitled "Voyelles." As Bowers implies, its vowel-colors are definite:

A black, E white, I red U green, O blue: vowels,
I will tell you some day of your hidden birth:
A, black hairy corset of the bursting flies
Which buzz around the cruel stench,

Gulfs of shadow; E, brilliance of vapors and tents,
Lances of proud glaciers, white kings, quivering flowers;
I, purples, spit blood, laughter of beautiful lips
In anger or drunk with penance;

U, cycles. divine vibrations of the viridian seas,
Peace of pastures scattered with animals, peace of the wrinkles
Which alchemy prints on great studious brows;

O, supreme Clarion full of a strange stridor,
Silence traversed by worlds and Angels:
—O, the Omega, the violet beam of His Eyes!

(Trans. John Porter Houston)

In a later prose poem, *Une Saison en enfer*, Rimbaud claimed rather playfully that "Voyelles" betokened a larger aesthetics of interrelationships: "I invented the colors of the vowels! . . . I fixed the form and movement of each consonant, and, with instinctive rhythms, I prided myself on inventing a poetic language accessible, at some time or another, to all the senses. I reserved translation rights"—a much-inflated claim in the view of John Houston: "[Rimbaud] here implies that 'Voyelles' contains an aesthetic doctrine, which it does not, and that even the use of consonants has been subjected to codification! These 'enchantments' belong to the supernatural and mythic world of *Une Saison en enfer* and have no literal meaning for Rimbaud's poetic practice."[53]

Cummings's vowel-colors are more precise than Scriabin's, less fanciful and more technical than Rimbaud's. On the same note that describes the color of various timbres, Cummings typed:

Vowel-Color			
	OO	(doom)	violet
	EE	(Deem)	white
	AY	(dame)	yellow
	O	(dome)	cobalt blue
	AI	(dime)	green

(Houghton notes, I[39] no. 294)

Another note, written on Camp Devens stationery and thus probably dating from 1918, bears a similar equation.

> Nile is black. Nail is yellow. Kneal is white. If there were such a thing as nool it would be violet. Thus:
>
> $$\bar{\imath} = \text{black}$$
> $$\bar{a} = \text{yellow}$$
> $$\bar{e} = \text{white}$$
> $$oow = \text{violet}$$
>
> (Houghton notes, I[21]10[186][54]

When compared to Scriabin's and Rimbaud's associations, Cummings's vowel-colors may seem no less arbitrary and subjective; indeed, the unrelatedness of all three examples implies that any pairing would be subjective. Yet, Cummings's vowel-colors are, for the most part, *internally* consistent, in that they build on other analogues he established between the various arts. We should recall, first, that he accepted the common notions about color and motion: that yellows, oranges, and reds seem to advance while blues, greens, and violets recede; and, second, that he likewise believed that some long vowels seem to advance ("tāen—advancing") while short vowels seem to recede ("shŏe—receding").[55] Thus, the most "advancing" color, yellow, should receive an advancing vowel, "ā"; the color that most recedes, violet, should take the most receding vowel, "oow."

In worksheets for one experimental "poem" of 1917[56] (really only a fragmentary line) Cummings apparently planned a vowel-color arrangement. The line (the syntax of which varies) is simply, "Teamsters huge with [or 'in'] leisure." Several worksheets graph the line;[57] but one also bears this construction:

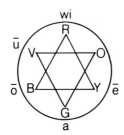

(Houghton notes, I[21] no. 47)

On the circle are six colors arranged in the usual sequence with complementaries diametrically opposed. A vowel accompanies each color except orange. Some of these pairings correspond to Cummings's other vowel-color pairings: blue takes "ō"; violet takes "ū." Yellow, however, receives "ē," whereas in two of the other three notes, it received "ā." Although the spatial arrangement Cummings planned is not clear from the graphs and syntactical orderings, it seems possible that he intended a syntactic structure that would account for the "coloristic" properties of the vowels—perhaps one, for example, that juxtaposed red ("wi") with its complement, green "a."

Cummings's other experimental poems do not explicitly address these vowel-color associations. The pairings, however, may have found their way into some of his published poems, not in determining structure, but in guiding the choice of a particular adjective to accompany color imagery. If the theory obtains, then an adjective will be chosen not merely for its semantic, visual, or musical contribution, but also for the specific coloristic effect of its vowels: advancing, long vowels for advancing colors, receding, short vowels for receding colors.

The results are inconclusive. Several early phrases align appropriate colors and vowels, but many other phrases—equally likely candidates in the same poems—either ignore or contradict the vowel-color scheme. A good example is "my eyes are fond of the east side" in its parade of colors on Allen street.

> stic-ky chromes and pretty-
> lemons and virginal pinks and wealthy vermillion and
> breathless-scarlet,dark colours like 'cellos keen
> fiddling colours colours cOOler than harps [. . . .]

Theoretically, such advancing colors as chrome yellow, vermilion, and scarlet should be paired with advancing, long vowels.[58] Here, they are not. But the long vowel "ē" in "keen fiddling colors" is perfect for the bright, forward timbre of the violin. And the capitalized "OO" emphasizes the cool, recessive timbre of harps.

There are other isolated examples of vowel-color pairings: "gluey twilight" matches the recessive "ue" to the mauves, purples, and violets of twilight; "Querying greys between mouthed houses curl" pairs the recessive "ou" in "mouthed houses" and "ue" in "querying" to the colorless gray of daybreak; "[I] feel your suddenly body reach / for me with a speed of white speech" emphasizes the advancing, reaching motion both in the color white[59] and in the long vowels "ē" ("me," "speed," "speech") and "ī" ("white")—just as Cummings linked long "ē" to white in his notes.[60]

Some pairings fulfill the theory only halfway. The lines

the mouth that sits between her cheeks
utters a thud of scarlet.   always
                         ("she sits . . .," &, Sonnets-Realities, XI)

nicely match the vowels and onomatopoeia of "utters a thud": a dull sound with a recessive vowel. But Cummings completes the clause with a bright, advancing color: scarlet. While scarlet might, in turn, have determined the long "ā" "always," it is an inappropriate color for "thud," *if* Cummings were linking the kinetic potential of colors, sounds, and vowels. "If" must, perforce, linger to keep the entire business speculative. What we can be certain of is that if Cummings followed his theory of vowel-color, he did so sporadically and unsystematically. Doubtless, many other considerations—semantics, imagery, and musical devices—preceded these vowel-color associations in his poetic priorities.

Visual-Harmonic Structure

In the "Poetry and Music" section, we observed Cummings's attempts to construct poetic "harmonics": vertical and diagonal columns of assonant vowels. In "Painting and Poetry," and in preceding chapters, we observed visual forms in his poetry. But in at least one experimental poem, Cummings sought to integrate these ideas. Like "Buffalo Bill's," which was composed a few months later, "city" (fig. 56) is shaped like an arrowhead pointing right.[61] Also like "Buffalo Bill's," its syntax takes the eye away from the arrowhead shape when "ab" of "abduct" returns to the left margin. But that one return was Cummings's only concession to conventional syntax, for he places "duct" at the extreme right margin to continue the diagonal. The bottom half adheres strictly to the shape by gradually reversing the word order to move from right to left: "sal / ute / thee."

More interesting, still, is the vertical-harmonic structure of this shape. "City" and "thee" are joined by long "ē"; "whose" and "ute" share an "oo" sound; "gestures," "soul," and "sal" each have a

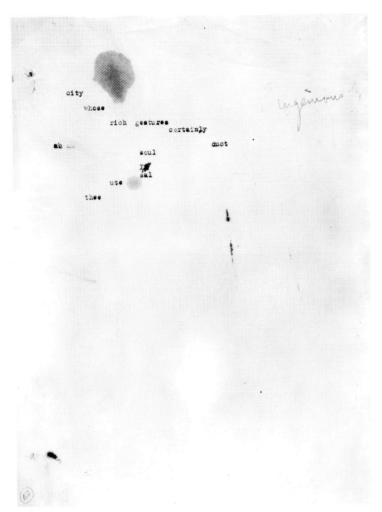

Fig. 56.
"city," c. 1916–17. The E. E. Cummings papers, the Houghton Library, Harvard University. By permission of the Houghton Library. Copyright 1982, The E. E. Cummings Trust.

sibilant *s*. These shared vowels and consonants vertically anchor the diagonal thematic progression, exactly as chords anchor a melodic progression by expanding its weight in vertical space. While, thematically, the poem says virtually nothing, its visual shape, thematic progression, and harmonic structure are nicely coordinated. The handwritten comment of Professor Briggs, to whom the young Cummings apparently showed this poem (and perhaps the other "Most Significant Pieces"), offers a fitting evaluation: "ingenious."

Does the published twin of this shape, "Buffalo Bill's" possess a similar harmonic structure? The worksheet on which Cummings developed the poem does not show evidence of harmonic order-ing (although it does try a musical term, "glissando").[62] But are the numerous vertical rhymes in the final version ("defunct" and "he," "break" and "a," "who" and "you," "smooth" and "blue—," "five" and "—eyed") entirely coincidental?

Nearly all of Cummings's theories and experiments in ana-logues seek the same goal and reach similar conclusions. Each theory attempts precise matchings among the properties of the separate arts and several theories find some form of poetic expression. But nearly always, Cummings backs away from these experimental forms, or modifies them substantially, in his published poetry. And perhaps wisely, too. For while these experiments are often "ingenious," they are also contrived and arbitrary orderings. They ignore discursive-ness, which Cummings was unwilling to do in his published poems, and they often neglect traditional poetic devices (figurative language, meter, etc.).

More important, these experiments attempt to cross what may finally be the unbridgeable gulf separating the arts: the unique-ness of form and expression in time and space that is intrinsic and inviolable to each art. This uniqueness might be seen as the "essen-tial core" of an art grounded in its particular dimension of time or space. For example, the essential core of a poem may be seen as its capacity to express an ongoing complex of meanings—even in one phrase—through a sequence of words. The sequence, though spatially presented on the page as descending lines of words, requires temporal apperception, as the reader moves from one word and line to the next. This linear progression and temporal apperception (or linear-temporal structure, for short) permits a poet immense freedom—*time*, really—to suggest verbal connotations, subsidiary ideas, and separate levels of symbolic, allusive, and allegorical meaning. More-over, as in the temporal arts of music and drama, the linear-temporal structure allows for *development*, as the poetic thought expands, shifts, even reverses itself, as it builds to an expressive or thematic climax. To alter a poem's essential core releases new structural, per-ceptual, and expressive possibilities. When Apollinaire, for example, transformed linear-temporal structure into a circular-spatial one in his *Calligrammes*, he achieved a simultaneity native to the spatial art of painting but not to the temporal art of poetry. In exchange for these new possibilities, however, some of the original ones (e.g., thematic complexity and development) are lost. C. M. Bowra, in *The Creative Experiment*, has observed an analogous limitation in nonsense poetry: "The trouble with 'trans-sense' is that, although it is often amusing and sometimes effective, its range is extremely limited. It succeeds only when it deals with irrational, unintelligible sensations, and these forms are so small a part of poetry that they can almost be discounted."[63]

In the largest sense, to alter the essential core of an art produces Einsteinian consequences: the art form itself is transformed into a different one possessing a different dimensional basis. Thus, poetry, stripped of its linear-sequential scaffolding and driven into free-floating spatiality by an Apollinaire or a Marinetti, becomes *word-painting*. For the poet, however, the problem is not one of definition but of pragmatism: how much artistic freedom—or technical facility—is lost or gained in violating the essential core? In the case of Cummings's poetic analogues, more freedom was lost than gained. To arrange vowels harmonically, he necessarily sacrificed the thematic flexibility of conventional syntax and constricted the visual possibilities of spatial arrangement. Vowel-color can determine an adjective, but only at the expense of ignoring several other, and perhaps sounder, considerations: semantics, imagery, figures of speech, musical devices, etc.

Should one conclude, then, that physical analogues among the arts are impossible or that Cummings abandoned the effort to find them? In both cases, no. For surrounding the inviolable core of an art is a broad periphery of possible elements, devices, and techniques that permit the poet any number of means—including borrowing from the other arts—to realize his end without curbing the essential expressiveness of his medium. Thus, a poem can employ the musical devices of meter, rhyme, and phonetic intensives, and the painterly qualities of imagery, synesthesia, visual structure, and linear movement, while still retaining all of its discursive complexity and development. This balance between the innovative periphery and the traditional core was the one Cummings finally adopted, incorporating all possible analogues from the other arts *consistent with* the complexity and flexibility of poetry's essential core. If his lines moved in several directions to reap the painterly benefits of dynamism and of planar solidity, they still worked within the essential linear-sequential framework that permitted them to develop, change, and conclude.

Ultimately, Cummings opted for more, not less, flexibility in his poetic techniques—precisely what his experimental analogues denied him. But his tinkerings must have proved valuable nonetheless in showing him just how far he could—and could not—go in integrating the arts. And his theories and experiments are valuable to us in revealing just how devoted the young Cummings was to *attempting* these integrations, to searching for analogues. Once again, they attest to the combined title, "poet & painter," by which Cummings referred to himself; they remind us that he was not two artists, but one.

Conclusion: The Paradox of Unity

█████ The preceding six chapters have presented and analyzed evidence to show that E. E. Cummings was not simply the romantic he made himself out to be, nor merely the poet the public thinks him to be. His hidden "selves"—cerebral aesthetician and lifelong painter—subvert Cummings's public persona to reveal a complex and sometimes paradoxical artistic personality.

As these new selves redefine the artist, so they revalue his art. The typographical innovations that proved so irritating and "unaccountable" to an R. P. Blackmur and like-minded critics are not at all autonomous tricks superfluous to the poem's import. Quite the contrary, these devices address fundamental concerns of Cummings's early aesthetics. The early paintings, likewise, are not the work of one who merely jumped on the Modernist bandwagon, for their techniques, too, derive from Cummings's aesthetic theories and are often analogous to the innovations of his early poems. It is, finally, to the early aesthetics that one must turn to find the theoretical basis and strategies underlying *both* the poems and the paintings. Thus, Cummings's concept of "seeing around" three-dimensional form produces techniques of juxtaposition that inform his colors, words, themes, and narrative and dramatic structures alike. The aesthetics of heightened perception inspires him to charge the elements of both poetry and painting with visual energy, while obscuring what is too easily recognizable in both arts. And the theoretical analogies considered in chapter 6 search even more boldly for parallels and informing models among the arts. This interconnectedness provides a context for what might otherwise be taken as isolated and seemingly arbitrary techniques in each art.

Yet, as so often happens, new insights raise new questions—questions about the way Cummings's various artistic "selves" cohere. How did he reconcile his public persona as a poet of feelings with his private and vigorous endeavors of the intellect? If he failed to reconcile thinking and feeling in his early aesthetic practice, then what becomes of the unifying principle of wholeness in his aesthetic philosophy *and* practice? More important, how do these tensions of division and unity affect his art, early and late?

To address these questions, we must first distinguish between the young artist of the teens and twenties who asked aesthetic questions and struggled for the answers, and the older artist who, increasingly, found those answers in a unified aesthetic philosophy of subjectivity and self-expression. For the young Cummings, the tensions between head and heart, wholeness and dividedness, snake like a fault line through his aesthetics and fissure his art. His published disdain for ratiocinative thought and praise for the spontaneous life of the feelings begins in his first published essay outside of Harvard, "Gaston Lachaise," continues through *The Enormous Room*, and becomes a dominant theme of his poetry. Nowhere in the early published work exists a comparable brief argued for the intellect. Indeed, the Lachaise essay offers what appears to be Cummings's theoretical attempt to reconcile his theory and practice: to use thinking to *negate* thinking. The carefully conceived techniques, and the aesthetic theories underlying them (not to mention the knowledge of the arts underlying both), all strive for effects the viewer and reader can *feel* instantaneously: a *sensation* of the whole surface, of whole form, of motion and interaction among all components of a work and between work and viewer. The artist's intellect thus becomes only a means to the aesthetic ends of wholeness and feeling.

A neat rationale. But how does it work in practice for the artist creating a work and for the viewer apprehending it? In some respects, very well indeed. Cummings's aesthetic calculations permitted him the one quality most important to his identity as an emerging artist: self-determination. Working out for himself the principles and practices of his "twin-obsessions," he achieved a heightened awareness of his aesthetic intentions. Like the skeptic from Missouri, he could take nothing for granted. To "do something FIRST" meant beginning with first principles: to determine for *himself* how the elements of each art worked, separately and in concert; to learn what had been done already by others that addressed his own predelictions;[1] to discover through experiment what was *not* possible (or effectual) in order to realize what was. That he determined from the outset to pursue two arts made clarity of purpose still more necessary. One cohesive structure of aesthetics precluded him from becoming two separate artists. And as his techniques in each art derived from a common structure, so they could cross-pollinate each other, a fact most noticeable in the visual immediacy and spatial complexities of the poems.

The rationale does not, however, address the artist's divided identity as the calculated creator of spontaneous effects, the thinker who espouses feeling. Nowhere is this unresolved divison more evident than in the troubled personality of the playwright Him—Cummings's dramatic self-portrait, in a play that culminates the artist's early period. From the viewer's standpoint, too, Cummings's rationale of making thinking the servant of feeling does not fully succeed in the early work. Certainly, one does *see* motion in the paintings and poems, and *feel* the sensuous elements composing the works in all their instantaneity before reductive thinking sets in. But one is also aware of the calculation behind these techniques. The unfolding spirals of *Noise Number 13*, the sweeping crescents of *Noise Number 1*, are dynamic, but also deliberate. The dislocated letters, words, and motifs in the poems flicker sensuously; indeed, for casual readers that is all they do. But serious readers soon realize that these elements, too, reflect a careful design and usually compose a discursive statement. At best, the sensuousness of these disjunctive particles—and of the reader's participation in reassembling them—resists only momentarily the inexorable pull of intellection. Perhaps Cummings's vast array of techniques strove for no more than these ephemeral, unsullied perceptions when "thinking abdicate[s] for a fraction of an instant in favor of the sensual enemy or NOW."[2] Yet their great achievement was to explode that moment—stretch it into spatiality—so that one's *experience* of the work becomes its real meaning.

Unresolved though these aesthetic contradictions were in Cummings's early work, they may finally have served the artist better than did the unified aesthetics of subjectivity and self-expression that goverened his later work. For it is certainly arguable that the later work lost in thematic complexity, inner tension, and (in the painting) formal rigor what it gained in the unity and consistency of single-mindedness.

This trade-off is most evident in the later painting. When Cummings chose, after 1926, to abandon his carefully determined Modernist aesthetics and to translate his subjectivist philosophy directly into an expressionistic technique of fast, loose brushwork, he succeeded in closing the aesthetic gap between philosophy and practice. But the results were decidedly mixed. Lacking the restraint of an external, rigorous aesthetics, the expressionistic paintings often wallowed in too *much* freedom, floundered on the painter's insecure sense of color and form. Only in watercolor, where the medium itself welcomed such spontaneity, was Cummings clearly successful in his expressionistic style. By contrast, his later naturalistic work (e.g., *Flowers and hat: Patchen Place*, (plate 12), even if stylistically conventional, is *technically* quite successful. It succeeds for the same reason that most of the early abstractions do: external aesthetics that Cummings had thoroughly assimilated (Modernism in the early period, naturalistic representation in the later) provided a rigorous check, a restraining counterbalance to his expressionistic excesses. Nor did naturalist aesthetics submerge Cummings's self-expression any more than Cézanne and Marin overwhelmed his Modernist abstractions. In both cases, these external models were merely the foundation on which Cummings built a personal style; on canvas, *his* personality dominates these sources. Thus, the *Self-portrait* of 1939 (fig. 29), although representational, becomes a distinctly personal—even autobiographical—statement about a feminized nature as the source and summit of the artist's creative vision. Like Frost, Cummings the painter did not flourish in playing tennis with the net down: His paintings benefitted from the oppositional tension of an established aesthetics *through which* his personality could emerge.

If a unified aesthetics of subjectivity permitted him too much freedom with a brush, it also allowed Cummings too much stylistic freedom, since its only demand was to paint as the emotion of the moment dictated. As the later painting oscillated among several styles—now expressionistic, now naturalistic, now quasi-Surrealist—Cummings failed to identify any one as *his*, through which he could develop and by which he could be recognized and judged, as indeed his poetic style was. And grounded as it was on a philosophical stance that grew ever more iconoclastic and isolated from its milieu, Cummings's subjectivist aesthetics provided his later painting a convenient refuge from public exposure. As he wrote his daughter late in his life, "the only thing—if you're some sort of artist—is to work a little harder than you can at being who you are: while if you're an unartist (i.e.aren't)nothing but big&quick recognition matters. . . ."[3] For Cummings, being "who you are" in *practice* meant not only painting as he saw fit, but also—and increasingly—avoiding the occasions that might challenge the fragile efficacy of that "who": namely, public exhibitions reviewed by professional critics. His failure to exhibit his later painting more often—an understandable failure, given the uninformed criticism of some earlier exhibitions, but a failure nonetheless—makes his comparison of "true" artistry (private self-expression) to "inauthentic" artistry (public recognition) self-justifying. Indeed, identifying self-expression with sheltered privacy permitted Cummings to paint to please *only* himself and to fall prey to privacy's inevitable concomitant of self-indulgence. Ultimately, the refuge of self became a prison, consigning the paintings to relative obscurity during his lifetime, shearing his public identity to a fraction of his real selves.

The later poetry was not so much prone to the risks of unrestrained subjectivity, but only because Cummings maintained the same thinking-feeling dichotomy that had governed the early poetry. He could pour all of his feeling into the poem's argument, while keeping the formal structure as abstract and cerebral as he wished; and he could continue to calculate his spontaneous effects. Thus, we find the interesting paradox of the poems in *no thanks* (1935) exhibiting what Rudolf Von Abele called the most "radical" and "experimental" techniques in Cummings's oeuvre, while expressing politically conservative and sentimental themes. Yet in the poetry following *no thanks*, thematic subjectivity does begin gradually to dominate the cerebral, typographical devices. As Von Abele notes, the later poetry is decidedly more "philosophical," less descriptive and presentational in purpose, and less typographically disjunct in technique than the early poems.[4] Moreover, the philosophical themes, as numerous critics have complained, tend to resolve and harden into the basic polarities of Cummings's philosophy: feeling versus thinking, spirit versus matter, "you and me" versus "mostpeople." While each poem conveying these polarities is uniquely crafted and often beautifully expressed, the themes themselves seldom vary. Nor does their tone of certainty waver, whether expressed as quiet reverence of the spiritual values Cummings worshipped or as mocking scorn for the worldly ones he reviled. Is not this increasing insistence of content over form also a victory of Cummings's subjectivist philosophy (from whence the themes emerge) over the objective detachment of his technique? And does not the increasing repetition of these subjective themes derive from an aesthetic philosophy from which inner tensions, inconsistencies, and uncertainties have been removed?

If so, then it would seem that as Cummings aligned his affective philosophy to his cerebral practice, he achieved aesthetic wholeness—but at considerable cost. By contrast, the early aesthetics, philosophically divided and even contradictory in places, produced poems and paintings that benefited from the intellectual rigor of their formalism and from the inner tensions of their themes—from, that is, the very dividedness of their aesthetic origins. Finally, however, the relative utility of the early and later aesthetics to Cummings's art in each period must await a thorough study of the later aesthetics vis-à-vis the painting and poetry they guided. Only then can posterity fairly judge the full achievement of this "poet & painter."

Appendix

Exhibitions Featuring Cummings's Art

DATE	GALLERY and TITLE	WORKS
Apr. 1917	Wanamaker's Gallery	geometric abstraction (sent)
Mar. 1919	Society of Independent Artists (hereafter: Independents)	*Sound* (Number 1), *Noise* (Number 1)
Apr. 1919	Penguin Gallery	*Sound Number 2*
Mar. 1920	Independents[1]	*Noise Number 5, Sound Number 5*
Mar. 1921	Independents	*Noise Number 10*
1921	Pennsylvania Academy of Fine Arts: "Exhibition of Paintings and Drawings Showing Later Tendencies in Art"	
July 1921	Wanamaker's Gallery	
May 1922	Brummer Galleries: "Modern Artists of America"	2 watercolors
Jan. 1924	Montross Gallery: *"The Dial* Collection"	*Sound Number 1*
Mar. 1924	Independents	*Noise Number 12*
Mar. 1925	Independents	*Noise Number 13*
Mar. 1926	Independents	*Ariel Acrobats*
Mar. 1927	Independents[?][2]	*Still Life*[?], *Portrait*[?]
Mar. 1928	Independents	*Nude*
1928	Salons of America: Spring Salon	1 drawing
Mar. 1929	Independents	2 portraits

DATE	GALLERY and TITLE	WORKS
Mar. 1930	Independents	*Garden-Madison Square, Garden-Madison Winter*
Spring, 1930	Salons of America: Spring Salon	
Dec. 1931	Painters' and Sculptors' Gallery: "E. E. Cummings and Group"	oils and watercolors, inc. *day, eyes, face, hair*
1931	Kokoon Art Club (Cleveland): one-man show	
Mar. 1932	Independents	2 portraits, 1 landscape
June 1932	Painters' and Sculptors' Gallery	7 oils, 27 watercolors
Dec. 1932	Painters' and Sculptors' Gallery: E. E. Cummings and William Jorgensen"	watercolors
Jan. 1934	International Art Gallery: one-man show	watercolors, sketches
Feb. 1944	American-British Art Center: one-man show	45 oils, 15 watercolors
Mar. 1944	American-British Art Center: one-man show	self-portraits
1945	Rochester (N.Y.) Memorial Art Gallery: one-man show	43 oils, 8 watercolors, 2 drawings
May 1949	American-British Art Center: one-man show	38 oils, 11 watercolors, 2 drawings

DATE	GALLERY and TITLE	WORKS	DATE	GALLERY and TITLE	WORKS
1950	Rochester Memorial Art Gallery: one-man show		Dec. 1976	Hirshhorn Museum: "E. E Cummings: The Painter as Artist"	68 paintings and drawings
1954	Rochester Memorial Art Gallery: one-man show		1976	Watson/DeNagy Gallery (Houston): one-man show	
Fall 1955	Chicago Art Center: one-man show	paintings, drawings	Oct. 1978	Tower Art Center, SUNY at Brockport College (Brockport, N.Y.): "Paintings by E. E. Cummings"	34 oils, 3 watercolors, 4 pencil drawings
1957	Fine Arts Gallery, Rush Rees Library, University of Rochester: one-man show		Feb. 1982	Gotham Book Mart	
1959	Worcester (Mass.) Art Museum: "*The Dial* and *The Dial* Collection"	*Sound Number 1,* ink drawings	Sept. 1982	University of Texas at Dallas and Dallas Public Library: "E. E. Cummings' Paintings: The Hidden Career"	28 oils, 5 watercolors, 1 ink drawing, 1 pencil drawing
Oct. 1963	Downtown Gallery (N.Y.C.): "Homage to E. E. Cummings" (memorial exhibition)		Nov. 1982	Dryden Galleries Ltd., Providence, R.I.: "Twentieth Memorial Exhibition of Paintings by E. E. Cummings 1894–1962"	
Mar. 1968	Gotham Book Mart (N.Y.C.): "E. E. Cummings: Sketches and Watercolors of the Twenties and Thirties"	35 watercolors, 12 ink drawings, 5 pastels, 5 pencil drawings	Jan. 1982	Gotham Book Mart	21 works in several media
Mar. 1971	The Arts Club of Chicago: "A Second Talent" (group show)		Jan. 1983	Nielsen Gallery (Boston)	
1972	Forum Gallery, Monroe Community College, Rochester, N.Y.: "Paintings, Watercolors, and Drawings by E. E. Cummings"		Feb. 1983	Gotham Book Mart: "The Art of E. E. Cummings"	*Acrobats*
Sept. 1973	Gotham Book Mart: "E. E. Cummings: Paintings and Drawings"		Jan. 1985	Gotham Book Mart: "E. E. Cummings: Charcoal-Ink-Oil-Pastel-Pencil-Watercolor"	
1975–76	"E. E. Cummings: An Exhibition of Original Paintings and Drawings" (traveling exhibition organized by Rushworth M. Kidder)	17 oils, 10 watercolors, 3 ink drawings, 6 pencil drawings, 1 charcoal	Sept. 1985	Rochester Institute of Technology: "Dr. James Sibley Watson: A Celebration"	

Notes

INTRODUCTION: The Hidden "Selves" of E. E. Cummings

1. Charles Norman, *E. E. Cummings: The Magic Maker*, rev. ed. (New York: Macmillan, 1964), p. 239.

2. Rushworth Kidder, "E. E. Cummings, Painter," *Harvard Library Bulletin* 23 (April 1975):119.

3. A number of recent exhibitions (see Appendix) and articles on Cummings's painting suggests that the import of his "other" career has begun to permeate academia and may eventually even prick that final bubble of artistic reputation: the biographical sketch in the literature anthology. Recent scholarship on Cummings's paintings was sparked by Rushworth Kidder's pioneering articles: "E. E. Cummings, Painter"; " 'Author of Pictures': A Study of Cummings' Line Drawings in *The Dial*," *Contemporary Literature* 17 (1976): 470-505; " 'Twin Obsessions': The Poetry and Painting of E. E. Cummings," *Georgia Review* 32 (Summer 1978): 342-68; and "Cummings and Cubism," *Journal of Modern Literature* 7, no. 2 (April 1979): 255-91.

Other discussions of Cummings's art may be found in the following: Norman, *Cummings: The Magic Maker*; Charles Norman, *E. E. Cummings: A Biography* (New York: Dutton, 1967), Chap. 11; Robert Tucker, "E. E. Cummings as an Artist: *The Dial* Drawings" and Dagmar Reutlinger, "E. E. Cummings and *The Dial* Collection," *Massachusetts Review* 16 (Spring 1975); 329-56; Frank Gettings, *E. E. Cummings: The Poet as Artist* (Washington: Smithsonian Institution Press, 1976); Richard Kennedy, *Dreams in the Mirror: A Biography of E. E. Cummings* (New York: Liveright, 1980); and Milton A. Cohen, *E. E. Cummings' Paintings: The Hidden Career* (Dallas: University of Texas at Dallas, 1982), "E. E. Cummings' Sleight-of-Hand: Perceptual Ambiguity in His Early Poetry, Painting, and Career," *University of Hartford Studies in Literature* 15, no. 1 (1983): 33-46.

4. For example, E. E. Cummings (hereafter E.E.C.) to Gabrielle David, 5 September 1949, *Selected Letters of E. E. Cummings*, ed. F. W. Dupee and George Stade (New York: Harcourt, 1969), p. 70 (hereafter cited as *Selected Letters*).

5. "Videlicet," *Arts Digest*, 1 December 1954; rpt. in *E. E. Cummings: A Miscellany Revised*, ed. George J. Firmage (New York: October House, 1965), p. 333 (hereafter cited as *Miscellany Rev.*).

6. "Post-Impressionism" was the categorical bin into which bemused critics of the day dumped *all* Modernist styles from 1885 on, no matter how disparate (e.g., A. J. Eddy's 1914 survey en-titled *Cubists and Post-Impressionism*). Thus, one of Cummings's abstractions at the 1920 Independents earned the uncritical praise, "a striking bit of post-impressionism" ("L'Art Pour L'Art Revels in Splash of Naked Truth," *New York World*, 12 March 1920, p. 8, col. 3).

7. E.E.C. to Edward Cummings, 22 May 1920, *Selected Letters*, p. 70.

8. Review of 1924 Independents, *New York Sun and Globe*, 6 March 1924, p. 16, cols. 2-3; E.E.C. to Edward Cummings, 5 December 1923, The E. E. Cummings Papers, Houghton Library, Harvard University, bMS Am. 1823.1(152). The unpublished letters, notes, manuscripts, drawings, and paintings quoted or reproduced in this book are done so by permission of the Houghton Library, Harvard University; by permission of the Harry Ransom Humanities Research Center, the University of Texas at Austin; and by permission of the E. E. Cummings Trust. All previously unpublished writings and visual art quoted or reproduced in this book are copyright by the E. E. Cummings Trust, 1982.

9. "Attractions in the Galleries," *New York Sun*, 20 May 1949, p. 23, cols. 6-7, my emphasis.

10. Unpublished notes, the E. E. Cummings Papers, Houghton Library, bMS Am. 1892.7(94). Hereafter, Cummings's unpublished notes in the Houghton Library will be cited as: Houghton notes. The numerical code refers to the Houghton Library call number of the volume containing this paper. Since the preponderance of citations in this book are to Cummings's unpublished notes—call number bMS Am 1823.7—I have abbreviated this call number to I. All other call numbers will be given in full. The number in parentheses or brackets refers to the volume number followed by the sheet number (if any).

Quotations from Cummings's notes and letters are reproduced as close to the original as possible with these exceptions: (1) lines arbitrarily broken in ways not vital to their meaning have been restored for greater clarity and economy; (2) my ellipses are bracketed to distinguish them from Cummings's; (3) illegible words are followed by [illeg.], semilegible words by [?]; (4) Cummings's deletions have been omitted unless they add important information; (5) all underlinings and other forms of emphasis are Cummings's unless otherwise noted; (6) closing periods have been added where necessary to indicate where a note or thought ends.

11. Kidder, "E. E. Cummings, Painter," 134.

12. Cummings's suspicion may not be entirely self-serving. Witness John Canaday's recollection of the monopoly held by Ab-

stract Expressionism in those years: "In 1959, Abstract Expressionism was at the zenith of its popularity, to such an extent that an unknown artist trying to exhibit in New York couldn't find a gallery unless he was painting in a mode derived from one or another member of the New York School" (*New York Times*, 8 August 1976, sec. 2, p. 1, col. 7).

13. Royal Cortissoz, review of Cummings's 1944 exhibition at the American-British Art Center, *New York Herald Tribune*, 27 February 1944, sec. 4, p. 5, cols. 3-4.

14. This criticism does not apply, however, to the considerable number of works painted in an exclusively naturalistic style. For, here, the painting's conformity to the details of the subject provided just that external discipline that Cummings's more expressionistic style lacked. As fig. 28 indicates, Cummings was quite accomplished in this mode. Nor does this criticism apply to Cummings's watercolors—his best medium—which benefited from such spontaneity. Chapter 1 sorts out Cummings's various styles.

15. Quoted in Norman, *Cummings: The Magic Maker*, pp. 288-89.

16. Gorham Munson wrote in 1923, "A complete study of Cummings should take penetrating account of his painting and drawing, and no estimate of his literary work can begin without noting the important fact that Cummings is a painter" ("Syrinx," *Secession*, no. 5 [July 1923]; rpt. in Stanley V. Baum, *E. E. Cummings and the Critics* [East Lansing, Mich.: Michigan State University, 1962], p. 9).

17. Cummings's notes contain fairly detailed studies of biology, geology and chemistry, and astronomy (Houghton Library), as well as extensive notes on the other subjects listed above. His other interests that appear in the notes would take a page to list. Richard Kennedy offers a sample of "the heterogeneity of his taste," ca. 1952, in *Dreams in the Mirror* (New York: Liveright, 1980), p. 438.

18. Kennedy, *Dreams in the Mirror*, p. 429. When Cummings's grown daughter, Nancy, mentioned to him some drafts of a poem she had happened on, she was greeted with a frosty silence. In the 1950s, he softened somewhat in permitting Norman Friedman to examine the numerous drafts of the poem "rosetree,rosetree" so as to document Cummings's compositional process for Friedman's study *E. E. Cummings: The Art of His Poetry* (Baltimore: Johns Hopkins Press, 1960), chap. 5.

19. Kennedy, *Dreams in the Mirror*, p. ix.

20. Kidder, "E. E. Cummings, Painter," 126.

21. Cummings's self-education in these two arts differs somewhat. Poetry, as he himself acknowledged, came more naturally to him and therefore required less study of fundamentals than did painting. Accordingly, his notes address far more theoretical attention to painting than to poetry (whose workshop was in the manuscript drafts and revisions of individual poems).

22. John Dos Passos, *The Best Times: An Informal Memoir* (New York: New American Library, 1966), p. 98.

23. Houghton notes, bMS Am. 1892.6(69) nos. 1-5.

24. E.E.C. to Edward Cummings, 10 December 1917,
quoted in Kennedy, *Dreams in the Mirror*, pp. 155-56.

25. Kennedy, *Dreams in the Mirror*, pp. 335, 411.

26. Charles Norman's phrase for the pastime painting Cummings was thought to pursue (*E. E. Cummings: A Biography*, p. vii).

27. R. P. Blackmur, the critic most influential in demeaning Cummings's standing as a poet, writes of these innovations: "extensive consideration of these peculiarities today [1931] has very little importance, carries almost no reference to the *meaning* of the poems. Mr. Cummings's experiments in typography merely extend the theory of notation by adding to the number, *not* to the *kind*, of conventions the reader must bear in mind" (Blackmur's emphasis). Blackmur finally dismisses the "peculiarities" as "irrelevant or unaccountable" ("Notes on E. E. Cummings' Language," *Hound and Horn* 4 [January-March 1931]; rpt. in Guy Rotella, *Critical Essays on E. E. Cummings* [Boston: G. K. Hall, 1984], pp. 109-10).

1. CUMMINGS THE PAINTER

1. Several factors contributed to Cummings's neglect of academic instruction. His parents, as Kidder notes, certainly did not encourage his study of art any more than they encouraged his practice of it ("E. E. Cummings, Painter," 120). Moreover, Cummings's own romantic temperament bridled at the submissiveness and conformity expected of an art student. But the most telling influence came from the heroes of his artistic pantheon, Cézanne and Lachaise. "For a Lachaise, as for a Cézanne, academies hold nothing beyond a knowledge of tools. For this reason, both men are intrinsically great geniuses," Cummings wrote in his 1920 essay on Lachaise. He thus accepted what he called "the conventional argument against art schools," namely, "that in the realization of academical ideals whatever originality the pupil may have had at the outset has been, if not entirely eliminated, at any rate irrevocably diluted." He concludes: "the man who by the gods has been fated to express himself will succeed in expressing himself in spite of all schools; . . . the greatest artist is the man whom no school can kill" ("Gaston Lachaise," *Dial*, February 1920; rpt. in *Miscellany Rev.*, pp. 16-17).

As we shall see below, however, Cummings's self-instruction in Modernist aesthetics was so diligent that his early painting skirted the same danger of derivativeness that he feared from academies. In a broader sense, the absence of formal instruction denied his painting not the factual knowledge that he could easily gain on his own, but the objective criticism of his painterly weaknesses that he could not.

2. Cited in Cummings's Harvard notes and the essay, "The Poetry of Silence" (1915), the E. E. Cummings Papers, Houghton Library, bMS Am 1892.6(94).

3. Cummings's well-marked copies of both books are in his papers at the Houghton Library.

4. For a thorough discussion of the influence of Thayer

and Damon on Cummings, see Kennedy, *Dreams in the Mirror,* pp. 78-82. Kennedy, however, underestimates Nagel's influence. As John Dos Passos writes, "It was Nagel who infected both Cummings and me with the excitement and experiments of the school of Paris. . . . It was in Nagel's room I saw my first copies of BLAST with Eliot's early poems" (*The Best Times,* p. 35). Cummings remained close to Nagel in Greenwich Village, where both artists lived and worked at their abstract paintings after leaving Harvard. Through Nagel, Cummings met Gaston Lachaise and Albert Gleizes.

5. E.E.C. to Rebecca Haswell Cummings (hereafter cited as R.H.C.), 19 February 1917 and 31 March 1917, the E. E. Cummings Papers, Houghton Library, bMS Am 1823.1(156).

6. Quoted in Malcolm Cowley, *A Second Flowering: Works and Days of the Lost Generation* (New York: Viking Press, 1973), p. 95.

7. E.E.C. to Edward Cummings, 5 December 1923, the E. E. Cummings Papers, Houghton Library.

8. Rushworth Kidder observes this also in "E. E. Cummings, Painter," 117.

9. E.E.C. to R.H.C., 2 March 1922, the E. E. Cummings Papers, Houghton Library.

10. E.E.C. to Elizabeth Cummings, 2 May 1922, the E. E. Cummings Papers, Houghton Library, bMS Am 1823.1(510).

11. E.E.C. to R.H.C., 18 June 1918, the E. E. Cummings Papers, Houghton Library.

12. The meaning of "types" is obscure. Rushworth Kidder describes them as "quick and often small oils and pastels of the characters who haunted the demimonde. . . ." (" 'Twin Obsessions,' " 343). But in the letter mentioning them, Cummings specifically identifies them as pastels, not oils, and does not divulge their content.

13. Cummings's reference in this note to *Noise Number 13* dates it no earlier than 1925.

14. "Conversation avec Picasso," *Cahiers d'Art* (Paris) 10, nos. 7-10, (1935): 173-78; rpt. in Herschel B. Chipp, *Theories of Modern Art* (Berkeley: University of California Press, 1969), p. 268.

15. E.E.C. to R.H.C., 4 July 1918, *Selected Letters,* p. 49.

16. Cummings does not specify the difference between "Sound" and "Noise," but one of his college notes distinguishes between the regular frequencies of musical notes and the irregular ones of noises (Houghton notes, bMS Am 1892.6[29] no. 12). We might surmise, then, that the "Sounds" refer to his calmer, more orderly patterns, while the "Noises" describe more chaotic or irregular abstractions. On this basis, I have identified *Sound Number 5* and *Noise Number 5* (plate 3, fig. 16). Cummings mentions both in a letter to R.H.C. (7 March 1920) and gives dimensions, but does not match title to dimensions. Although he had ample precedent among the Modernist painters (e.g., the Futurists and Kandinsky) in using synesthetic titles, his own proclivities were very much towards "the mutual explorings" of the arts, as the quotations above show.

17. Two other connections made "crazy quilt" an apt sobriquet: it was a play on Estlin's favorite comic strip, "Krazy Kat," and

a wry nod to the well-known satirical depiction of "The Original Cubist" as a grandmotherly quilter (*New York Evening Sun,* 1 April 1913).

18. E.E.C. to Edward Cummings, 25 November 1919, *Selected Letters,* p. 64.

19. Kidder, " 'Author of Pictures,' " 470-505; Hilton Kramer, "A Parenthesis to the Career of a Poet," *New York Times,* 16 March 1968, p. 26, cols. 1-3.

20. Kenneth Tynan, "Louise Brooks," *The New Yorker,* 11 July 1979, p. 72.

21. Houghton notes, I(15).

22. Few if any of Meier-Graefe's idiosyncratic views of Cézanne appear elsewhere in Cummings's notes besides the translation itself (Houghton notes, I[69b]). With no comprehensive edition of Cézanne's letters then available, the opinions that Cummings—and Wright before him—quotes must have come from Emile Bernard's *Souvenirs,* which was reprinted shortly before and during Cummings's stay in Paris. Cummings's phrasing of key quotations differs enough from Wright's to suggest that Cummings read both sources.

23. The list of colors Cummings cites in the elided passage of this letter conforms exactly to the hues and order of Cézanne's colors cited by Bernard (John Rewald, *Paul Cézanne,* trans. Margaret Liebman [London: Spring Books, 1958], p. 175).

24. Rpt. in Chipp, *Theories of Modern Art,* p. 22. As Cummings explained in his 1920 essay on Lachaise, what Cézanne had to "forget" were the "second hand ideas" of the academies about form and color in order to formulate his own ideas (*Miscellany Rev.,* pp. 19-20). But Cummings may also have intended "everything" to mean Cézanne's personal history. As Kidder has perceptively noted ("E. E. Cummings, Painter," 127), Cummings could not help but draw a parallel between Cézanne's determination to paint despite his father's resistance and Cummings's own struggle to do likewise despite Edward Cummings's increasing opposition.

25. The dedication is inscribed "To Paul Cézanne"; although in a separate folder (Houghton Library, I[21]) from the poems, it is on the same crumbly, yellowed paper with crude binder holes along the left margin as the experimental poems in volume 22.

26. Houghton notes, bMS Am 1892.6(29) nos. 10-11.

27. Houghton notes, bMS Am 1892.7(69-70) no. 96, bMS Am 1823.7(59) no. 63; "The Poetry of a New Era," Cummings Papers, Harry Ransom Humanities Research Center, University of Texas at Austin, p. 8.

28. Both Kennedy (*Dreams in the Mirror,* passim) and Kidder ("Cummings and Cubism," passim) apply the "Cubist" label loosely to Cummings's early painting. But as both admit, and as Cummings's Harvard essays on Modernist artists amply attest, he used such terms as "Cubist," "Primitivist," and even "Futurist," almost interchangeably. Thus his self-identification on an army form in 1918 as "a specialist in Cubism" (Kennedy, *Dreams in the Mirror,* p. 173) should not be taken seriously; in fact, as Cummings notes, the phrase came from an army clerk (E.E.C. to Sibley Watson, 30 Janu-

ary 1918, the Berg Collection, New York Public Library). While many of his early drawings do experiment with Cubist motifs and styles, they were essentially exercises in mastering and assimilating elements of extant styles into his own style.

29. "The Poetry of a New Era," 1916, Cummings Papers, Humanities Research Center, p. 10.

30. "Jean Cocteau as a Graphic Artist," *Vanity Fair,* September 1925; rpt. in *Miscellany Rev.,* pp. 99-100; Cummings Papers, Houghton Library, I(59) no. 112; "Picasso," *XLI Poems,* "Portraits," III.

31. E.E.C. to R.H.C., 24 April 1919, *Selected Letters,* p. 58.

32. E.E.C. to Edward Cummings, 26 June 1918, the E.E. Cummings Papers, Houghton Library.

33. "The Theatre: I," *Dial,* April 1926; rpt. in *Miscellany Rev.,* p. 14.

34. "The Adult, the Artist, and the Circus," *Vanity Fair,* October 1925; rpt. in *Miscellany Rev.,* pp. 112-13. Cummings's poetic evocation of the building, "at the ferocious phenomenon of 5 o'clock i find myself" (*XLI Poems,* "Portraits," IX) is analyzed in chap. 4.

35. Exhibition catalog for Watercolors and Oils by John Marin, Photo Secession Gallery, February 1913; quoted in Sheldon Reich, *John Marin* (Tucson: University of Arizona Press, 1970), vol. 1, p. 54.

36. E.E.C. to R.H.C., 4 July 1918, 5 October 1919, 25 November 1919, 9 January 1919, E.E. Cummings Papers, Houghton Library.

37. Dikran Tashjian, "E. E. Cummings and Dada Formalism," Chap. 8 in *Skyscraper Primitives: Dada and the American Avant-Garde 1910-1925* (Middletown, Conn.: Wesleyan University Press, 1975). Tashjian attempts to posit Dadaist influence on Cummings's poetic techniques by comparing them with Dadist poems allegedly composed earlier. Slippery verbs such as "appropriated" and "transformed" enforce a *post hoc ergo propter hoc* logic. Thus, even though "there is no evidence that Cummings ever saw or heard a [Raoul] Hausmann optophonetic poem. . . . Cummings appropriated [Hausmann's] informal experimentation for his own organic verse" (p. 170). Even were his logic persuasive, Tashjian's facts are not, since he dates Cummings's poems by their publication rather than their composition (which preceded publication by as much as a decade).

38. *is 5,* "One," XXXII.

39. Tashjian, "Cummings and Dada Formalism," 182, 165.

40. Kramer, "Parenthesis to the Career of a Poet," 26. Kramer did not see any of Cummings's most important early works, the *Sounds* and *Noises,* in the 1968 retrospective he reviewed.

41. E.E.C. to Edward Cummings, 18 June 1918, The E. E. Cummings Papers, Houghton Library.

42. "Independents Run Gamut in Art Show," *New York Sun,* 30 March 1919, p. 14, col. 3.

43. E.E.C. to R.H.C., 7 April 1919, 24 April 1919, *Selected Letters,* p. 58.

44. E.E.C. to R.H.C., 11 May 1919, 7 March 1920, The E. E. Cummings Papers, Houghton Library.

45. "L'Art Pour L'Art," p. 8, col. 3.

46. S. Jay Kaufman, *New York Globe and Advertiser,* c. March 1920; quoted in Kennedy, *Dreams in the Mirror,* p. 211.

47. *New York Evening Post,* 12 March 1920, p. 11, cols. 4-5.

48. E.E.C. to R.H.C., 29 January 1920; E.E.C. to Edward Cummings, 22 May 1920, 10 January 1920, The E. E. Cummings Papers, Houghton Library.

49. "Independents' Art Show Voluminous," *New York Evening Post,* 28 February 1921, p. 7, cols. 1-2.

50. In one letter, Cummings cites among his other artistic productions "the usual five million drawings a month." Eight months later, he refers to sending the *Dial* works selected "from some 400 drawings (pencil, brush, wash)" (E.E.C. to Edward Cummings, 17 April 1923, 5 December 1923, The E. E. Cummings Papers, Houghton Library). The Parisian drawings are easily datable by the serrated edge and "DURAL" watermark of their paper, the same paper Cummings used in several letters home.

51. Review of 1924 Independents, *New York Sun and Globe,* 6 March 1924, p. 16, cols. 2-3.

52. Cf. his equally rhythmic poem depicting, among other features, the "ta/ppin/g/toe" of a ragtime piano player (&, "Portraits," III).

53. *New York Sun and Globe,* 6 March 1924, p. 16, cols. 2-3.

54. Houghton notes, I(82) no. 1.

55. Norman, *Cummings: The Magic Maker,* p. 248.

56. Loren MacIver, quoted in Norman, *Cummings: The Magic Maker,* pp. 240-41.

57. "Words into Pictures," *Art News,* May 1949; rpt. in *Miscellany Rev.,* p. 329.

58. Kidder, "E. E. Cummings, Painter," 134.

59. Henry McBride, "Attractions in the Galleries," *New York Sun,* 20 May 1949, p. 23, cols. 6-7.

60. Kramer, "Parenthesis to the Career of a Poet," p. 26.

61. Henry McBride, "Attractions in Other Galleries," *New York Sun,* 3 February 1934, p. 9, cols, 1-2.

62. "Foreword to an Exhibit:II," in exhibition catalog for Cummings's one-man show, Memorial Art Gallery, Rochester, N.Y., May 1945; rpt. in *Miscellany Rev.,* p. 316.

63. "Fragile," "delicate," "charming," etc. mentioned in reviews in the *New York Sun,* 4 March 1944, p. 9, cols. 5-6; *New York Times,* 5 March 1944, sec. 2, p. 6x; *New York Sun,* 20 May 1949, p. 23, cols. 6-7; and *New York Herald Tribune,* 22 May 1949, sec. 5, p. 10, col. 3.

"Lacking boldness, craft," etc. mentioned in *New York Sun,* 3 February 1934, p. 9, cols. 1-2; *New York Sun,* 4 March 1944, p. 9, cols. 5-6; *New York Herald Tribune,* 27 February 1944, sec. 4, p. 5, cols, 3-4, and *New York Times,* 16 March 1968, p. 26, cols. 1-3.

64. Stewart Preston, *New York Times*, 22 May 1949, sec. 2, p. 12, col. 6; Brian O'Doherty, "Works by E. E. Cummings Are Shown in Exhibition at Down-Town Gallery," *New York Times*, 30 October 1963, p. 50, cols. 2-3. In questioning Cummings's diction, O'Doherty was obviously parroting R. P. Blackmur's well-known criticism that Cummings used too many general nouns.

65. *New York Sun*, 20 May 1949, p. 23, cols. 6-7.

66. "The Fable of a Painter Who Was a Writer," The E. E. Cummings Papers, Houghton Library, bMS Am 1892.7(94).

67. Houghton notes, bMS Am. 1892.7(94).

2. AESTHETIC UNDERPINNINGS: Wholeness and Feeling

1. Although the dating of the folders containing Cummings's notes at the Houghton Library is approximate and sometimes unreliable, biographical minutiae in the I(25) folders (envelopes, bills, etc.) confirm the Houghton's dating.

2. The third edition of Brill's *Psychoanalysis* (1922) uses pagination different from what Cummings cites.

3. A. A. Brill, *Psychoanalysis: Its Theories and Practical Applications*, 2nd. ed. rev. (London: W. B. Saunders Co., 1914), p. 67.

4. Barry Marks, *E. E. Cummings* (New York: Twayne Publishers, 1964), p. 116.

5. Houghton notes, I(15)3 and I(111) no. 4.

6. Cummings, "Gaston Lachaise," rpt. in *Miscellany Rev.*, p. 19.

7. "The Poetry of Silence," the E. E. Cummings Papers, Houghton Library, bMS Am. 1892.6(94) no. 4.

8. Robert Goldwater, *Primitivism in Modern Art*, rev. ed. (New York: Vintage-Random House, 1967), p. 255.

9. Kennedy, *Dreams in the Mirror*, passim.

10. E. E. Cummings, "I Take Great Pleasure in Presenting," *Vanity Fair*, February 1926; rpt. in *Miscellany Rev.*, p. 140. In this essay, Cummings equates "conscious" with "consciousness" and attributes both words to "psychologists."

11. Houghton notes, I(71) no. 57. This folder contains an autobiographical note written when Cummings was 28 (1922). References in the dialogue to the "bulge" of the color yellow also correspond to color theories Cummings described in letters to his mother in 1922, as chap. 4 shows.

12. Houghton notes, I(39) nos. 223-24.

13. In later notes, Cummings tends to place *his* values of "Actuality"—e.g., "truth," "IS"—at "right angles" to oppositions of their inferior counterparts in "Reality"—e.g., "fact vs. Fiction," "either-or" (Houghton notes, I[56] no. 5).

14. Cummings once wrote his editor: "what i care infinitely is that each poempicture should remain intact. Why? Possibly because, with a few exceptions, my poems are essentially pictures" (Norman, *Magic Maker: E. E. Cummings*, pp. 288-89).

15. Houghton notes, I(59) no. 74 and I(59) no. 108. These notes appear copied from a book, for the definitions lack Cummings's special biases.

16. "Why I Like America," *Vanity Fair*, May 1927; rpt. in *Miscellany Rev.*, p. 194. See also E. E. Cummings, *i: Six Nonlectures* (Cambridge, Mass.: Harvard University Press, 1953), p. 65.

17. E. E. Cummings, *The Enormous Room* (New York: Liveright, 1970) p. 186.

18. Houghton notes, I(59) no. 80.

19. E.E.C. to R.H.C., 11 September 1918, *Selected Letters*, p. 52.

20. *Selected Letters*, pp. 84-85. In *The Enormous Room* (p. 248), Cummings connected this destruction directly to feeling and art: "there is and can be no such thing as authentic art until the *bons trucs* (whereby we are taught to see and imitate on canvas and in stone and by words this so-called world) are entirely and thoroughly and perfectly annihilated by that vast and painful process of Unthinking which may result in a minute bit of purely personal Feeling. Which minute bit is Art."

21. Fittingly, Cummings quoted Keats's assertion in *i: Six Nonlectures* (p. 51) and referred to his own early, ornate, and self-conscious poetry as "my Keats Period" (Houghton notes, I[55] no. 54).

22. "Re Ezra Pound: II," *PM*, 25 November 1945; rpt. in *Miscellany Rev.*, p. 313.

23. Hyatt Waggoner, *American Poets: From the Puritans to the Present* (Boston: Houghton Mifflin, 1968), pp. 517-18; Dos Passos, *The Best Times*, pp. 86-87.

24. Although Waggoner claims that Emerson's Platonism was based in sensory experience, and thus paralleled Cummings's, the young Cummings would have had difficulty sympathizing with Emerson's tendency to treat sensory facts as symbols of higher forms: "[the poet] perceives that thought is multiform; that within the form of every creature is a force impelling it to ascend to a higher form" ("The Poet," quoted in Waggoner, *American Poets*, p. 329). Where Emerson's wholeness is hierarchical, binding the material world to the transcendental, Cummings's early sense of wholeness resides in the *sensory* consciousness of the artist and audience.

25. Henri Bergson, *Creative Evolution* (New York: Random House, Modern Library, 1944), pp. 124, 127.

26. Not all critics would agree that these *were* Cummings's predilictions. Rushworth Kidder cites three essays of the 1920s in which Cummings either praises intelligence ("Gaston Lachaise") or parodies the "uninhibited instinct" of the unconscious ("The Very Latest School of Art") or the "unanalyzability" of modern art ("Ivan Narb"). Kidder concludes that analytical "intelligence . . . became for him a requirement of all genuine aesthetic response" and "one defense against sentimentalism" ("E. E. Cummings, Painter," 124-26).

The meaning Cummings imputed to "intelligence," and its synonyms, however, was idiosyncratic. Lachaise, for example, represents "the intelligence functioning at *intuitional* velocity"; his work displays "absolute *sensual* logic" (*Miscellany Rev.*, p. 17, my emphasis). "Intuitional" and "sensual" have little to do with analytical intelligence; both are qualities Cummings attributes to feeling. "An intelligent process of the highest order," he continues, is "the *negation* on our part, by thinking *of thinking*" (p. 18, my emphasis).

The other two essays are not so much parodies of "uninhibited instinct" and "unanalyzability" as parodies of fakery, of pseudo-emotion (the false primitivism of Zorach), of those who imitate and misuse a method, medium, or idea they do not comprehend—pretenders who made Modernism an easy target of satirists. All three essays attempt to identify such fakery in order to distinguish it from genuine expressions of emotion.

27. *Miscellany Rev.*, p. 18; Houghton notes, I(71) no. 57.

28. "Gesture" is a term Cummings used frequently in his early writings to signify a sensuous creation. Chap. 3 discusses its meaning.

29. Houghton notes, I(55) no. 81. This note follows others dated "March 1945" in the same folder. By this time, Cummings's familiarity with Jungian theory was as extensive as his earlier knowledge of Freud had been. His library (now at the Houghton Library) includes seven books by Jung.

30. Houghton notes, I(55) no. 108.

31. Cummings's later poems may have espoused and emulated spontaneity, but they were not the products of it. Typically, they went through many drafts and transformations—sometimes hundreds, as Norman Friedman has shown of "rosetree,rosetree" (*Cummings: The Art of His Poetry*, Chap. 5)—drafts proving that, whatever the spontaneous *appearance* of the final product, Cummings crafted his poems with meticulous thought and planning.

3. PERCEPTION: Seeing the Whole Surface

1. *Selected Letters*, p. 85.

2. Cézanne to Emile Bernard, 23 October 1905, trans. John Rewald; quoted in letter, E.E.C. to R.H.C., 2 March 1922, the E. E. Cummings Papers, Houghton Library.

3. "Damn ideas, anyhow," Pound wrote in "Early Translators of Homer" and continued, "An idea is only an imperfect induction of fact" (rpt. in *Literary Essays of Ezra Pound*, ed. T. S. Eliot [New York: New Directions, 1954], p. 267).

4. Charles Norman, *Ezra Pound* (New York: MacMillan, 1960) 98-99; Ezra Pound, *Gaudier-Brzeska* (1916; reprint, New York: New Directions, 1960), p. 121; Norman, *Ezra Pound*, pp. 98-99.

5. "The Poetry of a New Era," Cummings Papers, Humanities Research Center, p. 39.

6. Cummings's denial appears in a letter to Rudolph Von Abele, 5 January 1955; cited in Von Abele, " 'Only to Grow': Change in the Poetry of E. E. Cummings," *PMLA* 70 (December 1955):917n. An earlier draft of "the / sky / was" attempts a more ambitious ideograph of a locomotive, incorporating the right-to-left syllable progres-

sions of the *faits* discussed in chapter 6, yet still reading from top to bottom (see *Etcetera: The Unpublished Poems of E. E. Cummings*, ed. George J. Firmage and Richard S. Kennedy [New York: Liveright, 1983], p. 37). It is significant that Cummings rejected this version for the more conservatively structured one he published in *XLI Poems*.

7. William Bates, *Better Eyesight Without Glasses* (1920; reprint, New York: Henry Holt, 1943). Most of Cummings's notes quoted in this chapter (Houghton notes, I[25] and I[27]) were written while he was in Paris, 1921-23.

8. Bates, *Better Eyesight*, p. 55. Cummings noted the converse of Bates's assertion: "a focus (or foci) are established [. . .] to the exclusion of the rest of the field" (Houghton notes, I[25] no. 65).

9. *Psychological Bulletin* 19, no. 10 (October 1922): 531-85.

10. This invitation to the spectator to complete the unfinished, or unrecognizable content is what Roger Shattuck calls "intimacy of Form" and considers an essential quality of all Modernist art (*The Banquet Years* [London: Jonathan Cape, 1969], p. 340).

11. Houghton notes, I(59) no. 59.

12. *XLI Poems*, "Portraits," VII.

13. *XLI Poems*, "Sonnets," IX.

14. *&*, "Sonnets-Actualities," XVI.

15. Houghton notes, I(25) no. 69.

16. Houghton notes, I(25) no. 149^v.

17. *Selected Letters*, pp. 63-64.

18. Among Cummings's drawings is a bill from Khouri's restaurant (95 Washington St., N.Y.C.) in Arabic.

19. The word turns up often in Cummings's published work: in such early poems as "conversations with my friend," "take for example this," "my naked lady framed," "since feeling is first," "some ask praise," and "after all white"; in the essay on Lachaise; and in the play *Him* (I, iv).

20. Houghton notes, I(27) no. 62.

21. "a blue woman with sticking out breasts hanging," *&*, "Sonnets-Actualities," XVI.

22. *is 5*, "One," XVI.

23. *&*, "Post Impressions," XI.

24. Kidder, "Cummings and Cubism," 283.

25. Houghton notes, bMS Am 1892.6(29)3 nos. 10-11; "The Latest Blast," the E. E. Cummings Papers, Houghton Library, bMS Am 1892.6(69) nos. 1-5; Pound, *Gaudier-Brzeska*, p. 43.

26. Houghton notes, I(25) no. 175. Here again, an idea was "in the air"—this time in the almost identical concept ("defamiliarization") of the Russian Formalist Victor Shklovsky (see *Russian Formalist Criticism: Four Essays*, trans. Lee T. Lemon and Marion Reis [Lincoln: University of Nebraska Press, 1965], pp. 11-12). Shklovsky's 1917 treatise "Art as Technique" anticipates both the perceptual problem and the solutions Cummings worked on in the early twenties. But with no English translation then available, Cummings could not have read it, although he may have learned of it indirectly.

27. E. E. Cummings, "Words into Pictures," *Art News*, May 1949; rpt. in *Miscellany Rev.*, p. 329.

28. Interestingly, Cummings felt then that the media of painting and music were not tied to representation as the medium of literature was. In the original form of "The New Art," he writes, "In 'Mlle Pogany' we can appreciate the significance of realistic sacrifices; in the [Five] Orchestral pieces of Shönberg we can enjoy the glory of one chord covering all the chromatics of the piano; but in 'Tender Buttons' the unparalleled familiarity of the medium precludes its use for the purpose of esthetic effect" (Houghton notes, bMS Am 1892.6[84] nos. 26–27).

29. &, "Post Impressions," I.

30. E. E. Cummings: An Exhibition of Original Paintings and Drawings, S.U.N.Y. College at Brockport, October 1978; Kidder, " 'Twin Obsessions,' " 345.

31. Ironically, he could have settled the matter, but did not. In a letter of 7 April 1919 to his mother, he paraphrases the befuddled director of the Penguin Gallery, "asking me if I minded his asking which side up my painting went?" Cummings never relates his answer.

32. Kidder, "Cummings and Cubism," 271; Kennedy, *Dreams in the Mirror*, p. 319.

33. This last ambiguity fittingly culminates several others: "the bugs crawling . . . up . . . everyone" and "everyone that's been there knows"; "knows what i mean" and "i mean a god damned lot of / people . . . ."

34. Louis Rus emphasizes the structural nature of these ambiguities in "Structural Ambiguity: A Note on Meaning and the Linguistic Analysis of Literature," *Language Learning* 6 (1955): 62–67. To leave the matter there, however, ignores the perceptual effects of the ambiguities that Cummings calculated in his notes. These effects were noted as far back as 1929, in Laura Riding and Robert Graves, *A Survey of Modernist Poetry*; rpt. in Baum, *Cummings and the Critics*, p. 41.

35. Houghton notes, I(27) no. 77.

36. "at the ferocious phenomenon of 5 o'clock i find myself," *XLI Poems*, "Portraits," XI; "inthe,exquisite;" &, 'Post Impressions," XIV; "my eyes are fond of the east side," &, "Post Impressions," XI.

37. Note, for example, such oils in *CIOPW* (New York: Covici-Friede, 1931) as: *portrait-face* (p. 58), *nude* (p. 49), *still life* (p. 73), *pipe* (p. 54), and *elephant* (p. 39).

4. "SEEING AROUND" FORM

1. Shattuck, *The Banquet Years*, pp. 333–34.

2. Shattuck, *The Banquet Years*, p. 349.

3. *Modern Painting: Its Tendency and Meaning* (New York: John Lane, 1915). Subsequent references to this book will be given parenthetically in the text. See, for example, Cummings's notes

I(39) nos. 300–400, passim. Wright also appears in the Harvard paper on El Greco (the E. E. Cummings Papers, Houghton Library, bMS Am 1892.6[106]) and the *Dial* essay on Lachaise (*Miscellany Rev.*, pp. 12–13).

4. Bernard, *Souvenirs Sur Paul Cézanne* (Paris: Société des trente, 1912). Cummings himself most likely owned a copy of Bernard's *Souvenirs*, for quotations from it (in wording slightly different from Wright's) recur obsessively in his notes. While Cummings recognized Wright's bias (see "Gaston Lachaise"), he doubtless accepted the somewhat dubious accuracy of Bernard's *Souvenirs* without question.

5. "One should not say 'modeling,' one should say 'modulation,' " Cézanne told Emile Bernard (Bernard, "Paul Cézanne," *L'Occident*, July 1904, 23–25; quoted in Wright, *Modern Painting*, p. 143).

6. Cézanne wrote to Bernard in 1904, "In an orange, an apple, a bowl, a head there is a culminating point; and this point is always—in spite of the tremendous effect [of] light and shade [and] colour sensations—the closest to our eye; the edges of the objects recede to a center on our horizon" (*Paul Cézanne: Letters*, ed. John Rewald, trans. Marguerite Kay, 4th ed. [New York: Hacker Art Books, 1976], p. 306; paraphrased in Wright, *Modern Painting*, pp. 149–50).

7. E.E.C. to R.H.C., 2 March 1922, the E. E. Cummings Papers, Houghton Library.

8. William Innes Homer, "Seurat and the Science of Painting," in *Seurat in Perspective*, ed. Norma Broude (Englewood Cliffs, N.J.: Prentice-Hall, 1964), pp. 150–52.

9. Houghton notes, I(25) no. 81.

10. Both Kennedy (*Dreams in the Mirror*, passim) and Kidder ("Cummings and Cubism") credit Cubism as the chief influence on Cummings's Modernist painting. The influence however, is exaggerated and misleading, as my discussion in chap. 1 attempts to demonstrate.

11. Rpt. in *Miscellany Rev.*, pp. 126–31.

12. Cummings's description of the French revue in another *Vanity Fair* article provides an excellent gloss on this process: "By the laws of its own standards, which are the irrevocable laws of juxtaposition and contrast, the revue is a use of everything trivial and plural to intensify what is singular and fundamental. In the case of the Folies Bergere, the revue is a use of ideas, smells, colors, Irving Berlin, nudes, tactility, collapsible stairs, three dimensions and fire works to intensify Mlle. Josephine Baker" ("Vive la Folie," September 1926; rpt. in *Miscellany Rev.*, pp. 162–63).

13. For a fuller explication, see Milton A. Cohen, "Cummings and Freud," *American Literature* 55 (Winter 1983): 591–610.

14. Frederick Hoffman, *Freudianism and the Literary Mind*, (Baton Rouge, La.: Louisiana State University Press, 1957), p. 52.

15. Nagel's psychoanalysis, in particular, impressed Cummings for its beneficial effect on Nagel's painting. It left Nagel "en-

tirely changed," Cummings wrote his mother, "he paints very finely now" (letter of 13 January 1922). Thayer's psychoanalysis later proved a failure, which Cummings satirized in the poem "listen my children and you" (*is 5*, "One," VII).

16. Among Freud's works he mentions reading in the twenties are *The Interpretation of Dreams, Wit and Its Relation to the Unconscious, A General Introduction to Psychoanalysis,* and *Totem and Taboo.* Cummings's copies can be found in the Houghton Library collection.

17. Houghton notes, I(55) no. 54.

18. Further in the quotation, Cummings describes his experience of Freudian reality as a plunging into "concrete (sex)." Hoffman (*Freudianism and the Literary Mind*, p. 63) notes that the bohemians of the Village misconstrued Freud for their own ends.

19. Kennedy, *Dreams in the Mirror*, pp. 103, 157, passim.

20. Ibid. pp. 246-47.

21. *Selected Letters*, p. 86.

22. E.g., "I Take Great Pleasure in Presenting," *Vanity Fair*, February 1926, and "The Secret of the Zoo Exposed," *Vanity Fair*, September 1926; both rpt. in *Miscellany Rev.*, pp. 137-40, 174-78.

23. Kennedy, *Dreams in the Mirror*, pp. 301-2.

24. Sigmund Freud, *The Interpretation of Dreams*, vols. 4-5 of *The Standard Edition of the Complete Psychological Works of Sigmund Freud*, trans. James Strachey, p. 318, n. 3. Although Cummings owned the Brill translation, Strachey's version is substantially the same as Brill's (Modern Library ed., p. 346, n. 1).

25. Freud, *Standard Edition*, vol. 4, p. 318, my emphasis. Cummings appears to paraphrase this passage when he states that the "opposition" between the rose's qualities and their antitheses exists "in terms of consciousness only," and that "secretly or unconsciously" these antithetical qualities "modify and enhance" the rose's qualities.

26. "Suites of color equaling progressive degrees of distance," recalls a similar note on Cézanne: "Cézanne DOES NOT MODEL. He proceeds by *contrasts of colors, submitted to a* CADENCE which has been established in advance, and which is autonomous with respect to the objects" (Houghton notes, I[22] no. 38, my emphasis). And in the same letter describing his painting "Chasms and bumps," Cummings also mentions using Cézanne's palette to "get form by colour" (E.E.C. to R.H.C., 2 March 1922 the E. E. Cummings Papers, Houghton Library).

27. Friedman, *Cummings: The Art of His Poetry*, pp. 96-97.

28. Kidder, " 'Author of Pictures,' " 478.

29. Alex Preminger, ed. *Princeton Encyclopedia of Poetry and Poetics*, enl. ed. (Princeton: Princeton University Press, 1974), p. 596.

30. Freud, *Standard Edition*, vol. 4, pp. 318, 295-96.

31. See, for example, his comments on primitivistic naïveté and children's art discussed in chap. 2 and in his essay, "Gaston Lachaise." Moreover, his poetry employs all manner of wordplay, including acrostics, palindromes, and juxtaposed anagrams (e.g., "gas / sags" in the poem "the bed" above, and "god / dog" in the poem "Who / threw the silver dollar . . ." [&, "N," IV]).

32. Sigmund Freud, *Wit and Its Relation to the Unconscious*, in *The Basic Writings of Sigmund Freud*, trans. A. A. Brill (New York: Random House, Modern Library, 1938), p. 674.

33. Freud, *Standard Edition*, vol. 11, p. 159 (my emphasis).

34. This detachment seems to contradict Cummings's aesthetic interest in overcoming barriers dividing viewer, artist, and subject. But his real subject in these poems is not the prostitute but the complex *experience* of having sex with her.

35. Houghton notes, bMS Am 1892.6(29) no. 5.

36. Houghton notes, I(39) no. 225.

37. John Peale Bishop, "The Poems and Prose of E. E. Cummings"; rpt. in Baum, *Cummings and the Critics*, p. 103.

38. Richard Kennedy, "Introduction," in E. E. Cummings, *Tulips & Chimneys*, ed. George J. Firmage (New York: Liveright, 1973), p. xiii. Cf. a similar technique in the "Newsreels" of Dos Passos's *U.S.A.*

39. Although, stylistically, "Post-Impressionism" is a meaningless term, Cummings uses it freely in his early notes and essays to cover all Modernist styles from Cézanne's to Picasso's. In doing so, he followed the common practice of his time, especially the well-meaning but hopelessly confused stylistic labels in Arthur Jerome Eddy's *Cubists and Post-Impressionism* (Chicago: A. C. McClurg and Co., 1914), a book Cummings owned and carefully annotated.

40. *Miscellany Rev.*, p. 10.

41. "The Adult, the Artist, and the Circus," *Vanity Fair*, October 1925; "You Aren't Mad, Am I?" *Vanity Fair*, December 1925; "The Theatre: I," *Dial*, April 1926; "The Theatre: II," *Dial*, May 1926; "Coney Island," *Vanity Fair*, June 1926; "Vive la Folie!" *Vanity Fair*, September 1926. All are reprinted in *Miscellany Rev.*

42. "Coney Island"; rpt. in *Miscellany Rev.*, p. 151.

43. "The Theatre: II"; rpt. in *Miscellany Rev.*, pp. 145-48.

44. In notes for *Him*, Cummings makes these perceptual-psychoanalytic connections explicit. Alongside of ideas relating the invisible mirror business to the conscious and unconscious (see n. 46 below) are notes on seeing around and the "breakable rose" from the burlesque essay (Houghton notes, I[59] no. 120).

45. As Richard Kennedy notes, Cummings's first draft of *Him* was cruder still in attempting to show "Freudian ideas in symbolic action" by having characters represent "consciousness or the ego," "the subconscious," etc. (*Dreams in the Mirror*, p. 290).

46. In *Wit and Its Relation to the Unconscious* (Brill trans., pp. 746-47, 761), Freud defines the nucleus of a dream as a repressed wish "that should appear foreign to conscious thinking or . . . supply consciousness with reinforcement from unknown sources."

In Cummings's notes appears this analogy:

the possession[?] of
sexual love, lust : desire to make children =

turning a mirror : looking into it
1.---------C[onscious]
        a mirror as an object, like the wall on which it
        hangs
2.   a mirror as images, reflections of objects
    --------Unc[onscious]

                          (Houghton notes, I[59] no. 120)

47. In the chorus scenes, for example, a backdrop shows the *painted* bodies of a doctor anesthetizing a woman; where the woman's head would be, Me's head appears. In scene 1, the doctor appears in person and hands Him a cigar. Me refers in act 1 (ii) to wanting "to decide something" and later says, "I've tried so hard not to talk about it and I'm sick with worrying—" (iv). Cummings confirms in notes entitled "The Structure of the Play" that "the chief theme . . . is pregnancy (Houghton notes, 1823.4 no. 15, quoted in Kennedy, *Dreams in the Mirror*, p. 504, n. 1).

48. E.g., Norman Friedman writes in *E. E. Cummings: The Growth of a Writer* (Carbondale: Southern Illinois University Press, 1964): "And, of course, her baby is born at the end." He cites as support a letter Cummings wrote him in 1961 stating: "Me's underlying ambition is to be entirely loved by someone through whom she may safely have a child" (pp. 55, 58). But Cummings's exegesis refers to Me's "ambition" to have a child, not to the fact of her having it.

49. Friedman is forced to interpret this response as Me's misunderstanding of Him's meaning (*Cummings: The Growth of a Writer*, p. 71)—an unconvincing explanation in view of the carefully detailed narration of the dream itself.

50. Him's realization dramatizes the autobiographical note above in which Cummings's "Keats period" (Beauty is truth, truth beauty") yields to the "reality" of Freud ("beauty has shut me from truth"). Note, also, the parallel between Him's artistic and human failings: in both cases, he cannot "give birth" to a new creation.

51. Simon O. Lessor, *Fiction and the Unconscious* (Boston: Beacon Press, 1957), pp. 142-43. Lessor cites Freud's similar views on the subject (p. 143 n. 26).

5. MOTION

1. It also closely resembles an unconscious process Freud termed "displacement"—a process that, as I have argued in chap. 4, Cummings both understood and exploited.

2. Cf. Cummings's descriptions of the unselfconscious art of children and primitives that "cannot be grasped until we have accomplished the thorough destruction of the world [i.e. adult logic]. By this destruction alone we cease to be spectators of a ludicrous and ineffectual striving and, involving ourselves in *a new and fundamental kinesis*, become protagonists of the child's vision" ("Gaston Lachaise"; rpt. in *Miscellany Rev.*, p. 18, my emphasis).

3. Houghton notes, I(39).

4. Houghton notes, I(I111).

5. The original version in Cummings's notes (Houghton notes, I[25] no. 162) is quite similar, with one significant exception: in place of the phrase "it is a *kinesis* fatally composed of . . . stresses," Cummings's original note stated, "it is a *poise* fatally or *accidentally* composed by . . ." (my emphasis).

6. *Tulips and Chimneys,* "La Guerre," II. In a later poem, "dying is fine)but Death" (*Xaipe*, 6), Cummings refined the equation of "death(being born)" to make "dying," the verbal, part of the cyclical process, while the noun "death" signifies the stasis and finality appropriate to thinking.

7. The ⟶ arrows in this quotation are somewhat misleading, since they accompany a sentence describing causality and should logically appear as → . Alongside of ⟵⟶ , Cummings placed an asterisk, noting that the ⟵⟶ moved "back & forth, is reflexive, or rebound."

8. Houghton notes, I(39) no. 46 and I(21) no. 149.

9. Contrary to the linearity of discursive logic, the logic of Modernist art, writes Roger Shattuck, "is circular and revolves around a point whose location is limitless. Apollinaire wrote his first 'calligraphic' poems literally in circles, the circles of expanding and contracting attention. (*The Banquet Years*, p. 38).

10. Houghton notes, I(111) no. 4.

11. Houghton notes, I(39).

12. Houghton notes, I(59) no. 63ᵛ.

13. "The Exhibitors to the Public," introduction to catalog of Futurist exhibition at Bernheim-Jeune, Paris, 5 February 1912; trans. rpt. in Joshua Taylor, *Futurism* (New York: Museum of Modern Art, 1961), p. 128.

14. In one college note, Cummings wrote, "the fallacy of the Futurists was that they could be modern thru disregard of the past—impossible" (Houghton notes, bMS Am.1892.7 [149] no. 3).

15. Houghton notes, bMS Am.1892.6(69) nos. 1-5.

16. "Wireless Imagination and Words in Liberty," *Lacerba* 1, no. 12 (June 1913): 121-24; excerpted in Rosa Clough, *Futurism: The Story of a Modern Art Movement. A New Appraisal* (1961; reprint, New York: Greenwood Press, 1969), p. 48.

17. "Wireless Imagination"; excerpted in Marianne Martin, *Futurist Art and Theory: 1900-1915* (New York: Hacker, 1978), p. 135.

18. "Wireless Imagination"; rpt. in Clough, *Futurism,* pp. 44-46, 48-49.

19. *Zang Tumb Tumb, Adreianopoli, Ottobre 1912* (Milano: Ediizione Futurists Di "Poesia," 1914); excerpted in Clough, *Futurism,* p. 52.

20. Cummings's only published work on either artist was his short review of Eliot's *Poems 1920* in the *Dial* ("T. S. Eliot," June 1920; rpt. in *Miscellany Rev.*, pp. 25-29). Although he sweated over this essay and left numerous drafts in his notes, the final version offers precious little analysis of Eliot's technique and, like the essays on Lachaise and Cocteau, simply bestows upon the artist's work such undefined terms of approbation as "intense" and "alive."

21. In *Dreams in the Mirror* (pp. 178-79), Kennedy men-

tions a 1918 essay on Joyce that Cummings "apparently submitted to the *Dial* before Thayer and Watson assumed control." But he does not cite his sources and says that only Cummings's Camp Devens notes for the essay remain. The notes quoted here may belong to sketches for that essay. In other fragmentary notes on *Ulysses*, Cummings complains of how difficult it is to "criticize" or even quote from the book and rationalizes: "there is everything to feel and nothing to say about the book" (Houghton notes, I[25] nos. 7–9, 60–61). Whether Cummings was temperamentally unable or simply reluctant to analyze the work of fellow writers is a debatable question; without doubt, however, his philosophy opposing thinking and favoring feeling contributed heavily to his critical silence.

22. E.E.C. to R.H.C., 17 May 1923, the E. E. Cummings Papers, Houghton Library.

23. Houghton notes, I(59) no. 27.

24. These notes on angles quote large sections of Wright, accompanied by Cummings's comments and diagrams.

25. Houghton notes, I(39) no. 304.

26. Houghton notes, I(25) no. 118.

27. Houghton notes, I(55) no. 90.

28. Houghton notes, I(25) no. 118.

29. The influence of both Matisse and Kandinsky on these speculative analogies is quite likely. In "Notes of a Painter" (1908), Matisse wrote, "There is an impelling proportion of tones that can induce me to change the shape of a figure or to transform my composition" (rpt. in Chipp, *Theories of Modern Art*, p. 134). Kandinsky was far more specific in analogizing the expressive effects of colors and shapes, e.g.: "It is evident that certain colors can be emphasized or dulled in value by certain forms. Generally speaking, sharp colors are well suited to sharp forms (e.g., yellow in the triangle), and softer, deep colors by round forms (e.g., blue in the circle)" (*Concerning the Spiritual in Art* [1912], *The Documents of Modern Art*, trans. Francis Golffing et al. [New York, George Wittenborn, 1947], vol. 5, p. 47). Cummings had read long passages of Kandinsky's work; whether or not he knew of Matisse's "Notes" is uncertain.

30. Cummings's appreciation of Lachaise's sculpture, particularly its towering proportions, is evident in his essay on Lachaise in the *Dial* (February 1920), and in letters to his parents in the late teens.

31. Houghton notes, I(27) no. 3.

32. *XLI Poems*, "Portraits," IX. When this poem was composed in 1918, the Woolworth Building was Manhattan's tallest and an architectural inspiration to Cummings. He praised it often in his notes and admired the way John Marin captured it in his dynamic watercolors and etchings.

33. Kennedy, *Dreams in the Mirror*, p. 181.

34. "Gaston Lachaise"; rpt. in *Miscellany Rev.*, p. 20.

35. Houghton notes, I(98); I(25) no. 109; I(59) no. 1.

36. Houghton notes, bMS Am. 1892.7(82) no. 1.

37. Houghton notes, bMS Am. 1892.7(70); quoted in Kennedy, *Dreams in the Mirror*, p. 180 (my emphasis).

38. *XLI Poems*, "Portraits," III.

39. R. P. Blackmur first raised this objection in "Notes on E. E. Cummings' Language," *Hound & Horn* 4 (January–March 1931): 163–92. His complaint, thoroughly justified, was that Cummings leaned heavily on a few words ("precise," "fragile," "skillful," "accurate," "distinct," etc.) that are "names for precise qualities" rather than being precise or concrete themselves.

40. Houghton notes, I(59) no. 1.

41. Norman Friedman has observed these transformations of verbs to nouns and adverbs to adjectives in *Cummings: The Art of His Poetry* (pp. 23–24, 105). But to my mind, he does not sufficiently stress the energy and dynamism Cummings effected by these transformations.

42. *is 5*, "Three," IV.

43. Draft of letter to Scofield Thayer, Houghton notes, bMS Am. 1892.7(69–70) (Camp Devens notes).

44. S. V. Baum, "E. E. Cummings: The Technique of Immediacy," *South Atlantic Quarterly* 53 (January 1954):78.

45. Houghton notes, I(39).

46. Dos Passos, *The Best Times*, p. 99.

47. Houghton notes, I(25) no. 199.

48. Alternatively, "tiny" can modify "boots" above ("of boots / tiny") leaving the quoted conclusion: "what shall death add?" Either way, the kinesthetic effect is the same.

49. *&*, "Seven Poems," I.

6. LIGHTS THAT FAILED: Interrelating the Arts

1. Houghton notes, bMS Am. 1892.6(29) no. 11.

2. These notes span Cummings's early period: from his last years at Harvard, 1915–16, through the 1920s (dated by references to Anne Barton, whom he met in 1925). The most intense periods of theorizing on analogues seem to have occurred during his Harvard years and his enforced confinements at La Ferté-Macé prison (October–December 1917) and Camp Devens (July 1918–January 1919).

3. Cummings's poetry, more than his painting, directly appropriated techniques from other arts. Consequently, the published poems provide the touchstone for his theories on analogues discussed below.

4. Adrian Klein, *Coloured Light: An Art Medium*, 3rd ed. of *Colour-Music* (London: Technical Press, 1937), chaps. 1, 3, 5, passim.

5. Joseph Chiari, *Symbolisme from Poe to Mallarmé* (1956; reprint, New York, Gordian Press, 1970), pp. 54, 101, 160–61.

6. Martin Turnell, *Baudelaire: A Study of His Poetry* (New York: New Directions, 1954), p. 30.

7. Quoted in Sven Loevgren, *The Genesis of Modernism: Seurat, Gauguin, Van Gogh and French Symbolism in the 1880s* (Bloomington, Ind.: Indiana University Press, 1971), p. 95.

8. "Notes Synthetiques" (ca. 1888); rpt. in Chipp, *Theories of Modern Art*, p. 61; "Diverses Choses 1896-1897"; rpt. in Chipp, *Theories of Modern Art*, p. 66.

9. Kennedy, *Dreams in the Mirror*, p. 82.

10. Klein's bibliography of relevant newspaper and magazine articles indicates that the subject of "colour-music" received increasing attention throughout the 1800s and crested in the 1890s with the demonstration of Rimington's color organ (*Coloured Light*, appendix).

11. Houghton notes, bMS Am 1892.6(84) no. 20.

12. Klein observes that Rimington's wavelength numbers for colors do not square with the data of numerous other scientists and theorists; in fact, Rimington's scale appears inverted (*Coloured Light*, pp. 125-28). But Cummingsnever pursued the technical analogy this far in his notes and never appeared to question the physical basis of Rimington's analogies.

13. Quoted in "The New Art," p. 18. The *Boston Evening Transcript* review, 24 March 1915, was also the source of Cummings's table comparing Scriabin's and Rimington's color-tone scales.

14. "Two Cases of Synaesthesia," *British Journal of Psychology* 7 (1914): 112-17.

15. Kandinsky, *Concerning the Spiritual in Art* (New York: George Wittenborn, 1947), p. 45. In a footnote to this passage, Kandinsky cites Scriabin's color-tone chart, noting that *Prometheus* "has given convincing proof to his [color-tone] theories" (pp. 45-46, n. 2).

16. Address to the Circle of International Artists, 1911; quoted in Martin, *Futurist Art and Theory*, pp. 92-93.

17. "Technical Manifesto of Literature" (1912) and *Zang Tumb Tumb*, p. 127, both quoted in Clough, *Futurism*, pp. 48, 51-52.

18. "Their subject is sounds," Cummings wrote in "The New Art" (p. 20), an example of "painting definitely encroaching upon music."

19. Introduction to catalog, Exhibition of Synchromist Paintings by Morgan Russell and Stanton MacDonald-Wright, Carroll Galleries, New York, 2-16 March 1914; quoted in Gail Levin, *Synchromism and American Color Abstraction 1910-1925* (New York: Braziller, 1978), p. 132.

20. Levin, *Synchromism and American Color Abstraction*, p. 23.

21. Klein, *Coloured Light*, p. 102.

22. Ibid., p. 105.

23. "A New View of Colour," *Cambridge Magazine*, 23 February 1918, 452-56; "The Analogy of Sound and Colour," *Cambridge Magazine*, 2 March 1918, 480.

24. Houghton notes, I(21) no. 186.

25. "The Poetry of a New Era," p. 6.

26. Actually, Cummings's parallels are skewed, since "shade" and "tint" are only two sides of the same element: value, or lightness-darkness. The two elements of "colors," therefore, cannot align evenly with the three elements of "sounds."

27. *XLI Poems*, "Portraits," VII.

28. Houghton notes, I(59) no. 42.

29. Houghton notes, I(59) no. 26.

30. Houghton notes, I(27).

31. Houghton notes, I(39) no. 117.

32. Houghton notes, I(59) no. 27.

33. Houghton notes, I(22) no. 21.

34. Rood recommended colors roughly equidistant from each other, or approximately 120° apart on his "contrast-diagram" color wheel. While in Cummings's triad, only two of the colors are equidistant from each other, the three colors (yellow-orange, green, and violet) are quite close to an example Rood cites with approval: "In this third triad [orange, green, and violet] the orange and violet are about 90° apart, but both are nearly equidistant from the green, and form, both of them, a good combination with it" (*Modern Chromatics* [1879; reprint, New York: Van Nostrand Reinhold, 1973], pp. 242, 244-45).

35. Houghton notes, I(25) no. 19.

36. "Technical Manifesto of Literature"; quoted in Clough, *Futurism*, p. 49.

37. Note that Cummings reserves the most self-integrated shape, the sphere, for first person—his beloved "i"—and borrows all three shapes from Cézanne's dictum to "treat nature by the cylinder, the sphere, and the cone."

38. Houghton notes, I(59) no. 30.

39. In *Dreams in the Mirror* (pp. 115-16), Kennedy dates the first of these poems from 29 June 1916 and states that Cummings's "consolidation" of his basic styles continued to January 1917. This is generally correct, although one of the poems ("city") may have been written before June 1916, while another ("teamsters") almost certainly dates from after 1 January 1917 (see nn. 56, 61 below). Thus, these poems date from the year of Cummings's first formal innovations. Recently, some of these poems have appeared in Richard Kennedy, "E. E. Cummings 1916: The Emergent Styles," *Journal of Modern Literature* 7 (April 1979): 175-204, and in *Etcetera: The Unpublished Poems of E. E. Cummings*, ed. George Firmage and Richard Kennedy (New York: Liveright, 1983).

40. *Tulips and Chimneys*, "Impressions," II.

41. "Cummings Miscellaneous," Harry Ransom Humanities Research Center, University of Texas at Austin. "Writhe and" appears in a category initialed "D.S.N." (which Richard Kennedy deciphers as "Designation Sine Nomine" [*Dreams in the Mirror*, p. 97]). Cummings later published about two dozen of the poems listed in the index, most of them of the D.S.N. free-verse group and subject to much revision. I thank Professor Kennedy for generously sending me a copy of the index.

42. Kennedy, *Dreams in the Mirror*, p. 122.

43. Richard Kennedy, "E. E. Cummings at Harvard: Verse, Friends, Rebellion," *Harvard Library Bulletin* 25 (July 1977): 286.

44. Kidder, "Cummings and Cubism," 283.

45. *Tulips and Chimneys*, "Portraits," VIII.

46. Including Schoenberg, Stravinsky, Debussy, and Satie —all discussed in "The New Art."

47. Kennedy, *Dreams in the Mirror,* p. 64.

48. In *Dreams in the Mirror* (p. 119), Kennedy considers this version the revision, but Cummings's footnote suggests otherwise: the other draft (fig. 53) achieves the harmonic structure this version lacks.

49. &, "Post Impressions," V.

50. *Tulips and Chimneys,* "Sonnets-Unrealities," III; &, "Sonnets-Actualities," V.

51. In order of citation: "but the other," *Tulips and Chimneys,* "Portraits," VI; "the dress was a suspicious madder . . ," &, "Post Impressions," XIII; and "of this wilting wall the colour drub," &, "Sonnets-Realities," XV.

52. Faubion Bowers, *Scriabin* (Tokyo: Kodansha International Ltd., 1969), vol. 2, p. 203.

53. John Houston, *The Design of Rimbaud's Poetry,* Yale Romantic Studies, 2d ser., vol. 2 (New Haven: Yale University Press, 1963), pp. 62, 178.

54. A third note, written at about the same time, offers a somewhat different equation:

$$\begin{array}{ccccccccc}
\text{white} & V & B & G & Y & O & R & B & \\
\bar{\text{i}} & \bar{\text{u}} & & & \bar{\text{e}} & & & & \text{o w}
\end{array}$$

analogy betw. keys in music & colors (tints)
$$\qquad \text{pitch} \qquad\qquad\qquad \text{Esp.—natural key (C)}$$
(Houghton notes, I[21] no. 35)

Another note compares green to the "u" of "thugs, buzz" (I[39] no. 294). From these variants, it seems that Cummings was least certain about "i" and most sure of "u" (always violet) and "o" (always blue).

55. These associations, however, do not square with Cummings's "scoring" of short vowels as high and long vowels as low. Logically, the more piercing high tones should "advance," and the blunter low tones "recede."

56. The worksheet for this poem (I[21] no. 47) bears several New York City addresses of contractor-repairmen, whose assistance Cummings might have sought after moving to New York in January 1917.

57. Houghton notes, I(21) no. 47, I(21) no. 188.

58. These pairings offer further reason why "lilac shrieks and scarlet bellowings" is "impossible": the contradiction between the advancing "ē" of "shriek" and the recessive color of "lilac"; viceversa for "scarlet bellowings."

59. Cummings is somewhat contradictory on whether white should be considered a color. In one note (I[39] no. 119) he refers to white as a "hue" and as a fusion of all hues. In several other notes,

however, he contrasts white, gray, and black unfavorably to colors. Some early paintings use variants of white as an advancing color (e.g., *Open window*).

60. In order of citation: "my small headed pearshaped," &, "Post Impressions," VII; "nearer . . ," &, "Sonnets-Realities, X; "when i have thought of you somewhat too much," &, "Sonnets-Actualities," VI.

61. The handwritten comment, "ingenious," on this poem matches the handwriting of Dean Briggs, Cummings's poetry professor at Harvard in 1916, who annotated many of Cummings's extant college papers on the arts. Thus, "city" could have been written any time in 1916 while Cummings still lived in Cambridge. Rushworth Kidder has found the news story announcing Buffalo Bill Cody's death (dated 10 January 1917) that inspired Cummings's poem (" 'Buffalo Bill's'—An Early E. E. Cummings Manuscript," *Harvard Library Bulletin* 4 [October 1976]: 375).

62. Houghton notes, I(21) no. 80.

63. Quoted in Harold Osborne, *Aesthetics and Criticism,* (Westport, Conn.: Greenwood Press, 1955), p. 265.

CONCLUSION: The Paradox of Unity

1. Unlike his absorption of Modernist painting, which derived from his independent study of the artists, paintings, and styles and from his working out of their aesthetics, much of Cummings's assimilation of poetic traditions came through organized courses at Harvard, such as the "English Versification"course of 1916 that required him to compose works in various genres and inspired him to imitate the styles of various poets (Kennedy, *Dreams in the Mirror,* pp. 91-92).

2. Houghton notes, I(27) no. 74.

3. E.E.C. to Nancy Cummings, 7 September 1959, *Selected Letters,* p. 263.

4. " 'Only to Grow,' " 924, 929-33.

APPENDIX: Exhibitions Featuring Cummings's Art

1. Although a reviewer for the *New York World* identifies one of Cummings's entries as *Soft-Shell Crab Defending Its Young,* the catalog of the Independents shows no such title. Probably, it was a humorous subtitle added by Cummings.

2. Cummings mentions his intention to send these two works to the 1927 Independents (E.E.C. to R.H.C., 7 January 1927). The 1927 Independents catalog, however, does not list Cummings.

Selected Bibliography

Manuscripts and Papers

Austin, Tex. The Iconography Collection of the Harry Ransom Humanities Research Center, University of Texas at Austin. E. E. Cummings collection.

Cambridge, Mass. Houghton Library, Harvard University. E. E. Cummings papers.

New York, N.Y. Berg Collection, New York Public Library. E. E. Cummings papers, J. Sibley Watson Archive.

Major Collections of Cummings's Art

Barrington, R.I. Luethi-Peterson Camps, Inc.

Brockport, N.Y. State University of New York College at Brockport Foundation.

Cambridge, Mass. Houghton Library, Harvard University. E. E. Cummings papers (drawings).

New York, N.Y. Metropolitan Museum of Art. *The Dial* collection.

Rochester, N.Y. Memorial Art Gallery of the University of Rochester.

Articles and Books on Cummings's Art

Cohen, Milton A. *E. E. Cummings' Paintings: The Hidden Career.* Dallas: University of Texas at Dallas and Dallas Public Library, 1982.

Gettings, Frank. *E. E. Cummings: The Poet as Artist.* Hirshhorn Museum exhibition. Washington: Smithsonian Institution Press, 1976.

Hjerter, Kathleen G. *Doubly Gifted: The Author as Visual Artist.* New York: Abrams, 1986, pp. 108–11.

Kennedy, Richard, S. *Dreams in the Mirror: A Biography of E. E. Cummings.* New York: Liveright, 1980.

Kidder, Rushworth M. " 'Author of Pictures': A Study of Cummings' Line Drawings in *The Dial.*" *Contemporary Literature* 17 (Autumn 1976): 470–505.

———. "Cummings and Cubism: The Influence of the Visual Arts on Cummings' Poetry." *Journal of Modern Literature* 7, no. 2 (April 1979): 255–91.

———. "e. e. cummings: American Poet and Painter," *Christian Science Monitor,* 25 November 1974.

———. "E. E. Cummings, Painter." *Harvard Library Bulletin* 23 (April 1975): 117–38.

———. "Precision Creating Movement." *Christian Science Monitor,* 9 November 1977.

Norman, Charles. *E. E. Cummings: The Magic Maker.* Rev. ed. New York: Macmillan, 1964, chap. 11.

Porter, Wakefield. "The Paintings of E. E. Cummings." *Harvard Wake* 5 (Spring 1946): 75–76.

Reutlinger, Dagmar. "E. E. Cummings and *The Dial* Collection." *Massachusetts Review* 16 (Spring 1975): 353–56.

Tucker, Robert. "E. E. Cummings as an Artist: *The Dial* Drawings." *Massachusetts Review* 16 (Spring 1975): 329–53.

Reviews of Cummings's Exhibitions and Articles Mentioning His Submissions to Exhibitions

Note: This section is in chronological order; an asterisk indicates significant coverage.

"Independents Run Gamut in Art Show." *New York Sun,* 30 March 1919, p. 14, col. 3.

*Review of 1920 Independents. *New York Evening Post,* 12 March 1920, p. 11, cols. 4–5.

"L'Art Pour L'Art Revels in Splash of Naked Truth." *New York World,* 12 March 1920, p. 8, col. 3.

"Independent Art Show Teaches a Moral Lesson." *New York Sun,* 14 March 1920, p. 15, col. 1.

Kaufman, S. J. *New York Globe and Advertiser,* c. March 1920.

"Independents' Art Show Voluminous." *New York Evening Post,* 28 February 1921, p. 7, cols. 1–2.

*Review of 1924 Independents. *New York Sun and Globe,* 6 March 1924, p. 16, cols. 2–3.

*K. G. S. "An Experimentalist's Exhibition." *New York Times,* 6 December 1931, sec. 2, p. 8n, cols. 7–8.

*Review of December 1932 exhibition. *New York Times,* 11 December 1932, sec. 9, p. 10.

*McBride, Henry. "Attractions in Other Galleries." *New York Sun,* 3 February 1934, p. 9, cols. 1–2.

Devree, Howard. "A Change of Case." *New York Times,* 4 February 1934, sec. 9, p. 12x.

*Cortissoz, Royal. Review of 1944 exhibition at American-British Art Center. *New York Herald Tribune,* 27 February 1944, p. 9, cols. 5–6.

*McBride, Henry. "Hands Across the Sea. The British Discover E. E. Cummings to be a Painter." *New York Sun,* 4 March 1944, p. 9, cols. 5–6.

"Briefer Mention." *New York Times,* 5 March 1944, sec. 2, p. 6x.

*McBride, Henry. "Attractions in the Galleries." *New York Sun,* 20 May 1949, p. 23, cols. 6–7.

P. V. B. Review of 1949 exhibition at American-British Art Center. *New York Herald Tribune,* 22 May 1949, sec. 5, p. 10, col. 3.

Preston, Stewart. Review of 1949 exhibition. *New York Times,* 22 May 1949, sec. 2, p. 12, col. 6.

*Review of 1949 exhibition. *Arts Digest* 23. no. 17 (1949): 19.

O'Doherty, Brian. "Works by E. E. Cummings Are Shown in Exhibition at Down-Town Gallery." *New York Times,* 30 October 1963, p. 50, cols. 2–3.

*Kramer, Hilton. "A Parenthesis to the Career of a Poet." *New York Times,* 16 March 1968, p. 26, cols. 1–3.

Kooi, Cynthia. "E. E. Cummings' Hidden Career Viewed." *Plano Daily Star-Courier,* 25 August 1982, sec. C, p. 1.

*Marvel, Bill. "Poetandpainter': A New View of Cummings' Art." *Dallas Times Herald,* 6 October 1982, sec. E, pp. 1, 12.

*Kutner, Janet. "E. E. Cummings' Other Life." *Dallas Morning News,* 27 October 1982, sec. C, pp. 1–2.

Gray, Channing. "What's Left of E E Cummings." *Providence Journal-Bulletin Weekend,* 12 November 1982.

"Bookish." *New York Times,* 17 February 1983, "Going Out Guide."

*Rankovic, Catherine. "Poet and Painter: Review of Exhibit at Nielsen Gallery." *Boston Ledger,* c. March 1983.

Articles and Books on Cummings's Aesthetic Theories and Experiments and on the Relations Between His Poetry and Painting

Brown, Slater. Review of *Tulips and Chimneys. Broom* 6 (January 1924): 26–28.

Cohen, Milton A. "Cummings and Freud." *American Literature* 55 (Winter 1983): 591–610.

Friedman, Norman. *E. E. Cummings: The Art of His Poetry.* Baltimore: Johns Hopkins Press, 1960.

Gidley, Mick. "Picture and Poem: E. E. Cummings in Perspective." *Poetry Review* 59 (1968): 179–95.

Kennedy, Richard S. *Dreams in the Mirror: A Biography of E. E. Cummings.* New York: Liveright, 1980, chapts. 6–15.

———. "E. E. Cummings 1916: The Emergent Styles." *Journal of Modern Literature* 7, no. 2 (April 1979): 175–204.

———. Introduction to *Etcetera: The Unpublished Poems of E. E. Cummings.* Edited by George J. Firmage and Richard S. Kennedy. New York: Liveright, 1983.

———. Introduction to *Tulips & Chimneys: The Original 1922 Manuscript with 34 Additional Poems from "&".* Edited by George J. Firmage. New York: Liveright, 1973.

Kidder, Rushworth M. " 'Buffalo Bill's': An Early E. E. Cummings Manuscript." *Harvard Library Bulletin* 4 (October 1976): 373–83.

———. *E. E. Cummings: An Introduction to His Poetry.* New York: Columbia University Press, 1979.

———. "Poem into Picture: The Genesis of Cummings' 'i am a little church.' " *Contemporary Literature* 21 (1980): 315–30.

———. " 'Twin Obsessions': The Poetry and Painting of E. E. Cummings." *Georgia Review* 32 (Summer 1978): 342–68.

Mullen, Patrick B. "Cummings and Popular Culture." *Journal of Popular Culture* 5 (Winter 1971): 503–20.

Munson, Gorham B. "Syrinx." *Secession* 5 (July 1923): 2–11.

Riding, Laura, and Graves, Robert. *A Survey of Modernist*

Poetry. London: William Heinemann Ltd., 1929.

Rus, Lewis C. "Structural Ambiguity: A Note on Meaning and the Linguistic Analysis of Literature." *Language Learning* 6 (1955): 469–78.

Von Abele, Rudolph. " 'Only to Grow': Change in the Poetry of E. E. Cummings." *PMLA* 70 (December 1955): 913–33.

Williams, William Carlos. "E. E. Cummings' Paintings and Poems." *Arts Digest* 29 (1 December 1954): 7–8.

Bibliographies and Collections of Critical Essays on Cummings's Poetry

Baum, Stanley V. *EΣTI: eec; E. E. Cummings and the Critics.* East Lansing: Michigan State University Press, 1962.

Dendinger, Lloyd N., ed. *E. E. Cummings: The Critical Reception.* Introduction by Dendinger. New York: Burt Franklin, 1981.

Firmage, George James. *E. E. Cummings: A Bibliography.* Westport, Conn.: Greenwood Press, 1974.

Friedman, Norman, ed. *E. E. Cummings: A Collection of Critical Essays.* Englewood Cliffs, N.J.: Prentice-Hall, 1972.

Lozynsky, Artem. "An Annotated Bibliography of Works on Cummings." *Journal of Modern Literature* 7, no. 2 (April 1979): 350–91.

Rotella, Guy. *Critical Essays on E. E. Cummings.* Boston: G. K. Hall, 1984.

———. *E. E. Cummings: A Reference Guide.* Boston: G. K. Hall, 1979.

———. "E. E. Cummings: A Reference Guide Updated." *Resources for American Literary Study* 12 (Autumn 1982): 143–88.

Index

Note: Page numbers in italic indicate illustrations.

Milton A. Cohen is Associate Professor of English and Education at the University of Texas at Dallas. Dr. Cohen, who received his M.A. degree from Indiana University and his Ph.D. from Syracuse University, has written *E. E. Cummings' Paintings: The Hidden Career* in addition to several articles on Cummings.

The manuscript was edited by Christina Postema. The book was designed by Joanne Kinney. The typefaces for the text are Century Expanded and Geneva Light. The display faces are Geneva Medium and Bold. The book is printed on Mead's Black and White dull enamel and is bound in Holliston Mills' Crown Linen over binder's boards.

Manufactured in the United States of America.